Heidegger's Language and Thinking

D0143824

Heidegger's Language and Thinking

Robert Mugerauer

Humanities Press International, Inc.
New Jersey ◇ London

First published in 1988 by Humanities Press International, Inc.,
Atlantic Highlands, N.J., and 3 Henrietta Street, London WC2E 8LU.

©Robert Mugerauer, 1988

Reprinted in paperback 1990

Library of Congress Cataloging-in-Publication Data

Mugerauer, Robert.
  Heidegger's language and thinking.

  Bibliography; p.
    1. Heidegger, Martin, 1889–1976.   2. Languages—
Philosophy—History—20th century.   3. Thought and
thinking—History—20th century.   1. Title.
B3279.H79M76   1988   193   86–27188
ISBN 0-391-03667-X (Pbk.)

British Cataloguing in Publication Data

A CIP record for this book is available from the British Library.

The following publisher has generously given permission to use extended quota-
tions from copyrighted works: From *On The Way to Language*, by Martin Heidegger.
Translated by Peter D. Hertz. Copyright 1971 by Harper & Row, Publishers, Inc. From
What is Called Thinking? by Martin Heidegger. A Translation of *Was Heisst Denken?* by
Fred D. Wieck and J. Glenn Gray. Volume Twenty-One of the Religious Perspectives
series edited by Ruth Nanda Anshen. Copyright 1968 by Harper & Row, Publishers,
Inc. From *Discourse on Thinking* by Martin Heidegger. A Translation of *Gelassenheit* by
John M. Anderson and E. Hans Freund. Copyright 1966 in the English translation by
Harper & Row, Publishers, Inc.

All rights reserved. No reproduction, copy, or transmission of this publication may
be made without written permission.

Printed in the United States of America

TO TOM CUNNINGHAM

a true and magnanimous man

LIBRARY
ALMA COLLEGE
ALMA, MICHIGAN

Contents

Preface

My purpose is simple. I want to read and understand Heidegger in a way which is true to what he says: all philosophical thinking, even the severest and most prosaic, is in itself poetic, yet never is poetry.[1] At the least, this means that thinking belongs inseparably to the language in which it occurs.

Exhortations to recognize the bond between thinking and language and to read Heidegger with the apposite twinned vision are familiar. For example, in *The Philosophy of Martin Heidegger*, J. L. Mehta says:

> The manner in which Heidegger handles language, both in the writings of the earlier phase and in those of the later, is inseparably bound up with what he has to say and must therefore be taken as an intrinsic part of the method or "way" of his thinking.
>
> In these later writings what is thought and said becomes inseparable from the individual and unique language and manner of saying it; not only does the thought and the utterance merge into one but the particular language employed and the thought content expressed become indissoluble.[2]

Similarly, Albert Hofstadter, in his introduction to the translation of Heidegger's essays called *Poetry, Language, Thought*, writes of the language of Heidegger's thinking: "The style is the thinking itself."[3] And George Steiner, in his *Martin Heidegger*, holds that we cannot avoid confronting the point: "No aspect of Heideggerian thought can be divorced from the phenomenon of Heidegger's prose style."[4]

Though the thesis, then, lies clearly before us, it still needs to be examined. For example, even two recent major works that are especially sensitive to Heidegger's special uses of language proceed through his complete works in order to elaborate Heidegger's theory of language and poetry and, therefore, must pass by individual works too quickly to demonstrate the thesis which concerns us here.[5] Thus, what often has been described has not yet been instantiated. That is the aim of this book: to begin to flesh out the principle by an exegesis of three of Heidegger's works, *Discourse on Thinking*, "A Dialogue on Language," and *What Is Called Thinking?*

An apology may be in order. I proffer little scholarship, but not because of any lack of respect for it. Think of what Heideggerian scholarship accomplishes: it reviews, organizes, and integrates a vast and constantly growing mass of literature; it presents overviews and summaries of Heidegger's work; it traces the development of specific, often difficult, themes; it correlates Heidegger's views with those of earlier or foreign philosophers, poets, and religious figures; it evaluates Heidegger's philosophy. Clearly, all this is important.

Yet, I venture something more modest—and, perhaps, prior. I want to try to let Heidegger's works be; I want to devote a close, careful reading to his texts. The attempt to hear and think about what Heidegger says is, at the same time, the attempt to find a way whereby those texts can speak for themselves and reveal themselves. The reading achieved here also points out how we might approximate a fuller understanding of these works, and thereby how we might approach Heidegger in general.

The thesis that Heidegger's thinking and the language of his thinking belong together is specified in three ways in this book. First, I have tried to show that Heidegger's thinking and language are the same. That is not to hold that they are identical, but that, for example, they proceed by way of a figural unity rather than by way of concepts and that Heidegger homologizes what the works accomplish and what they tell. Secondly, I endeavor to demonstrate that Heidegger both says and shows that thinking and saying (or language) themselves are the same. This claim involves their essential nature and the way they gather together what belongs together. For all this, Heidegger's work does not merely have a formal unity. Rather, the wedding of insight and style intends to move the reader, to persuade him not only of the truth disclosed during the conversation on a country path, during the dialogue between the Japanese citizen and the inquirer, and during the lecture series, but also of the way he might learn to let *aletheia* (unconcealedness, or truth) occur in his or her own thinking. Thus, the first two features generate a third: finally, (1) how Heidegger thinks and says (2) what he thinks and says, (3) act heuristically and rhetorically to teach us to think and interpret thinking and saying. Together, all three specific movements show that Heidegger's language and thinking accord with what is, and especially with the event of thinking and saying.

In addition, I offer this reading to commend the general approach which holds that philosophical works, like literary works, are wholes, in that their composition and thoughtfulness, like husband and wife, are given both at once, or not at all, and that only as a result of such union is there fruitful issue. As Louis H. Mackey says, "In one extravant word: every philosopher is a poet, and ideally every student of philosophy should be a literary critic. The intellectual substance of a philosophical essay will emerge only in conjunction with a careful analysis of its form as imaginative writing."[6]

Of course, this book not only intends to demonstrate the fecundity and truth of the hypothesis that philosophical works are holistically meaningful and should be read accordingly, it also springs from that hypothesis. That is, the specific, detailed reading presented here begins with the assumption that *Discourse on Thinking*, "A Dialogue on Language," and *What Is Called Thinking?* are sensible wholes. But, this does not result in a vicious circle, merely working out and asserting a conclusion that already has been assumed. Rather, the double action of interpretation exhibits how it is possible to read at all. Simply put, the specific theses, announced above and demonstrated below, do not appear *ex nihilo*; they result from and confirm an attitude or approach to the text. Indeed, the exegesis—and only exegesis—could show the assumption wanting, for with the ideal of wholeness as the measure, a careful reading could show the text to be nonsensical. The general thesis makes it possible to approach what at first appears impenetrable, confused, or even incoherent; the specific, practical reading exhibits some of the text's sense, and insofar as a convincing or substantial meaning is made explicit, so far also is the assumption's truth. We do not, all at once, pull ourselves up into meaning by metaphysical bootstraps. Understanding is much more ordinary. It is like asking a stranger for directions in a foreign country: an initial trustful assumption is necessary for us to have a chance to go where we want. Of course, whether we actually do becomes clear only later, when we either get more lost or find our way home.

Finally, a word needs to be said concerning the use of English translations in approaching Heidegger, especially if we intend to examine the fusion of the substance and style of his work. An apparently obvious question is, how can we find the unity of what he says and thinks in German, if we read him in English? But, unless we do all our thinking and speaking about Heidegger, as well as all our reading, in German, how else would we find him except by way of translation? That is, the issue becomes not whether to use translations, but how to use them thoughtfully, as a way of questioning.

Learning to hear a thought originally said in another language is what Heidegger himself teaches about when, for example, he speaks in German about Greek and Japanese thinkers. We learn to hear a thinker by jumping over to what he says and thinks from where we are. And, where are we? Many learners, both students and scholarly teachers, are native English speakers. We begin our learning by way of English. That also is why all good trans-lation is an interpretation and possibility of going-over, the same as all genuine reading, learning, and thinking in any language are. When used thoughtfully as a means to questioning and beginning to think, English translations help make it possible for us to leap across to the original German, which we always keep in mind. English, because it is our language, carries us across what sepa-rates, toward Heidegger's language and thinking.

Acknowledgments

An early version of chapter 1 appeared in *The Southwestern Journal of Philosophy*, 8:1 (February 1977).

I would like to thank Grand Valley State Colleges and St. Edward's University for faculty development funds supporting the preparation of this book. Dr. Irwin C. Lieb and Dr. William Livingston, successive Vice-Presidents of Graduate Studies at the University of Texas at Austin, graciously appointed me Visiting Scholar—which provided wonderful access to colleagues and research materials. Special thanks is due to Brian Craddock for his friendship and thoughtful help in preparing the final manuscript. Judith A. Camlin and the copy editor at Humanities Press International, Inc., have contributed a good deal to treating Heidegger's difficult and subtle language with respect and clarity.

CHAPTER ONE

Learning to Read and Think: *Discourse on Thinking*

It seems a reasonable question: "Does Heidegger make sense?" His etymologies disturb the scholar; his method of "argument" wrests a moan from the logician; his talk of will, releasement, region, and horizon offend the clear-headed; words often appear to be shuffled together in combinations so various that they strike even the sympathetic reader as attempted poetry or word magic. (See, for example, pp. 66–67.)[1] These difficulties and more await the reader bold enough to open even so thin a volume as *Discourse on Thinking*—one of the least imposing of Heidegger's works. But anticipating difficulty can help. It can encourage readers to be uncommonly alert; it can ready them to deal with the unexpected or unusual.

I take it that one of the reasons Heidegger wrote the *Discourse* was to invite us to think. And if we are aware of the difficulties of reading and thinking, we might fairly assume that Heidegger was aware of them, too. Indeed, we might assume he was more aware of them than most of us are. Further, if I or anyone else claim to be able to help us read Heidegger, we must *discover* some clues as to how to go about it and then pass them on. I say "discover," rather than "invent," because I believe that Heidegger himself shows us how he is to be read.

Parts of *Discourse on Thinking* do not make obvious sense, but they *do* make sense. The translation has two parts—a "Memorial Address" and a "Conversation on a Country Path about Thinking." I want to show that the book is reflexive: "Memorial Address" tells us how to read "Conversation"; it provides us with

1

pointers that help us make our way through the conversation and to think along with the scholar, scientist, and teacher whose conversation it is. I am not contending that "Memorial Address" only tells us how to read, or that "Conversation" is merely raw material for the approach. But in addition to being more, they are at least this. And that is enough for my modest task.

To show this I will cite seven passages from "Memorial Address" that act as guides to reading and thinking and indicate how they illuminate "Conversation" and help us understand not just the book, but also, since meaning is transitive, what the book is about—thinking.

> 1. Let us not fool ourselves. All of us, including those who think professionally, as it were, are often enough thought-poor; we are far too easily thought-less. Thoughtlessness is an uncanny visitor who comes and goes everywhere in today's world. For nowadays we take in everything in the quickest and cheapest way, only to forget it just as quickly, instantly. (44–45)

Is Heidegger suggesting that professors of philosophy are guilty of thoughtlessness? At the least, he is asking us to reflect on what we do and on how we do it.

To begin, we need to examine our assumptions. For example, don't we expect Heidegger to be simple; aren't we annoyed when he is not. However complex or sophisticated his arguments are, we expect him to stick to his point and lead us straightforwardly to what he has to say. We try to teach students to stick to the point, to state a thesis, then prove it. If this is to be a discourse on thinking, then what is to be made of the opaque talk of willing and non-willing, horizon and region, advancing and withdrawing? So we assume that Heidegger is about a simple task, however intricate the single theme may be; we expect him to *tell* us about thinking.

This assumption, however, is hasty. Though Heidegger does in fact tell us about thinking, his primary concern is to exhibit thinking; the "end" of the address is not so much to tell us this or that, as it is to engage us in the process of thinking.

Heidegger does not intend to satisfy our desire to understand by being told about something. He wants, in fact, to call this assumption about the nature of understanding into question insofar as it involves "what is put before us as if sheltered amid the familiar and so secured" (65).

What we take as the standard mode of thought, or even as the only legitimate mode of understanding, is characterized as logical-scientific or representational thinking. But Heidegger calls this mode of thinking into question by *exhibiting* the difficulties it results in. He shows how it *fails* as the characters (including the scientist) fail to re-present the nature of thinking. For example, the scientist, as a *persona*, admits at one point, "But at the same time, I know less and less what we are talking about. We are trying to determine the nature of thinking. . . . With the best of willing I cannot re-present to myself this nature of thinking" (62). That is, when the characters try to use logical-scientific thinking to understand thinking itself, they do not succeed. Thus, the book does not proceed straightforwardly to specify the nature of thinking; rather, it shows how such an attempt breaks down, or better, how it does not lead where the characters intended it to. If this is true, sections which appear to be superfluous because they do not directly re-present the nature of thinking indeed do not re-present it. But they are not superfluous because of that; they *exhibit* precisely that failure. (And this is not, I contend, because these passages are not good attempts at re-presentation, but because even good attempts are often inappropriate.)

But, we might object, though the characters fail, we needn't. Perhaps. Heidegger is less interested in telling readers that representational thought fails than in leading them to raise the issue, to examine it, and to consider alternative strategies. Heidegger, then, has drawn us in: we hope to get clear of our difficulties as we too *try* to represent what is going on in the conversation and try to understand the nature of thinking. But Heidegger has "warned" us that it is likely that we also shall fail with this method. At the least, then, some of the difficulties and failures in the conversation are deliberate; they manifest the limitations of logical-scientific thinking and reflexively indicate that this mode of understanding may be inappropriate for readers reading this work. If they try to use a method on "Conversation" that fails in the conversation itself, they, too, shall fail to understand the nature of thinking and the conversation.

The way that the conversation "begins" is another signal that Heidegger intends to do more than state something about thinking; it suggests that he wants to involve the reader in this task. When we join it, the conversation is already underway. In fact, it continues a discussion that has been going on for some time. (For example, the characters refer to things they have said before.) This indicates (1) that what is being discussed is not a discreet or isolated matter, but an aspect of a larger topic; (2) that the reader is asked to plunge into a conversation that has been going on who knows how long, since the time of Heraclitus?; and (3) that we might expect that the end of this particular conversation is not the end of the conversation itself. If so, our assumption that Heidegger is going to tell us about thinking is too simple; it is, in its way, thoughtless. Our assumption, or hope for a quick answer (which may even be why we chose this slight volume instead of *Being and Time* or *What Is Called Thinking?*) interferes with our understanding of what we are reading.

But Heidegger suggests that there may be another way of thinking and reading, besides the logical-scientific mode, that is not as quick, but that is more appropriate:

> 2. At times meditative thinking requires a greater effort. It demands more practice. It is in need of even more delicate care than any other genuine craft. But it must also be able to bide its time, to await as does the farmer, whether the seed will come up and ripen. (47)

Heidegger anticipates his readers' impatience. Following his metaphor, one can say that impatience over the direction that the conversation takes is as inappropriate as irritation over the time it takes a seed to germinate. The fruitful way to get at the whole work involves our overcoming our urge to get quick results by finding an assertion to hold on to, carry off, and verify. Thus, meditative thinking, the thinking perhaps appropriate to the nature of thought and to this conversation, would involve an active waiting—a possibility that emerges in clearer form near the end of the conversation:

"A patient noblemindedness . . . would be the nature of thinking" (85).

This too would make the characters' apparent dawdling and the anxiety it creates in readers understandable. For example, in the course of the conversation ideas often emerge only to be dropped or to be held off until much later, as when, toward the end, the scholar is on the verge of naming "a word which up to now seemed to be appropriate to name the nature of thinking and so of knowing," (88) but the word is held off again and again. (In fact, it was first mentioned in a previous conversation.) To return to Heidegger's metaphor, it seems that after planting, there needs to be an active "worrying" about the crop before it comes clearly into view. In fact, once the word is spoken after the delay, the scientist calls it "an excellent name for designating the nature of knowledge" since it expresses "the character of advancing and moving toward" (88). The process does not stop there, however; once it is named, the word is taken back and reinterpreted and retranslated.

The apparent delay in progress manifests a deliberate restraint, which is necessary if the thought is to come out. It may be that to read we have to restrain ourselves, to let the character of this meditative thinking, for example, emerge in its own time.

But even if "there are, then, two kinds of thinking, each justified and needed in its own way," as Heidegger claims, (46) when is meditative thinking appropriate? And why would it be appropriate in reading the conversation? A third passage offers a clue:

3. Meditative thinking need by no means be "high-flown." It is enough if we dwell on what lies close and meditate on what is closest; upon that which concerns us, each one of us, here and now; here, on this patch of home ground; now in the present hour of history. (47)

We needn't look to other texts to find out the referent of "that which concerns us here and now. Heidegger shows us by what he gives us—the nature of thinking is what concerns us . . . here and now." We should meditate on thinking. But there is something even *closer*, so close that we may not see it at first glance. Indeed, it is closer because it is between us and thinking. I refer to the book that we are reading, to the conversation *through which* we think about the nature of thinking. Thus, what is closest here and now is our reading and thinking. It is enough if we meditate on them.

If this is so, Heidegger's pointers are reflexive. If the book is about thinking, and it is, then Heidegger indicates that we need to meditate on the nature of thinking to understand it; but we also need to meditate on the conversation itself and on our own reading and thinking here and now.

Again, it is a matter of attending in a careful way to what we are already doing. Thinking and reading are already close by for us. Whether we actually understand Heidegger or try falteringly, whether we agree or not, we already see thinking and reading in one way or another. To help us meditate on thinking and reading, then, the conversation would have to keep our own assumptions and differences close. And it does. The characters—scientist, scholar, and teacher—embody the ways we might think and the sorts of things we might think about. Though this is too complex to elaborate or show conclusively here, note that the scholar typically (but not exclusively) brings the tradition to bear on the issues; he distinguishes and clarifies historical meanings of terms; he is concerned with time as continuity; he remembers. The scientist is concerned with calculative thought, with time and causality, and with spatial relations (for example, the topology of horizon and region). The teacher appears to know the path better than the others; he typically guides the conversation to deeper, surer thought (though he doesn't direct the course of the discussion). This indicates that, in addition to the re-presentational thought noted in the third passage above, several modes of thinking function heuristically in the conversation. It can be argued, then, that throughout "Conversation" the successes and failures of the characters exhibit fruitful strategies of thinking and reading their difficulties. For example, they make the same sorts of mistakes over and over and they forget insights painfully won; this may be inescapable in thinking and reading that are underway (as opposed to reported thought that is already over and distant from us, a difference that is exhibited in the tentative character of conversation). Meditative thinking, then, is also difficult to attempt or sustain, and it has limitations. This brings us to the fourth passage:

> 4. But—it is one thing to have heard and read something, that is, merely to take notice; it is another thing to understand what we have heard and read, that is, to ponder. (52)

Before Heidegger can motivate us to try to understand, he must make us take notice. We notice that we read and think, but do we understand what that is? Do we examine the ground of our reading and thinking, our facile use of words? To bend us toward such notice, he throws things in that disturb our train of thought. Most likely he disturbs us, not from thought, but into it. For example, after what appears as a breakthrough in the conversation when the *scientist* achieves meditative thinking and undertakes the important task of indicating how he did it—to clarify what happened and facilitate the attempts of others—the talk of thinking as movement on a path comes to a halt, or, at least, a rest. A shift takes place to what seems a new topic, the use of words to designate and name.

But this is not a distraction. It points out that what was noticed (that we are aware that we use language and names) was not understood. The issue has to be faced: are the thinking and reading that are going on arbitrary? Are the insights gained and held in language so much vapor? How are they justified, or how are they possible at all? Again, it would be naive to expect a quick, simple solution to this issue. What is crucial is that Heidegger has thrown us against it; he has forced us to take into account what we had been using without question. If this is so, without providing any answers to what is raised as something that has to be understood if the reading and thinking here and now are to make any sense, what may have seemed superfluous or inappropriate becomes more meaningful. Seemingly annoying and distracting passages make sense, at least in part, as means to Heidegger's "end ": they incite us to ponder reading and thinking. And their inclusion here may serve as an example. We cannot wait for someone else to reveal what we do not understand. We need to make an effort to raise such matters for ourselves.

If this is so, what appear to be obstacles may help us see more about the nature of meditative thinking. While logical-scientific thinking is getting on with its business, meditation holds its place; it examines what is being done and how it is possible. That is, as noted in "Memorial Address," we forget to examine the grounds of modern scientific thinking, for example (50). We tend to be satisfied too easily. We need to pass beyond the grasp that suffices for use, for reckoning. Such a passing is, to a large extent, what happens within the conversation in the talk about horizon and transcendence. Much of the scholarly and logical thought frustrates characters and readers alike because it does not provide clear definitions. While it is clear that talk about "horizon" and "transcendence" refers to representational thought, they are not clearly represented to us—neither in a sentence or section of the conversation, nor, I believe, in any reader's coherently and consistently worked-out definitions of all the relevant texts. Such definitions *are* worth trying, but are, in themselves, inadequate. That is, if readers do not try to represent as clearly as they can such concepts, they do not do their part—they must struggle as heroically as the characters do. But what is the meaning of the difficulty (at best) or the impossibility of a clear understanding of horizon, that is, of its clear definition and relation to other concepts? Suppose the characters or readers successfully presented a final definition; what would we have? I imagine we would not just notice it; rather, we would assume that we had understood. And I believe that Heidegger is too concerned with his readers to leave them with this impression. He could have, but he does not because he wants us to really understand. That is, he wants us to see that what we take as understanding is only noticing.

Thus, when he appears to summarize the result of the conversation about horizon, transcendence, and representational thought, he begins to push beyond it, "to suggest that in this way what lets the horizon be what it is has not yet been encountered at all" (64). Ideas which seem fragmentary, inconsistent, or confused are that way to keep us from believing that we understand when we do not (that is, when we work out a consistent definition); they incite us to see what does have to be understood and prod us to try to ponder where we would otherwise have left off, content. The conversation, then, does not pretend to give us understanding, as if that were something that could be handed over if only the characters were clearer or more decisive. At the least, the conversation aims to shatter this illusion. The conversation is concerned instead with pushing us toward understanding.

Consider, for example, whether we notice or understand the formal aspects of the conversation that is immediately before us. To begin a list of significant features that need to be understood, we must try to answer a number of questions: (1) Why are there just these three characters (scientist, scholar, and teacher)? (2) What dramatic roles does each one play, or what would a detailed analysis of each consist of? For example, how is the teacher different: does he learn the way the others do? (3) How is it that the characters change in the course of thought, so as to increasingly trust, support, and complement one another, especially when one notes the relation of "con-versation" to a change in state or mode of thinking? (4) How do we deal with the various ways in which time appears, for example, as duration and continuity? (5) Can we unravel the senses of "relation," a pervasive, crucial idea throughout "Conversation"? (6) How do the uses of nouns and verbs mirror the emphasis on process and experience, for example, in the shift from "region" to "that-which-regions" and "regioning"?

How, then, do we go about understanding? What is involved in trying to understand meditatively? Does Heidegger help readers see how to go about it? A fifth passage may once again act as a guide:

5. Meditative thinking demands of us not to cling one-sidedly to a single idea, nor to run down a one-track course of ideas. Meditative thinking demands of us that we engage ourselves with what at first sight does not go together at all. (53)

The conversation appears to abandon clear and simple thinking. The first line of the conversation sets the tone: "Toward the last you stated that the question concerning man's nature is not a question about man" (59). We are then led through, among other

concepts, willing and non-willing, acting and waiting, responsibility and letting-be, movement and rest, coming near and yet remaining distant. As if this were not difficult enough, what do these
pairs of seeming contradictions have to do with one another? Do
they simply compound the mist, and intimate obscurity as a
substitute for insight?

If we read in light the passage quoted above, we may see that
when one begins to think meditatively, the simple thread must be
rejected from the outset. That is, suppose we begin by holding, for
example, that to understand thinking we should inquire into humankind, specifically into how one wills things to be (a psychology
of representation, perhaps) and into how this is the first of a series
of events by which he grasps and uses objects. But if we begin that
way our thought is, in fact, fixed. We won't engage ourselves with
what thinking really is because we have already decided what it is
and aim only to let the idea run its course (*dis-cursis*). But Heidegger, by writing as he does, blocks such a process; he says no to it.[2]

Rather than following a simple thread, Heidegger unravels a
rope made of diverse strands. Conclusions are reversed; what is
said is undone; it's like *Waiting for Godot*. The reader endures, as the
characters do: "Again this restless to and fro between yes and no.
We are suspended as it were between the two" (75). As example,
one of many: near the end of "Conversation" the characters come
closer to their goal and yet are more distant; they have and don't
have what they seek. As they put it, "Then perhaps we can express
our experience during this conversation by saying that we are
coming near to and so at the same time remaining distant from
that-which-regions; although such remaining is, to be sure, a
returning" (86).

This is frustrating, but not merely for the reader; the characters, too, find their grasp dissolving: "Meanwhile this formulation
has proved ambiguous" (59). In the conversation, however, the
ambiguity is deliberately preserved. Multiple senses are not reduced, but are cultivated and held in tension. Thus, the reader
need not try to reduce these meanings, but to follow their elaboration. But this does not mean giving in to a hash of confused
meanings. As the scientist in the discussion continues to press for
single, clear thoughts, so must the reader; as the whole cast of

characters indicates, however, there is more to be thought than any singular sense provides. Thus, the conversation is not antiscientific: "That means you would not discard the traditional view of the nature of thinking" (63). Instead, it insists on more than scientific thought can provide. The drive toward univocal meaning is not rejected here; rather, it is one aspect yoked to others, which together generate the sense of the conversation—as the tensed meanings in a metaphor result in its plural sense.

I only note here that this yields an obvious reason why Heidegger chose a conversation and not a lecture. The form forces the reader to consider diverse ideas and approaches through the diversity of the characters.

It appears, then, that with the seemingly contradictory items Heidegger intentionally presents a fuller, though less obvious, meaning than a single thought can. In fact, *Discourse on Thinking* gives another name to this tension of diverse ideas: "releasement," (54) or "*Gelassenheit.*" This is the title of the German edition of *Discourse,* and, I believe, a central concern of the whole work. Indeed, the conversation indicates that this is the nature of thinking itself![3]

But again, the conversation does more. Beyond saying that thinking essentially involves tensed double vision, "Conversation" does what it says. The characters come to think (and think about thinking) by engaging themselves in the process of struggling through what does not seem to fit together. At another level, the book requires readers to do this, too. That is, because its form invites him to abandon single-mindedness and engage himself in the process, the book *finally* does not say what thinking is, though it *does* go some way toward doing that; it actually attempts to get readers to think what thinking is by prompting them to attempt to unify what is seemingly contradictory.

This implies that the meaning readers seek to discover in thinking, while close at hand, is neither simple nor obvious. "Memorial Address" provides another pointer here:

6. *The meaning pervading technology,* for example, *hides itself.* But if we explicitly and continuously heed the fact that such hidden meaning touches us everywhere in the world of technology, we stand at

once within the realm of that which hides itself just in approaching us. That which shows itself and at the same time withdraws is the essential trait of what we call the mystery. I call the comportment which enables us to keep open the meaning hidden in technology, *openness to the mystery*. (55)

This hint, like the others, can help us to make sense out of what may appear confused or nonsensical in "Conversation" by telling us how to read it.

This involves more than just a theoretical insight about mystery, such as the idea that thinking does not amount to a subject–object relation. Consider the meaning of thinking, which is at present hidden in "Conversation": it is hidden since it resists being sought as an object by representational thought. If the reader seeks the hidden meaning of thinking (and, reflexively, the meaning of "Conversation"), he will "seek to clarify how far this is possible, or perhaps even necessary" (58).

To begin, we recognize that looking for the meaning of thinking as an object might involve trying to locate it. This touches one of the reasons we are bothered by this book: we may be irritated because we cannot find where the meaning of thinking, or anything else, is given or, assuming it is not our fault, because the meaning isn't here to be found. That is precisely the point. The meaning is not located between the covers of the book. Yet it is near; it pervades the whole book from beginning to end. That is, the meaning of thinking is present in the process of the conversation and in the process of meditative reading. We cannot look for meaning as for an object, then, and so should not expect to locate any answers *in* this book; rather, the meaning is there all along and the book may provide the time for us to engage in the process of discovery by interpretation—interpretation guided by the course of the conversation itself.

The process of thinking does not amount to a defining, nor is its meaning found *in* any definition. That is, it does not become a conclusion which we might seize and record, leaving behind what came before.

Like the reader, the characters labor to describe. And as in the passage below, they fail, exhibiting another aspect of how we have access to meaning:

Scientist:	Then we can't really describe what we have named?
Teacher:	No. Any description would reify it.
Scholar:	Nevertheless it lets itself be named, and being named it can be thought about. (67)

We think, then, not by objectifying, defining, or describing (though thinking involves these activities and goes beyond them): we think by letting ourselves into the meaning, which hides itself. And we do this by getting underway, trying to understand what we notice by engaging ourselves with what does not ordinarily seem to go together, by practicing the approaches hinted at in passages four and five above. That is, we think, or find meaning, in and through the process already presented.

The characters in "Conversation" begin as best they can; they struggle with representational thought and overcome it, improving in meditative thinking as they go on. "The occasion which" leads to the right sort of comportment to meaning "was more the course of the conversation than the representation of the specific object we spoke about" (69). Again, the point is reflexive: readers will gain the meaning not so much through what is specifically said at any point, but by letting themselves struggle with the conversation as it takes its own course. The process involves a struggle with each word as it comes: "We can hardly come to releasement more fittingly than through an occasion of letting ourselves in" (69). Just as the representational thinking of the characters changes in the process of releasement in the conversation, so the "silent course of this conversation that moves us" (70) is our occasion to let ourselves into thinking.

For a specific example of how this approach works we might consider how to make sense out of the section at the end of "Conversation" that deals with Heraclitus's word. The section seems as odd as any, as overwrought. While waiting and speaking of the nature of thinking in regard to the nearness of distance, the scholar hints at what might be a resolution: "Probably this can no longer be said in a single word. Still I know a word which up to now seemed to me appropriate to name the nature of thinking and so of knowing" (87). And just as an insight seems near, it recedes: the conversation goes on for a page and a half as the scholar talks mysteriously about his thought, before he says the word, *Angchiba-sie*. And even after the word is heard, after Heraclitus's word is given, it is far off, for the traditional interpretation indicates that it tells of the nature of modern scientific thought, not meditative thinking at all. But during the course of the conversation, the interpretation changes to allow the truth to come out another page and a half later. The entire section indicates that while what "is spoken" does not change, what "is heard" does change in the course of conversation: Heraclitus's word remains as near and as far as it has been for 2,500 years, but we can come to think it and understand its meaning. And the activity of the three pages, indeed the whole conversation, is indispensible to this interpretation; indeed it *is* the interpretation itself. That is, by actively waiting and working through the conversation, the characters are, and the reader may be, able to uncover the meaning—to creatively discover the meaning which is there, but which was as hidden and access-able as Heraclitus's word: "Such hidden meaning touches us everywhere" (55).

Whether there is meaning, then, is not the issue. What is important is the *way* the meaning is presented and *how* we must respond to discover it. Thus a seventh hint for the reader:

> 7. Perhaps today's memorial celebration will prompt us toward releasement toward things and openness to mystery. Both flour-ish only through persistent, courageous thinking. If we respond to the prompting . . . (55 and 58)

Consider how "Conversation" does what *Discourse* says: the conversation *"persists"* or "goes on" in several ways even in the last words. The final section exhibits a movement around, both in regard to *Discourse* itself and reality. "Conversation" closes as the threesome *returns* to the town, the site of their being called to conversation, of Heidegger's call home to commemorate the com-poser, and of the composer's calling. The closure then is a return, well matched with the final words "from whence we are called" (90).

The end of "Conversation" moves us back to origins. Again, we learn from the placement of Heraclitus's waiting words at the end of "Conversation." We find a key in what was there all along, indeed, in what was near for the longest time. The movement of thinking, then, moves around to the origin of our thinking.

The end of "Conversation" also takes us back to *its* beginning: the penultimate line treats human nature, as did the first line. But further, the end returns us to the beginning of the book. In fact, the end of "Conversation" seems odd, even in light of the rest of the book. The conversation apparently ends with the scholar's calm sentence which "summarizes" and rounds off their new understanding: "the word could rather, so it seems to me now, be the name for our walk today along this country path" (89).

But they go on for a final page, growing more poetic. They rhapsodize in harmony as they celebrate their insight. This praise of meditative thinking is a thanking. It echoes the beginning of "Memorial Address" which begins: "Let my first public word in my home town be a word of thanks" (43). What was thinking all along, begins and ends in thanking—a thinking that responds to a calling. (Notice all in "Conversation" that has to do with thinking as return, homecoming, and thanking.)

The formal structure of the *Discourse* is rounded off here. To simplify, it could be illustrated thus:

"Memorial Address"		"Conversation"
1	2	1 and 2
thanking	human nature and meditative thinking	thanking, thinking, and human nature

But its formal closure does not result in a hermetic verbal creation: rather, it opens out beyond the realm where humans create words and their meanings. Indeed, it takes us beyond asking questions such as which pole (man or that-which-regions) comes to which. Thus, the end of "Conversation" (for example, the dense section, "He is released to it in his being insofar as he originally belongs to it. He belongs to it insofar as he is *appropriated* initially to that-which-regions and indeed, though this itself." (73 ff.) leads us to try to understand together the nature of humankind and that which appropriates us.

If all this is so, the work is complex and in its way "complete." It reposes. And yet, and precisely because of this, the word *complete* rings out to be heard, read, and elaborated as we continue the conversation. As the seventh passage indicates, meditative thinking involves prompting.

In fact, prompting lies at the heart of *Discourse*. In "Memorial Address," Heidegger responds to the prompting of Conradin Kreutzer by "thinking of the origin of his work, the life-giving powers of Heuberg homeland" (56). This, in turn, leads to "Conversation": the conversation on a country path about thinking is a response to "Memorial Address." The country path is the extension of "Feldweg" alluded to at the start of "Memorial Address." The conversation picks up where the address leaves off, with the themes of the nature of man and of meditative thinking. Just as "Memorial Address" has a public, memorial setting which calls attention to and emphasizes man and society, "Conversation" is social, too. It is social in two different ways. First, there is a real response to the prompting because it is a conversation rather than an address to an audience: several people persist in thinking together. But while more social in this sense, it is also withdrawn from the town, from the social issue of technology, for example. While human nature is still emphasized, then, and the role of individuals enhanced, neither appears primarily in a social setting, but in a "cosmic" context, as it were. At the least, the surrounding countryside is the setting for society and its problems. Thus, "Memorial Address," in which Heidegger responds to Kreutzer, "strikes new roots" (57) in "Conversation." But there is more, for the reader is drawn in: he is asked to respond to Heidegger. This provides further proof that the address provides hints to the reader; as Heidegger responds in "Memorial Address," the reader might well respond to "Conversation."

The conversation, and the reader's thinking contribute to the

project: "The issue is the saving of man's essential nature. Therefore, the issue is keeping meditative thinking alive"(56).

"But once meditative thinking awakens, it must be at work
unceasingly and on every last occasion—hence, also, here and now
at this commemoration" (53). The reader is called on to begin to do
his part, to respond by thinking properly. And he does that by
reading properly.

If meditative thinking must go on, we become clearer about
why Heidegger refuses to tell us something simple that we can
easily understand and just as easily forget. He is trying to teach us
an art because we are the ones who must now respond. Hence the
conversation with all its devices aims at showing us the art and how
to practice it; hence follow all the indirect means he uses to get us to
do it. He recruits and trains the reader: we either declare the book
nonsense and pass on or we stop and learn how to think meditatively. "Conversation" then does not stop or conclude; rather, it
persists.

Recall the section dealing with Heraclitus's word. It was first
seen to mean "going toward," but was reinterpreted to mean
"moving-into-nearness" (88–89). That is what "Conversation"
itself does by giving readers insight into what thinking is and what
it prompts them to do by reflexively showing them how to understand and pursue thinking.

CHAPTER TWO

Heidegger's Thinking and Language Concerning Saying: "A Dialogue on Language"

Heidegger's "A Dialogue on Language" appears to be a laby-rinth: the discussion leads readers into a tangle of thoughts in which they become lost. Consider the first ten pages. First there is a conversation about a Count Kuki, an acquaintance of the speakers. The next section is harder, since it is more philosophical: it questions the application of European aesthetics and language to Japanese art and experience. Still, enough is enough. Some lines of "A Dialogue on Language" disorient us because, as in the passage below, their trail vanishes before our eyes:

Inquirer:	Without this theological background I should never have come upon the path of thinking. But origin always comes to meet us from the future.
Japanese:	If the two can call to each other, and reflection makes its home within that calling . . .
Inquirer:	and thus becomes true presence. (10)[1]

How can one make sense of such talk? How does it fit in with the parts of the dialogue that make more obvious sense—if, indeed, it does fit in? Worst of all is the suspicion this throws on the rest of the dialogue. Can we trust the meaning and outcome of anything here when such sections, which become more frequent, appear incoherent?

I want to examine the difficulties of the dialogue (some of which are only apparent, some of which are deliberate) to show

how "A Dialogue on Language" itself results from three distinct sub-dialogues, all going on at once within it; to show how these three dialogues work against and with one another to form a unified work; and to show what the final complex meaning is and how it effects the reader.

1. A REPORT

The dialogue immediately draws the reader in by unfolding the story of Heidegger's early thinking and its relation with East Asian thought. This account of part of Heidegger's development appeals to the reader's natural interest in biographical and historical information. It is a choice moment: we are made privy to what really happened. Our curiosity about familiar and often charming details would be motive enough to pursue the report; but the fact that these incidents really *are* important in the history of Western thought and that they may help us to understand Heidegger's thought, provides a more important, intellectually substantial, incentive.

In fact, the dialogue reports a report. A Japanese man and Heidegger (ostensively in the role of inquirer) meet to discuss events in Heidegger's intellectual career and his discussions with Count Kuki. But, since the complex events often involved many other thinkers and took place some thirty years before, no one person has the whole story. Accordingly, in order to fill in and clarify matters, the Japanese man reports what he and others in Japan were told by Kuki, and in turn, Heidegger himself appears as the chief witness of past events. The story is pieced together only gradually.

The Japanese man begins by recalling their mutual friend, Count Kuki, who had studied with Heidegger for several years. Because Heidegger has fond memories of Kuki, who died prematurely, he is pleased to have photographs of the grave and the grove in which it lies. The grove, part of a twelfth-century temple garden in Kyoto established for meditation, is seen to be a fitting place for Count Kuki because he persistently reflected on "*Iki*" and, after his return from Europe, lectured on the aesthetics of Japanese art. In those lectures, he used European concepts of aesthetics concepts to identify what was of concern, since the Japanese thought their language was incapable of properly representing aesthetic objects.

In fact, Heidegger adds, he and Kuki often had discussed the propriety of the East Asian use of European conceptual systems. For example, they questioned whether aesthetics, which grows out of European philosophy, might remain finally alien to East Asian thinking and, in turn, whether the East Asian might be led astray by European concepts.

But this possible impropriety involved them even as they reflected on it. Though he had not explicitly discussed it with Kuki, Heidegger had already noted the dangers inherent in their attempted encounters, even in their informal discussions at Heidegger's home, where Count Kuki was not silent as he was in formal seminars.

Heidegger noted, for example, that even though he was cut off from understanding *Iki* because he did not know Japanese, the real danger was not due to an inability to use language, for Kuki was fluent in several European languages. Rather, the danger stemmed precisely from correctly translating the Japanese subject matter into a European language, because then the language of the dialogue falsified that subject matter and destroyed the possibility of articulating its nature.

Despite these obstacles, the Japanese scholar has ventured to come to Germany because of Kuki's apparent success at dialogue with Heidegger, a success evidenced by Kuki's constant reference, in workshops at Kyoto University, to those dialogues. In fact, Count Kuki himself had been prompted to work with Heidegger even before *Being and Time* had been published because several Japanese professors were already acquainted with Heidegger. After World War I, these Japanese professors, including the revered Tanabe, went to Freiburg to study phenomenology with Husserl, when Husserl's assistant, Heidegger, weekly discussed Husserl's *Logical Investigations* with them. (By that time Husserl no longer regarded the work as an introduction to phenomenology. And it was because phenomenology presented the possibility of saying what he wanted to, that six years later Heidegger dedicated *Being and Time* to Husserl.) At that same time, in 1921, the Japanese professors also attended a class that Heidegger gave titled "Expression and Appearance." It was the transcript of this course, which they took back to Japan, that later influenced Kuki to study with Heidegger in Marburg. Indeed, as reported by the Japanese professors and confirmed by Heidegger, the questions of language and Being already were important to him.

But, Heidegger adds, because the relationships were unclear at the time, the themes of language and Being remained in the background, as did those of poetry and art, though the poetry of Hölderlin and Trakl was constantly before him. As for his initial impulse to philosophy and the book he inscribed "my first guide through Greek philosophy in my *Gymnasium* days," Heidegger tells us:

> And still earlier, during my last years in the *Gymnasium*—to give a date, in the summer of 1907—I came up against the question of Being, in the dissertation of Husserl's teacher Franz Brentano. Its title is "On the manifold meaning of being according to Aristotle"; it dates from 1862. The book came to me as a gift from my fatherly friend and fellow Swabian, Dr. Conrad Grober, later to become archbishop of Freiburg. Then he was vicar of Trinity Church in Constance. (7)

Thus, though he was concerned with the themes of language and Being from the start, in retrospect Heidegger adds that the fundamental flaw of his *Being and Time* may be that he spoke of Being too soon. He was more cautious concerning language: it was seven years after the appearance of *Being and Time* and a full twenty years after his doctoral dissertation that he raised the question of language in class and at the same time made public his interpretation of Hölderlin's hymns. Though he offered a lecture series in the summer of 1934 on logic, he wasn't able to articulate his thought for another ten years. Interestingly, some of these lectures on Hölderlin were later translated from the German by the same Japanese scholar Heidegger is speaking with in this dialogue. Thus, the Japanese scholar, who also has translated several of Kleist's plays, directly knows both Heidegger's work and Kuki's.

Heidegger, unsatisfied with the explanation of Kuki's interest in him, pursues the reason for the special attention which the Japanese professors, and especially Kuki, gave to the transcript of that particular course, "Expression and Appearance." According to Kuki's explanations, as reported by the Japanese, the interest had to do with "hermeneutics" and "hermeneutic," words which Heidegger remembers initially using in a later course, in the summer of 1927, when he began the first drafts of *Being and Time*.

What Heidegger meant by *hermeneutics* obviously needs elaboration and perhaps correction.

Although Heidegger notes that the answer to why he used the term "hermeneutic" is given in the introduction to *Being and Time* (section 7c, pp. 58 ff.),[2] he goes on to say that originally he became familiar with the term in the course of his theological studies, particularly in his work concerning the relation between the word of Holy Scripture and theological-speculative thought. In fact, his theological background was crucial to his path of thinking. Later, he recognized that same source in the work of Wilhelm Dilthey and Schleiermacher.

To further clarify Heidegger's specific use of the term and its interest to Kuki, the Japanese scholar wonders whether Heidegger uses "hermeneutic" in a broad sense to indicate the theory and methodology of interpretation in general, including that of art. Actually, Heidegger explains:

> In *Being and Time*, the term "hermeneutics" is used in a *still* broader sense, "broader" here meaning, however, not the mere extension of the same meaning over a still larger area of application. . . . In *Being and Time*, hermeneutics means neither the theory of the art of interpretation nor interpretation itself, but rather the attempt first of all to define the nature of interpretation on hermeneutic grounds. (11)

Thus, the connection between Kuki's work and Heidegger's emerges: the Japanese wanted a means to "give a higher clarity to what endows [their] art and poetry with their nature," that is, to *Iki*; what Heidegger "meant to say with hermeneutics must somehow have illuminated *Iki* more brightly for Count Kuki" (13). Even at that time, Heidegger had sensed as much, though he had been unable to follow Kuki's insights because "the language of the dialogue was European; but what was to be experienced and to be thought was the East Asian nature of Japanese art"(13).

Heidegger was aware of their procrustian treatment of the East Asian experience because of "the manner in which Kuki explained the basic word *Iki*. He spoke of sensuous radiance through whose lively delight there breaks the radiance of something suprasensuous"(14). This apparent distinction between a sensuous and suprasensuous world, which seems to correspond to the basic distinction of Western metaphysics, enables Heidegger to more fully "understand how great the temptation was for Kuki to define *Iki* with the help of European aesthetics, that is as [Heidegger] pointed out, define it metaphysically" (14).

But, it was not primarily the Japanese who had difficulty understanding Heidegger's ideas. In fact, despite inherent difficulties, the Japanese appreciated Heidegger's thinking about Being and nothingness in a way that the metaphysically oriented Europeans did (or could) not. As the Japanese scholar says, "To us, emptiness is the loftiest name for what you mean to say with the word 'Being'" (19).

Just as it was dangerous for Kuki to interpret *Iki* metaphysically, so Heidegger's use in the lecture "What is Metaphysics?" of the name "Being," which belongs, after all to the patrimony of the language of metaphysics," (19) was the occasion for great confusion. For example, Europeans mistakenly interpreted Heidegger's treatment of Nothingness as nihilistic.

The attempt at mutual understanding leads them to discuss more fully that crucial lecture series of the twenties, "Expression and Appearance." Heidegger notes that, actually, the course was rather controversial and that, at that early stage of his career, he was unclear himself. It would seem that the use of the pair of terms, "expression and appearance" indicated the metaphysical sphere even if, for example, he did not use "expression" in "the narrow sense of sensuous appearance" (38), to refer to "phonetics and the written forms of words, which are generally conceived to constitute the expressive character of language" (35). Here, he says, "language, as sense that is sounded and written, is in itself suprasensuous, something that constantly transcends the merely sensible. So understood, language is in itself metaphysical" (35).

But such an account is too simple. Heidegger would have used the term "expression" not only because he thought of language with metaphysical distinctions, but because he thought the reverse also is true: language appears in metaphysical guise only where it is already thought by means of experience, which refers back to the "I,"as in Dilthey's *Erlebnis*. And, just as "expression," as the "utterance of something internal, . . . refers to the subjective," the contrasting term, "appearance," "names the objective" since, following Kant's usage, "appearances are the objects of experience" (36). Actually, the use of these terms did not commit Heidegger to either the metaphysical sphere or the subject/object relation. At the time, he asserts, it was just this thinking of language within the circle of metaphysics and expression and appearance which he tried to leave behind by calling into question the guiding notions themselves.

Despite the problems of the early lectures, the Japanese evidently did understand Heidegger's efforts to recover original questions. In fact, they often dwelt on the question that Heidegger put to Tanabe—"why it was that we Japanese did not call back to mind the venerable beginnings of our own thinking, instead of chasing ever more greedily after the latest news in European philosophy."

Curiously, this information results in a new puzzle. Since, as just explained, Heidegger moved beyond metaphysics and the aesthetics grounded in it, and since Japanese thought apparently was closely related to Heidegger's, how could Count Kuki, who seems to have grasped all this unusually well, have expected Heidegger's thought to help in aesthetic problems? Heidegger suggests a solution, identical to that just reached to explain his own use of seemingly traditional metaphysical terms. Like Heidegger himself, Kuki "used the European rubric 'aesthetics,' but what he thought and searched for was something else . . . *Iki*" (42).

Thus, the discussion reports what both Heidegger and Kuki thought in order to get a truer account of what they meant and were attempting. Moreover, this clarification, which aims to transform versions of what they apparently said into an accurate story of what they really meant, indicates that their paths were parallel.

But "A Dialogue on Language" does not just report what Heidegger and Count Kuki said and thought. The discussion which unfolds between them in the context of an already given past is articulated in a style which exhibits this "unfolding between, in the midst of." The very form of the account replicates the story it attempts to clarify: both "unfold."

Consider the mode of language and its corresponding purpose: the discussion moves within the language of report which aims at accurate correction; we hear inquirer and witness. The Japanese scholar says, "What matters to me is to hear from your own lips an—if I may say so—authentic explanation." (11) Heidegger modestly relies, "I will be glad to do as you ask. Only do not expect too much." (11) Because the Japanese scholar believes Heidegger is "mistaken" (34), Heidegger "will gladly add a few remarks, to dispell the illusion," saying "it may indeed have looked that way. In fact, however . . . quite the reverse" (9). The revisions also expand to deal with the confusions of Heidegger's critics (19–20).

Testimony by a credible participant in the intellectual events is sorely needed because even when much of what Heidegger thought was, by his own admission, "veiled and inaccessable" (11), "flawed" (7), "the occasion for very great confusion" (19), "most imperfect" (6), and the result of "only an obscure if not confused intimation. Such youthful capers easily lead to doing injustice" (35); "much had to remain unclear in those lectures" (36).

To complicate matters, neither Heidegger nor Kuki were able to fully understand one another's ideas. Heidegger had only a distant inkling of what Kuki meant by *Iki* and "never could follow him in his insights" (13). Nor did Kuki succeed in explaining Heidegger's ideas satisfactorily (9). As a result, layers of misunderstanding built up.

But the dialogue does not merely utilize language appropriate for a report; it also unfolds a giving of accounts in a fuller way. That is, the dialogue moves toward a finally correct version of events and meaning by elaborating two major alternatives, and this double *structure* develops and relates details at several levels of complexity.

That the meeting of East and West on an apparently "mu-tual" concern can succeed or fail is posited implicitly by the two alternative manners of encounter which appear in the dialogue, one of which could guarantee credibility and historical accuracy, the other of which would falsify and destroy those projects. One alternative appears in language characterized by calm and re-straint; the other by haste and threat.

Consider the ominous alternative which the dialogue presents as the speakers discuss the normal course of events surrounding the meeting of East and West. Here Europe appears as rich and powerful, while Japan, needing help, is bent before Western power. The weaker Japanese "have to call on European aesthetics to aid us . . . because since the encounter with European thinking, there has come to light certain incapacity in our language" (2): the Western "technical world sweeps" the East Asian "along," but that does not yield a true encounter (3).

The whole enterprise is cast in terms of danger and violence: "But I have a constant sense of a danger which Count Kuki, too, could obviously not overcome," says the Japanese scholar. "Yet a far greater danger threatens. It concerns both of us; it is all the more menacing just by being more inconspicuous" (3). And Heidegger replies, "Now I am beginning to understand better where you smell the danger. The language of the dialogue con-stantly destroyed the possibility of saying what the dialogue was about," (5) "even though the danger remains" (8).

It appears that in the inescapable encounter (2, 3), language itself prevents dialogue (13) and forces the Eastern experience into European terms (14); it is the very power of Western thinking with its metaphysical distinctions which is "the source of that danger of which we spoke" (14). This conflict is not accidental or avoidable. Rather, "the confusion that has arisen must be endured. Indeed, perhaps for long, and perhaps only in this way, that we painstak-ingly labor to unravel it" (20, 21).

In sharp contrast to this encounter based on metaphysics and its resultant technological power, the dialogue unfolds an alternate manner of encounter that is beyond exploitation and command. Here there is lively movement. The conversation recounts that the exciting dialogue between Heidegger and Kuki was like a "spontaneous game" (4). The individuals' experiences are congruent. Kuki's thought involved "sensuous radiance" and "lively delight" (14); while translating, the Japanese scholar was overcome by "the German language" as if by a "waterfall" (24); in his course, Heidegger experienced the "quickening" of the "attempt to walk a path," (6) he attempted to "leap" beyond "the predominant circle of ideas" and the "well-worn tracks of traditional thinking" (36).

But this exuberance is wedded to restrained deliberation: Heidegger "kept silent for twelve years" (6) about the theme of language and Being, which, as a result, stayed "in the background" between his dissertation and the even later publication of *Being and Time* (7, 8). Unlike language that functions as a tool in the struggle for subjective power, Heidegger's language, congruent with restrained insight, is not at all used "willfully" (11). His position is presented as preferable to the distorting alternative, yet it is properly modest, as befits one testifying on his own behalf.

These two alternative manners of encounter are embodied by two distinct sorts of characters in the dialogue. One group, notably including Heidegger's critics, speaks or acts destructively in the hasty, illusory, fruitless manner of the violent encounter. This faceless group includes, for example, those who claimed that Heidegger's talk of "overcoming metaphysics" implies a destruction" or a "denial of metaphysics" and a "childish presumption and a demeaning of history" (20, cf. 9, 19).

In clear contrast, the dialogue's second cast is composed of familiar individuals and fondly presents characters whose modest, complementary natures correspond to the positive mode of encounter, which associates them with the Japanese, Count Kuki, and Heidegger.

Here we have the cozy circle of pupils and teachers, friends and family. Even a brief sketch of the characters indicates their close relationships. We know that the central figures, Kuki and Heidegger, were close acquaintances because, for example, their private dialogues at Heidegger's house were spontaneous games at which Kuki's wife wore festive garments (4). Kuki, who died early, now has a lasting place in Heidegger's memory; Kuki's Japanese teacher, Nishida, worked for a year on the epitaph, his "supreme tribute to his pupil" (1). The circle is expanded: Kuki, Heidegger, and Nishida are embraced by the thoughts of the present Japanese dialogue partner and his friends and, thereby, by the tradition of the twelfth-century priest Honen. The present Japanese scholar's "visit is especially welcome" (8) because he already has translated some of Kleist's plays and several of Heidegger's works, including his Hölderlin lectures. And recall the old professional relationships and friendships between the Japanese scholar's "compatriots" (5), including Tanabe, Husserl, and Heidegger.[3] Further, Heidegger's thinking is connected through the gift from Archbishop Grober, "my fatherly friend and fellow Swabian," (7) to Husserl's teacher Brentano. From Brentano's work on Aristotle, paths lead to Duns Scotus, biblical studies, Dilthey, and Schleiermacher. In sum, the dialogue describes a close group within venerable traditions and presents Heidegger and his Japanese partner in a positive, flourishing encounter.

Further, this intimate group of characters operates within domestic scenes appropriate to their calm task. The dialogue opens with an evocation of the grove that holds Kuki's grave, a grove established in the twelfth century in the temple garden of the then imperial city of Kyoto (1). This initial reference to a dignified, ancient site establishes the next setting, Heidegger's house, as a place for a parallel, secular reflection (4). In turn, this leads us to another, broader scene, the region of language itself (4), and specifically to "Language, the House of Being" (5). Thus, we have the reliably homely as a setting respectively for the fond memory of Kuki, for the earlier discussions between Kuki and Heidegger, and for the present dialogue on language.

Heidegger was trying to fit phenomenology "back into the place that is properly its own within Western philosophy" (9), and to bring "metaphysics back within its own limits" (20). The latter task is a common one, joining Freiburg and Kyoto—though it raises further, similar issues. In the elaboration of the story, the attempt to arrive at a correct version depends on the reliability of the witnesses. Accordingly, the witnesses are presented as familial and eminently honorable, and they gain further reliability from the homely, trustworthy scenes.

The success of the present conversation hinges not only whether there can be a "dialogue from house to house," but on two specific issues: whether Europeans "dwell in an entirely different house than East Asian man" (5) and whether the Japanese partner can follow Heidegger's thought on hermeneutics, since the Japanese is not "at home" in theology (itself the site of hermeneutics), though Heidegger is (10).

Despite difficulties, we would expect that the prospect of success would be great for two members of such a convivial tradition, in such an exemplary setting, modestly aiming at a correct report. Indeed, the "prospect that attracted Kuki" (42) may now be handled more successfully both by the present Japanese interlocutor than it was by his earlier compatriots because, as Heidegger says, he has a "keener ear for the questions that I addressed to your compatriots almost thirty-five years ago" (8) and by Heidegger himself because by his own admission, "even though the danger remains that is necessarily implied in our using the German language for our dialogue, I believe that I have meanwhile learned a little more, so that now I can ask questions better than several decades ago" (8). In fact, in the course of their report of events and ideas, they do understand the past better; for example, things become clearer which before were merely surmised (24).

Now all these facets of the dialogue are congruent with one another and with what the dialogue says. The language of this report, which aims to correct the story of the past, is distinguished from falsifying and hasty talk by its calm, yet joyful restraint and its prudent attention to the inherent dangers of the conversation. The dialogue establishes a complex, value-laden identification: the Japanese interlocutor and Heidegger belong to a warm tradition of kindly teachers and friends and converse in the shelter of a series of domestic sites with an inevitably bright prospect. Not only does this style of differentiation and identification fill in what the report says but, and at the same time, means to persuade us that the report is authentic. That is, the identifications posit that the discussion between Heidegger and his Japanese partner is itself an accurate account by witnesses of the right sort of character—calm and of impeccable pedigree. Eschewing misunderstanding and dominance, they successfully engage one another and the past, thereby achieving the proper encounter of East and West. Thus, by means of its stylistic devices, the dialogue is presented in the image of and as the guarantee of the report it gives.

There are further congruencies between structure and content. For example, the reporting is arranged in a sequential "swing back and forth." The account concerning Heidegger, Kuki, and their work evolves as the discussion moves back and forth between Heidegger's and the Japanese's information and interpretation. The dialogue swings back and forth between past and present, East and West, and from the East's wild chase after the West to a proper translation of the Western into the Eastern. The principals also move back and forth in their roles: Heidegger is the inquirer when he asks the Japanese interlocutor about Kuki's thought on *Iki* and about why "Expression and Appearance" was important for that thought; then the Japanese is the inquirer when he asks Heidegger about hermeneutics. To understand Kuki and what happened between Heidegger and Kuki, we need Heidegger; to understand Heidegger we need the Japanese interlocutor, and so on, back and forth. Thus, the dialogue not only reports and clarifies what went on earlier; in addition, its structure witnesses the account which it gives.

But there is a unity of form and content at yet a deeper level. What we call content is in fact an abstraction of the whole. Here, in abstract, we find that the discussion tells us that and how hermeneutics and the lecture on "Expression and Appearance" unfolded from the Western tradition of theology and metaphysics into Heidegger's work. In a parallel movement, hermeneutics and the lecture also unfolded the nature of *Iki* for Count Kuki. The report itself witnesses the process of tradition unfolding by way of positive, helpful encounter and translation.

Formally, to abstract from the whole in another way, the work itself unfolds. There appear to be eleven major moments in the dialogue. Of course, these might be construed differently, into seven or thirteen; but while the precise number is important, it is not as crucial as the fact that such an unfolding, in phases, is going on. The relation of the particular incidents would remain largely unaffected by cutting at different joints (and one might even hope that insight into their relationships would be enhanced by finer discriminations). Consider, in sequence, the incidents which unfolded as the story was told:

1.   Kuki's work with *Iki* and aesthetics
   2.   The question of language differences and the encounter between East and West, between the Japanese partner and Heidegger
      3.   Heidegger's work on "Expression and Appearance"
         4.   The Japanese partner's translation of Heidegger's works
           5.   Heidegger's thought on hermeneutics
             6.   Kuki's ideas on *Iki*
           7.   Heidegger's thought in "What is Metaphysics?"
        8.   The Japanese partner's translation of Heidegger's works
      9.   Heidegger's work on "Expression and Appearance"
   10.   The question of the Japanese relation to the West
11.   Kuki's thought on *Iki*

Clearly these are symmetrical: the last five repeat the first five in reverse order; the sixth (Kuki on *Iki*) is the central point and corresponds to the beginning and end. I would not insist on this as *the* symmetry of the structure. In fact, several others present themselves immediately. Note just one of the obvious ones. If we abbreviate Kuki's thought as *a*, the mutual encounter or translation of the Japanese and Heidegger as *b*, and Heidegger's thought as *c*, we have the symmetrical pattern: *a,b,c,b,c,a,c,b,c,b,a*. Though, as noted, different structural symmetries would emerge depending on our discriminations of particular events, the major point, which would seem to remain constant through any variation, is that the structure does not merely posit ideas in strata; rather, it gracefully unfolds the story. Again, calm and gracious movement unfolds.

Moreover, formally Kuki's thought is at the beginning, center, and end; nested within these parameters is the encounter of East and West, of the Japanese and Heidegger. Within that we find the work of Heidegger and the Japanese interlocutor themselves. The form of the discussion, then, exhibits that the past ideas and events, which are the subject matter reported between Heidegger and the Japanese, nonetheless already contain Heidegger and his Japanese partner. Structurally, Heidegger and the Japanese appear as already within, as part of, what goes on between them. And this structural truth fuses with what the account explicitly says. For example, structure and statement coincide in their report of Heidegger's and Kuki's use of "hermeneutics" which *presupposes* a relation between them and the facts of the matter. Formally, the work does what, as a report, it tells. Its structure, in the largest sense, is an image of the truth it means to present. The outcome of all this is a truth greater than that of any, or all, of the specific incidents that which emerges out of them. The structural report shows that while Heidegger and the Japanese have past ideas and events between them as subject matter and how they have come to share these ideas, the two figures actually already move within it; what they unfold is already presupposed. To repeat the truth which the whole witnesses, *they already are within what they have between them.*

The effect of all this on the reader is subtle, yet powerful. It *satisfies.* Both the correctness of the report itself and the emergent truth about encounter with the past sustain and finally fulfill the reader's interest. Further, because the details are crafted so as to cohere, the work leads the reader through a resolved, yet dynamic pattern. Movement through it results in understanding and pleasure; participation in its completion yields satisfaction.

Even so, the work continues to make demands on attentive readers. For example, though its form aims to guarantee its veracity, insofar as unbiased testimony is crucial to establish the truth of the story, many points still require historical, scholarly investigation.[4]

In addition, and less obviously, readers need to explore the assumption on which the report hinges, that the speaker in the dialogue who is called "Inquirer" is actually Heidegger. We must question the assumption simply to avoid being naive about the report's credibility and, more crucially, to avoid seriously misunderstanding the dialogue by assuming that one dramatic character or voice in a complex work speaks directly for the author of the whole—a point long familiar to literary critics.

Historical and biographical data are used one way in a courtroom or in a straightforward biography, and in quite other ways in a literary fiction. How is it used in this philosophical composition? Precisely what use such information has in "A Dialogue on Language" and how it should be understood is neither obvious nor settled in the work itself. Rather, these questions are *raised* seriously by this facet of the dialogue. (The effect of T.S. Eliot's notes to the "Wasteland" and Spurgeon's notorious biography of Shakespeare remind us of the importance of the issue.) As a result, the reader finds himself already contained within a puzzle which he needs to solve in order to understand what apparently are statements about the past, and, finally in order to encounter and understand the dialogue as a whole and Heidegger himself. For clearly, this complex use of the historical surely is deliberate on the part of such a careful composer as Heidegger.

However, even if readers are satisfied with the accuracy with which the story is fitted together and interpreted, insofar as they allow the thoughts about *Iki* or hermeneutics to be reported and, as a transcript, thereby relegated to the past, readers fall prey to the danger of the false encounter they have so often been warned against. Here the report will be merely a source of booty for the violent to bear away. Thoughtful readers will give up merely idle curiosity and greed for quick answers and, instead, will attempt to understand what *Iki* and hermeneutics really are. That is, the dimension of dialogue that historically corrects will provide the motive for understanding the ideas themselves, which still bear on the present and into the future.

By exhibiting itself as only moderately important and interesting, once it has successfully engaged the reader, the report points beyond itself. It beckons readers in and then orients them so that they can see what is really important for the Japanese and the inquirer; that is, that they both function as inquirers and thinkers who *do* work to ask, understand, and answer seminal questions.

Further, "A Dialogue on Language" expands the role of inquirer to involve readers. The rich exchange of thought between the two primary inquirers opens the role to readers; indeed, it invites them to participate in the dialogue by thinking along. More than that, beyond providing an opportunity to merely follow the thinking, it challenges them to think through what the two speakers think together. The dialogue is appealing on this level because it does draw readers into the important matters at hand, encouraging each to join in the process of puzzling issues out as a third partner in the dialogue.

In short, from the first level, a second emerges: what the Japanese and Heideggerian inquirers think. As "A Dialogue on Language" moves from reporting to thinking, readers must move too, to think the interplay of what the speakers have to say.

2. A THINKING

The interplay of thought between the inquirer and his Japanese partner has two major movements, each of which has three minor movements. In the course of these six phases of their thinking, each speaker prompts the other to think his own thought more deeply; each responds to that prompting as best he can.

Here the Japanese interlocutor and the inquirer attempt a genuine encounter, a far more difficult task than recounting and clarifying the meaning of past events and thoughts. They begin by raising as what they now must think the question of what *Iki* and aesthetics mean; at least this much must be understood if they are to achieve a thoughtful relation. It appears that East and West say the same thing each in his own way:

| Japanese: | We say *Iro*, that is, color, and say *Ku*, that is, emptiness, the open, the sky. |
| Inquirer: | This seems to correspond exactly to what Western, that is to say, metaphysical doctrine says about art when it represents art aesthetically. The *aistheton*, what can be perceived by the senses, lets the *noeton*, the nonsensuous, shine through. (14) |

But just this apparent similarity endangers thought, both by falsifying what is thought and by stopping thought in a convenient "answer." Because the speakers understand that *Iro* and *Ku* mean more than "the sensuous" and "suprasensuous," they bring the essential meaning of Japanese thought into question and expand the inquiry through metaphysics and aesthetics.

It turns out that the great Japanese film *Rashomon*, which the inquirer takes as a paradigmatic presentation of the Japanese experience of art, is understood by the Japanese speaker to be a striking example of the Europeanization which falsified experience and thought. The Japanese speaker finds the film realistic. By this, however, he does not mean it is a detailed or insistent presentation of the sensuous as the metaphysical language of aesthetics would indicate; rather, he means to say that in the film the Japanese world is captured as an object, and even more importantly, is already *experienced* as an object in the European or American manner, in order to be so appropriated. The film's so called aesthetic quality is irrelevant here because the Japanese world has been distorted insofar as it has been reduced into photography, and by means of this specific technology forced into the general frame of European thinking.[5]

As the result of this and several similar experiences, the thinkers realize that they are misunderstanding one another because of their assumptions. This allows them to begin to hear each other and think together. For his part, the Japanese reveals the experience of the Japanese world by speaking of the *No* drama: "To allow you to see, even if only from afar, something of what the *No*-play defines, I would assist you with one remark. You know that the Japanese stage is empty" (18). The emptiness is the scene, which, because it demands unusual concentration, requires only a subtle addition for a dramatic effect, as the Japanese speaker exhibits by evoking a mountain landscape: he "slowly raises his open hand and holds it quietly above his eyes at eyebrow level" (18). This too, however, only opens the question further, for it is not clear what gesture is, or what the essence of emptiness is, or whether emptiness can at all be understood as the same as 'nothingness' in "What Is Metaphysics?" for example.

To think genuinely, then, without falling prey to the danger of falsifying the thoughtful experience of the Japanese, requires non-metaphysical thinking. Though thinking by way of European meta-physical conceptualization cannot be avoided completely, it can be overcome (22, 25).

Just as the Japanese speaker helped both speakers move bey-ond the level of report and correction to thinking itself, and even beyond metaphysical thinking, Heidegger does the same. The experience and insight are reported as they reverse roles. Earlier, Heidegger had inquired into *Iki*; now he thinks about hermeneu-tics. He immediately indicates a level more important than the record of what he or other thinkers said. Concerning that first clarification of the past, Heidegger admits, "we did not get very far with an explication of hermeneutics. I told you stories, rather, showing how I came to employ the word" (28). What is needed is "a more precise explanation of hermeneutics" (29), not because of any historicist or antiquarian interest, but "because the explana-tion may issue in a discussion" (29).

In a deeper sense, this historical nature of every thinking dialogue is not, however, in need of all those enterprises that report things from the past about the thinkers and what they have thought in the manner of historiography (31). That is, Heidegger goes into the past, but now he engages "in dialogue with his forebears" (31) in order newly to think the subject matter. Thought by way of etymology and past thinkers is termed "hermeneutics," which, as the noun *hermeneus* suggests, relates to the god Hermes, the divine messenger who brings the message of destiny. Similarly, Heidegger tells us that the verb "*hermeneuein* is that exposition which brings tidings because it can listen to a message. Such an exposition becomes an interpretation of what has been said earlier by the poets who, according to Socrates in Plato's *Ion* (534e), *hermenes eisin ton theon*—'are interpretors of the gods'" (29). Thus, hermeneutics means first hearing a message, then bearing and interpreting it. Thinking this original sense of hermeneutics enables Heidegger to think nonmetaphysically. Hermeneutically thought, Being itself—the two-fold of presence and present beings—calls and claims man, even as it veils itself; in turn, man "realizes his nature as man by corresponding to the call of the two-fold, and bears witness to it in its message" (30).

The *relation* of the *two-fold* and *man* is hermeneutical; accordingly, this relation prevails in and is borne up by language. As the Japanese speaker puts it, "But if language is the basic trait in hermeneutically defined usage, then you experience the reality of language from the start differently from the way one does in metaphysical thinking" (34). Similarly, here relation is not thought in a formal sense or in terms of the logistics of useful function, but in an entirely different way which understands that man, in his essence, "belongs within a needfulness which claims him . . . hermeneutically—that is to say, with respect to bringing tidings, with respect to preserving a message" (32). Further, the two-fold is not thought by way of subject and object of "mental representation" which contrasts present beings and presence itself as two pre-given objects. Rather, the two-fold is "the sway of usage" (33) in which man as man and what calls on him are both given at once. At the second level, the dialogue is a genuine thinking, which, though historical (hermeneutical), passes beyond the level of historiography and chronicle, and, at the same time, beyond its obvious alternative, traditional atemporal metaphysical thought. Heidegger and the Japanese speaker establish this third sort of thinking by thoughtfully moving back along the path of the first two (both were held in the first level—which chronicled past events and metaphysical thought).

This makes sense of the refusal to compare and contrast Heidegger's ideas with those, for example, of the Greeks, Descartes, or Kant, who embodies the view of thought as representative objectification. Instead, the dialogue partners continue attempting to understand previous thinkers and, beyond that, to thoughtfully experience language and the relation of man and the two-fold. "Our own thinking today is charged with the task" (39) of thinking, in its origin, the appearing of appearance, for example. In Greek thought, appearance is a "basic trait of the presence of all present beings, as they rise into unconcealment" (38). That is, what is needed is the attempt to think what has so far been unthought—the very coming about of the unconcealedness—in the realm of hermeneutical relation where "man is the message-bearer of the message which the two-fold's unconcealment speaks to him" (40).

Next, since the Japanese speaker senses a kinship with this thinking, the dialogue again turns to consider emptiness. The Japanese speaker ties the two together by saying that the site of the kinship, "shown to us in *Ku* which means the sky's emptiness" (46), is boundlessness. Apparently, the Japanese speaker and the inquirer come closer together as they move beyond conceptual language "toward a transformation of thinking" (42), which occurs as a passage from the site of metaphysics to another, beyond naming. The thinking of this dialogue is self-consciously hermeneutical then, for embodied by their asserted kinship within the site of the undefined, the thinkers try to place the sites in discussion (42) by thinking them and the passage between them.

This requires rethinking *Iki*. Since there may be a kinship between Japanese and Heidegger's thinking, where the latter "in leaving behind metaphysics, also leaves behind the aesthetics that is grounded in metaphysics" (42), Count Kuki's thought on *Iki* remains to be understood.

Accordingly, Heidegger and the Japanese speaker need to rethink what Kuki achieved and how he strove toward his goal by way of aesthetics. And in order to bring the difference as well as the similarity between *Iki* and aesthetics into view, they must think from a different vantage point, that is, nonaesthetically. To do so, they think aesthetics by way of what they already have thought, the subject-object relation. Once imposed, the subject-object framework results in a specific understanding. Where the concept of "subject" dominates the experience of the art work, it will be treated, even defined, in reference to the artist's creativity and virtuosity; where the concept of "object" dominates, the work will appear as his product, ready for "the art business" (43) and museums.

How then can the Japanese speaker think *Iki* without falling "into the clutches of aesthetic ideation" (43)? On the one hand, he begins to think *Iki* on its own terms by hesitantly translating *Iki* as the "gracious" (43); on the other, he does "attempt to detach *Iki*, which we just translated with 'grace', from aesthetics, that is to say, from the subject-object relation. I do not now mean *gracious* in the sense of a stimulous that enchants . . . that is, not in the realm of what stimulates, of impressions, of *aisthesis*" (44).

The Japanese speaker explicates the nonmetaphysical meaning: "*Iki* is the breath of the stillness of luminous delight" (44). That is, delight is thought hermeneutically; it is "of the same kind as the hint that beckons on, and beckons to and fro" (44).

Or, graciousness would be the source of all presence "in the sense of the pure delight of the beckoning stillness" (44). In short, the Japanese speaker thinks *Iki* the same way Heidegger thinks 1) the hermeneutical relation of the two-fold's sway and the usage of man and 2) the occurrence as unthought. Though *Iki* is the proper aim of the Japanese partner, his thought comes together with Heidegger's, or better, shows itself to be parallel. And because each needs the other's prompting in order to hear and speak his own thought, they help each other toward originary thinking.

But the dialogue does not merely elaborate and ornament these bare bones of thought. Indeed, this skeleton is itself an abstraction from the complex, unified whole. Similarly, we can distinguish, as a congruent abstraction, the formal dimension. Yet, the resultant complementary argument and form are of little interest in themselves, save as mnemonic and heuristic aids; their incompleteness hints at their coincidence in a vital source. Put another way, understanding the "ideas" requires understanding their organization and embodiment and that the unified work is not actually made of separate aspects; taken together both point to the origin from which they were derived.

To begin, consider the style of the second level of thinking. Again, we find two alternative sorts of language which embody two sorts of encounter and exhibit their difference. From a position out of and beyond metaphysics, Western metaphysics itself appears to have determined its own hostile mode of encounter with the East; in contrast, nonmetaphysical thought about language and art provides for a fruitful encounter between the partners in the dialogue.

The dialogue uses the language of military conquest to understand the usual meeting of the metaphysical West and the East. For
example, we find the sure and swift "triumphal march of Reason"
(15), the "complete Europeanization of the earth and of man"
(15), which in its grand scale is everywhere and unavoidable and
"all consuming" (16). Indeed, "in the face of modern technicaliza-
tion and industrialization of every continent, there would seem to
be no escape any longer" from European conceptual systems (3).

An "attack on the nature of language" takes place as logic
becomes logistics (25); Europeanization "attacks at the source of
everything that is of an essential nature." For example, "the real
nature of East Asian art is obscured and shunted into a realm that
is inappropriate to it" (14).[6] The subject matter grasped by such
aggressive reason becomes a mere object to be disposed of, or in the
final reduction, to be appraised, bought, and sold, once in the
"clutches of aesthetic ideation" (43). In a parallel way, those
subject to reason are in peril: as the Japanese say, the danger is
"that we will let ourselves be led astray by the wealth of concepts
which the spirit of the European languages has in store, and will
look down upon what claims our existence, as on something that is
vague and amorphous" (3).[7]

But, for all its power, such grasping, imperialistic thinking
"destroys the possibility of saying" what is at hand; for all its
speed, "the technical world which sweeps us along must confine
itself to surface matters" and "for this reason a true encounter with
European existence is still not taking place, in spite of all assimila-
tions and intermixtures" (3). The European idolization of reason
and its concealed descendents fail to achieve any true encounter,
and this includes the first level of this dialogue, motivated by
curiosity for "inside," correct biographical detail. "Thirst for
knowledge and greed for explanations never lead to a thinking
inquiry. Curiosity is always the concealed arrogance of a self-
consciousness that banks on a self-invented *ratio* and its rationality.
The *will* to know does not *will* to abide in hope before what is
worthy of thought" (13).

In sharp contrast, the dialogue presents the speakers' attempt at a truely thinking encounter in modest terms. They neither engineer nor travel on a *via imperia*; rather, they "follow a faint trail" (41), a "path" (e.g. 21, 22), a "trail or bypath" (26), which is no more than "an almost imperceptible promise" (41). This pathway is slowly established by individual steps which themselves fade away: "Every thinking step only serves the effort to help man in his thinking to find the path of his essential Being" (34); each former standpoint is "merely a way-station along a way" (12). Unlike progress on the road of Western reason, movement along this path always remains tentative, slow, and cautious (5, 8, 16, 21).

Here thinkers speak "clumsily enough" (5) and express themselves inadequately (16). For example, after all his years of thinking about language, Heidegger does "not yet see whether what [he is] trying to think of as the nature of language is *also* adequate for the nature of the East Asian language (8). The difficulties lie between the speakers and that of which they think and also between the speakers themselves. Naturally, Heidegger notes, "much had to remain unclear" (36); "how is one to give a name to what he is still searching for?" (20) Even when he can articulate what he understands, he admits that he is "not certain whether you have your eye on the same" (12). Not surprisingly, this path opens up "most easily if from the very outset we do not demand too much" (23).

In further contrast to the conceptual grasp which fractures its object, this restrained way touches its subject matter delicately: "Thanks to that concentration, only a slight additional gesture on the actor's part is required" (18); Heidegger's phrase, "Language the house of Being" "touches upon the nature of language without injury" (22); "his gaze into the nature of language does not fasten upon" its parts (35). This thinking "corresponds to the call" (30) and "leaves the defining something in full possession of its voice" (22).

This thinking is the way of encounter because it lets be and hears. For example, the trusting thinker "must guard all the more carefully the ways toward the nature or reality of language" (25), by taking care to be non-willful, non-arbitrary, and humble (11, 26, 28). Clearly, so understood, the thinker is no virtuoso who aims to dazzle by means of his subjective creativity. Thus, the Japanese speaker and the inquirer may truly encounter one another insofar as they abandon the swift road of proud, controlling conceptual thought to cautiously seek the path which touches its subject matter by letting it be. "This," says the inquirer, "is what our language calls 'hesitate.' It is done truly when slowness rests on shy reverence. And so I do not wish to disturb your hesitation by urging you on too rashly" (28).

The dialogue presents and contrasts, then, two modes of encounter between East and West by means of two clusters of images and metaphors: the metaphysical, technological encounter appears in militant and commercial language; the nonmetaphysical encounter in tentative and familiar terms. But this is not arbitrary. These two specific groupings in just these specific relationships exist because this level of the dialogue is grounded in an even deeper formal structure. Behind these two clusters of images and metaphors, there is an organizing principle that both guides their elaboration and holds them, in their difference, in unity.

Consider the nature of the conceptual relation that shows itself most clearly in the formal metaphysical thinking and calculus of mathematics, logic, and their derivatives (technology, logistics, and commercialism) (32, 42). Actually, this relation is a specific form of "gathering" (*Versammlung*).[8] Note the description of conceptual thought: a chief capacity is its "delimiting power to represent objects related in an unequivocal order above and below each other" (2). The dialogue specifies this causal sequence, which lies at the heart of scientific thought, in both its logical and temporal aspects. For example, the partners speak of "a confusion *grounded* in the matter itself and linked with the use of the name 'Being'" (19). They also suggest that "because this language itself *rests on* the metaphysical distinction between the sensuous and the suprasensuous, in that the *structure* is supported by the basic elements of sound and script on the one hand, and signification and sense on the other" (15), "you are no longer *basing yourself* on the subject-object relation" (37).

In fact, movement and relation along the straight, swift highway of metaphysics and the resultant service roads of science, technology, and aesthetics exemplify a fundamental causal and temporal "gathering up and down." Further, what is here gathered, is *already* included as a necessary principle. For example, "In appearance as Kant thinks of it, our experience must already include the object as something in opposition to us" (37). Because it bundles together what already pre-exists, this metaphysical thinking is, at base, a re-presentation: "To experience in this sense always means to refer back—to refer life and lived experience back to the 'I'. Experience is the name for the referral of the objective back to the subject" (35–36). The organizational principle behind all this, then, is *gathering as bundling into a hierarchy what is pre-given.*

In contrast, the hermeneutic relation shows itself in homely patterns. Recall the grave in the temple grove which sets the scene and tone of the dialogue, the question of the site of *kinship* between their thought, their concern with a "dialogue from house to house," and "language as the house of Being" (5). All this also manifests a gathering, but here we find gathering as the calling and responsive touching of what already is together (what unfolds) and of what yet only thereby comes together (what only occurs together at the same time). For example, in thinking the house of Being, the partners do not mean that the "house is a shelter erected earlier somewhere or other, in which Being, like a portable object, can be stored away" (26). Rather, this is by way of the two-fold, "which, as far as I can see, cannot be explained in terms of presence, nor in terms of present beings, nor in terms of the two. Because it is only the two-fold itself which unfolds the clarity, that is, the clearing in which present beings as such, and presence, can be discerned by man" (33).

Further, whereas the metaphysical gathering operated verti- cally, ordering things above and below each other, the dialogue's second sort of gathering *gathers* what belongs together *within and without.* What is thought here moves in and out of openings and clearings (21, 23, 30, 38, 39, 41). This formal principle is elaborated by the details and enables us to understand them. For example, think of the seeming contradiction, or nonsense, involved when the speakers talk about the site of the gathering both as homely and as undefined, boundless, and emptiness itself. Actually, the first way of speaking emphasizes that which is within reflection; the second, that which is without. (That which is outside reflection is the site within which reflection is; in turn, the site is already and only given within reflection.) The speakers, then, think the realm of gathering in a way which altogether avoids the categories of conceptual thought: it is neither precise in the manner of conceptual representation, nor yet "vague and amorphous"; rather, gathering belongs to the realm of mystery (3, 12, 16, 41).

The true encounter of the Japanese speaker and the inquirer with one another and with what is to be thought takes place by means of this second sort of gathering. Specifically, the dialogue provides three extended thoughts which move by way of, and thereby exemplify, this *gathering within—thought of as calling and responsively touching what is already together and what yet only thereby comes together.*

This organizing principle initially manifests itself when the speakers think beyond—that is, beyond their first level historical-biographical report—by returning back to what was earlier. They also go further forward by going back in a second, different way. Specifically, "gathering within" occurs as the thinkers move between past and future in an attempt to originarily think *Iro* and *Ku* as they attempt to bring metaphysics back within its limits (10–12, 20–21, 33–34, 36, 42).

Thus, Heidegger's thought does not aim to ignore, much less to destroy, the past. Rather, "it speaks out of a thinking respect for the past" (34) in its efforts to "recover the things of the past in a more originary form," which means "to fetch, to gather in, to bring together what is concealed within the old" (36).

Japanese: In what sense do you understand "originally famil-
              iar"? You do not mean what we know first, do you?
Inquirer: No, but what before all else has been entrusted to our
              nature, and becomes known only at the last. (33)

Or again, in a marvelous section which does what it says in the movement of two pages, the Japanese speaker and the inquirer move beyond a biographical account. (The beginning of the section is marked off from the surrounding dialogue by its notably different language.)

Inquirer: But origin always comes to meet us from the future.

Japanese: If the two call to each other, and reflection makes its home within that calling . . .

Inquirer: . . . and thus becomes true presence. (10)

Inquirer: . . . And ways of thinking hold within them that mysterious quality that we can walk them forward and backward, and that indeed only the way back will lead us forward.

Japanese: Obviously you do not mean "forward" in the sense of an advance, but . . . I have difficulty in finding the right word.

Inquirer: "Fore"—into that nearest nearness which we constantly rush ahead of, and which strikes us as strange each time anew when we catch sight of it.

Japanese: And which we therefore quickly dismiss again from view, to stay instead with what is familiar and profitable.

Inquirer: While the nearness which we constantly overtake would rather bring us back.

Japanese: Back—yes, but back where?

Inquirer: Into the beginning.

Japanese: I find this difficult to understand, if I am to think in terms of what you have said about it in your writings up to now.

Inquirer: Even so, you have already pointed to it, when you spoke of the presence that springs from the mutual calling of origin and future. (12)

This section speaks of thinking as movement forward and backward; further, it moves forward by going back to the thought it started with two pages earlier. The thinking, then, is both what is spoken and the movement of that speaking.

Here, the dialogue itself clarifies the relation between the first and second levels of discussion. Heidegger's thought moves forward by going back to the past, but not by merely reporting that past. Though it is indeed already within a report of the past (the first level of the dialogue), genuine thought (the second level) returns to think in an originary way what is unthought in the report, however correct that report is. That is, thinking gathers the thinkers within what is already there (the record of the past that they are discussing), and yet both the thinkers and the past really emerge as such only insofar as they come together, in other words, only when past and present thoughts enter into one another.

A second manifestation of the organizational principle "gathering within" is found in the dialogue's "two-way thought," that is, in the thinking which proceeds by double movement, to and fro. Language which appears confusing or contradictory actually embodies the complex principle (it gathers what is already together; at the same time, it gathers what only comes together in the gathering) without reducing it to a simple linear process. Actually it hints at an experience. Notice how the inquirer and his Japanese partner speak about "bearing," "hint," "gesture," and "the two-fold."

People, as messengers, can interpret only because they already hear and *bear* messages and tidings (29). The gathering together of message and messenger, within one another, is thought in terms of bearing. As Heidegger puts it, "Because what truly bears, only bears itself *toward* us . . . though we bear only our share to its encounter. While that which bears itself toward us has already borne our counterbearing into the gift it bears for us" (18–19).

In turn, gesture is gathered together with bearing. Clearly gesture is not thought in a metaphysical-conceptual manner: the style of the thinking shows this. The speakers state that the gesture considered here will not even appear to be such to Europeans (18). This gesture, the Japanese speaker notes, is "something that may not even be called gesture any longer in the sense of which I understand your usage" (16).

Inquirer:	And yet, the word "gesture" helps us experience truly what is here to be said.
Japanese:	Ultimately, it coincides with what I have in mind.
Inquirer:	Gesture is the gathering of a bearing.
Japanese:	Thus you call bearing or gesture: the gathering which originally unites within itself what we bear to it and what it bears to us. (18–19)

Thus, gesture is thought of as a gathering-within that proceeds by moving back and forth (in the manner of the messenger and message). The hand, in true gesture, "is suffused and borne by a call calling from afar and calling still onward, because stillness has brought it" (16). But, the gathering within, thought as a calling, is not by any means a mere bundling together of previously given objects: rather, it is the gathering of what belongs together and of what only comes together and is truly itself in the gathering. This is why they say: "However, with this formulation we still run the risk that we understand the gathering as a *subsequent* union . . . instead of experiencing that all bearing, in giving and encounter, springs first and only from the gathering" (19).

Further, because such ideas hint at the nature of language, the Japanese speaker and the inquirer think the nature of hinting itself, but in a way that does not "elaborate the notion of hinting into a guiding concept in which we then bundle up everything" (24). Instead, it is thought of as a gathering together in movement back and forth: "You are thinking of hints, as belonging together with what you have explained by the word 'gesture' or 'bearing'" and as belonging apart "from signs and chiffres, all of which have their habitat in metaphysics" (26). Actually, hints "are enigmatic. They beckon to us. They beckon *away*. They beckon *toward* that from which they unexpectedly bear themselves toward us" (26). Further, hints are thought within the site of gathering (a site that as already noted, is both familiar and boundless). In this contrast they think of the movement of hints not as willful, sequential control, but as gathering within the mysterious. "Hint" becomes a freeing word (24), and "hints need the widest sphere in which to swing where mortals go to and fro only slowly" (27).

Hints, gestures, and bearing all come together as they belong together with the two-fold, and the two-fold is gathered together with them in the thinking. The two-fold is thought, then, in terms of the double-directioned gathering: the two-fold is what makes its claim on people in calling them to their essential being, "with respect to bringing tidings, with respect to preserving a message" (32). Thus, "man is really as man when needed and used by what calls on man to preserve the two-fold" (32). This two-fold cannot be explained in terms of the relations between—previously grasped—man, Being, or beings. They already belong together: "The two-fold has always already offered itself to man, though its nature remained veiled. Man, to the extent he is man, listens to this message" (40); but, as noted above, they only occur in the occurrence of the gathering.

Inquirer: This is why we may no longer say relation to the two-fold, for the two-fold is not an object of mental representation, but is the sway of usage.

Japanese: Which we never experience directly, however, as long as we think of the two-fold only as the difference which becomes apparent in a comparison that tries to contrast present beings and their presence. (33)

There is a third and final example of thinking which elaborates the figure "gathering within." We again find the double movement back and forth in the thinkers' thoughts concerning the Greeks. At first appearance, these sections seem confused and belabored. In fact, though they are complex, they are simply a triple development of the basic double motion found in "gathering within what already belongs together." That is, the third thinking, which proceeds by way of the double movement, itself goes over the path three times.

This double motion of thought first appears in the statement that the inquirer *does* and *does not* attempt to think appearance in the Greek sense. *Yes*, he does attempt to think appearance in the Greek sense insofar as this involves a "no," that is, insofar as he does not think of it *via* the objectivity of Kantian thought or the subjectivity of Cartesianism. These latter paths do not lead to thought in the Greek sense. At the same time, *no*, he does not think it in a Greek sense, for he does not aim only to return to Greek thinking or to try to understand the Greeks better than they did themselves. Thus, both his "yes" and "no" lead to a "no" and explain the sense in which he does not use "appearance" in a Greek sense. Yet, despite the "no" that comes from both the "yes" and "no," a "yes" comes, too: "it has something in mind that is correct" (38). The task is "to think what the Greeks have thought in an even more Greek manner" (39).

Next, another double step unfolds. The task of thinking appearance, for example, in the Greek sense means that the thinker already is within the Greek tradition. But Greek thought itself already is within the midst of what is to be thought (presence as appearance, for example), and this includes what is unthought. Therefore, the inquirer and the Japanese speaker think a Greek thought in a Greek way and yet do not intend their thought to be Greek.

Heidegger's thoughts and the Greeks' are together within what is to be thought and within the tradition; yet, they are separate, since, although already within what is to be thought, they come together in thinking differently what is the same (39).

There is one more double movement. Their attempt to "pursue more originally" (39) involves the double swing of gathering: Heidegger thinks the unconcealedness that *already prevails* in the thought of being present as appearance, yet, at the same time, the unconcealedness (as unthought occurrence) and originary thinking occur together.

Thus, the entire thought about appearance by way of its relation to Greek thought is a fugue woven of double movements: it moves through "yes" and "no," through what is thought and unthought, through thoughts which belong within thoughts, and through the concealed unconcealing.

To summarize, the second level of the dialogue is moved by a general organizational principle: it unfolds "within" or "between." This master figure has been shown to lie behind the speakers' thinking of encounter (which has the opposite possible goals of conquest or letting be), the character of the thinkers, the scene, the separation of metaphysical thinking from the Japanese speaker and the inquirer, and (in the three specific manifestations) this double movement of gathering.

The movement is not up and down or merely back and forth as it would be in the dominant metaphors of the metaphysical tradition; rather, this further movement to and fro results in a complex structural nesting "within/between." Consider the six phases of this level of discussion: (1-a) the apparent similarity of *Iki* and aesthetics is questioned, which leads to (2-b) a split between the Japanese speaker's foreground world of objects (thought by way of *Rashomon*)[9] and his background world which yields the relation of

Japanese emptiness and Heidegger's nothingness (thought by way of *No* drama); this division is kept in (3-c) where European conceptual thought is thought as distinct from hermeneutics which, in light of the tradition, opens up the relation of the two-fold and man, that is, the sway of usage. Remaining within these thoughts the dialogue further develops (4-c) the realm of object and subject in regard to Descartes and Kant, but attempts to leap beyond them, by way of originative thought of Greek appearance, to think the two-fold and man. In (5-b), reaffirming the kinship of their thought at the site of the boundless, the Japanese speaker and the inquirer think the transformation of thinking beyond metaphysics, then finally return again, but now in a deeper way because of the thoughtful distinction resulting from the transformation, to do what Kuki did: (6-a) think *Iki* apart from aesthetics and in the realm of hermeneutic relation.

The pattern exhibited is clearly *1-a, 2-b, 3-c, 4-c, 5-b, 6-a.* (Of course, this might be divided differently, depending on which thoughts were taken together or on which were seen as dominant or inclusive. Then the thought might appear to have five divisions and it might be grounded, for example, *a, b, c, b, a.* But, in any case, the basic sequence and pattern would remain.) Initially, the pattern appears to result from the movement to and fro; or, the pattern may seem circular (*a, b, c,* then back around *c, b, a*). Finally, however, the movement to and fro, newly back to where it started, embodies the dominant *figura*—the relation, gathering "between" and "within." (Recall that the second level thinking in its six phases takes place within and derives from the context of the first level.) Graphically, we have the pattern of gathering within represented on p. 52.

Further, the *figura* behind the diverse, often apparently turgid language organizes the details of what is said in a way that not only unifies the meaning, but allows the exhibition of the full meaning of thinking: thinking as a "gathering within." In other words, the second level of discussion says what thinking is, but, it also does that thinking, that is, it is an instance of it. It says that thinking is a gathering within, which means that it (1) brings together, holds together, and passes beyond (2) what already belongs together. At the same time, in the course of the six phases just analyzed, the

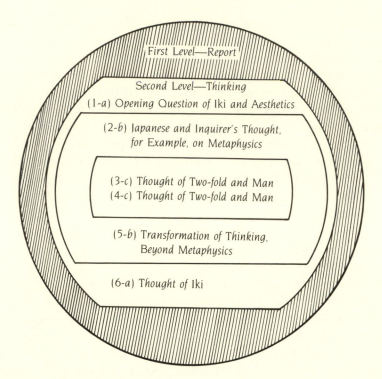

dialogue actually (1) brings together, holds together, and passes beyond (2) what already belongs together. For example, in the first half of the second level of the dialogue, the opening questions (*1-a*) of *Iki* and aesthetics are brought together and clarified even as they already belong together. (This second level takes place within and derives from the first level; what is already reported, for example, *Iki* and aesthetics, is now newly rethought.) Then, (*2-b*) the thought and experience of the inquirer and the Japanese, which already belong together, are held together with the now distinguished metaphysical realm. Next, (*3-c*) the third phase moves within the ideas already together in the second (*2-b*), but the thinkers think the relation of the two-fold and man more fully, beyond concep-tual-objectifying thinking. The second half of this level of dialogue moves back along this path: it stays within the ideas which already are thought together. Along the way, the speakers also come to understand (*4-c* and *5-b*) both originary and metaphysical thinking as they did not before. As a result, for the first time metaphysical thinking is really brought together with the nonmetaphysical in the thought of the sway of usage. Further, because the speakers develop these thoughts as they move through them to return to their starting point (*6-a* returns to *1-a*), they pass beyond the understanding of the first part to clarify *Iki* in a manner not possible when it was first introduced. Thus, thinking as gathering within is a return which intends to reach and hold the "originarily familiar."

This fusion of the dialogue and the nature of thinking is a marvelous accomplishment. Yet, there is even more. The whole second level of the dialogue not only *bodies forth* what thinking is, but, beyond that, what the thinking intends: *the hermeneutical relation itself*. This happens because in the very course of speaking of and achieving (1) the bringing together, holding together, and passing beyond (2) what is already together, it complexly replicates the sway of usage—which earlier was thought as the relation of the two-fold and man (33). More precisely, the dialogue explains how in the sway of usage ("relation") there is (1) a clearing in which man is called, claimed, and brought together with the message which he holds fast—bears and carries—and within which he further penetrates as he interprets or thinks that message and also thinks (2) how man and the two-fold already belong together. Man bears the message because he has heard it; he responds to what has already offered itself (40). (For example, Heidegger's course "Expression and Appearance" is an instance of this because it "already was on a trail which was a promise" (41). Further, the dialogue systematically shows the two thinkers in each of these specific "relations" with the two-fold (and its central message of the sway of usage), as the analysis of this section already has shown. Thus, in the second level of discussion, the dialogue thinks and tells of the hermeneutic relation; at the same time, the exfoliation of that thinking and telling exhibits the hermeneutic relation. That is, it is an image of the truth it intends—the sway of usage.

Here, each thinker tells his own thoughts to the other; the other helps him to hear his own thought. Each one's thought shows itself as an echo coming back from the other. What is said is not objectified by being forced into the sphere of metaphysical thought or by being reduced to a "fact" to be reported or corrected; rather, it is let be, as it is thought. Thus, unlike the initial objectification of the reported lecture courses or that apparent in *Rashomon*, the second level of discussion holds thoughts to memory, and rethinks them, just as the photo of Count Kuki's grave in the grove held his memory together with the thinkers and spurred this dialogue. That is, the dialogue itself is the site of thoughtful reflection. Earlier, the Japanese speaker reported that the teacher Nishida worked for a year on the epitaph of his pupil, Kuki, and that the grave was in a grove which was the site of deep meditation; so, too, the thinking conversation of the Japanese speaker and the inquirer is "grown out of memory of Count Kuki" (15), and, the inescapable encounter of East and West is itself "searching reflection" (2). The thinkers succeed, then, insofar as they help each other (33).

To be sure, the formal unity of the successful thinking pleases the reader, for who would not delight in watching the speakers help each other to speak and, at the same time, develop their own thoughts? But, for all that, the second level of the dialogue is only the beginning of thought. The thinking is complex and unfinished; more is hinted at than is systematically developed. Thus, the reader is drawn in. The reader, too, puzzles out the thought. That is, to grasp the thinking at this level, one must think along with the Japanese speaker and the inquirer, and, since the thought is incomplete, think beyond what is spoken in the dialogue. In short, the dialogue aims to move the reader toward a nonconceptualizing thoughtfulness where he or she may participate with Heidegger and the truth that the dialogue presents. Insofar as this is achieved, the reader, already gathered into the dialogue, is brought together with it in the course of moving through and beyond it. Here the dialogue is not simply between the principal thinkers, the Japanese speaker and the inquirer; rather, the dialogue is between all the participating thinkers and what is to be thought. Thus, the dialogue shows itself as an illuminating, gathering gesture by means of which the thinkers (especially Heidegger) help those who try to think.

3. A SAYING

Still, explained or experienced in this way, the dialogue does not fully satisfy. The language of the dialogue often is unclear and self-consciously mysterious. It frequently confuses and troubles those who do try to think along. If we do not give up, however, we may notice that the same sections which seem obscure are also evocative: their tone is promissory. Further, there are pointers in the discussion which indicate that there is more here than is obvious (more, for example, than what the thinkers tell us). For some at least, such passages will raise the question, what further level of meaning or fuller experience do the second level of discussion and the sections of difficult language hint at?

Several times thinkers indicate that it is not they, but something undefined (possibly called "the same")[10] to which they entrust themselves and which displays itself and guides the dialogue (13, 28, 30); that the word for what is to be thought is still lacking today (8, 22); that it is this word itself which hints at and says what is essential (23, 24, 27).

The inquirer and the Japanese speaker attempt, then, to pass beyond what they themselves are able to say; they attempt to hear the nature of language through what words say. To do this is difficult: it requires that the thinkers hold themselves back, when, for instance, the inquirer asks his Japanese partner whether there is "in your language a word for what we call language" (23).

Finally, after a self-controlled "shy reverence" (28) which allows the word to emerge, the time is ripe. The Japanese speaker names the word for language: "*koto ba*" (45).

"*Koto ba*," then, speaks "for what we Europeans call language" (45). *Koto* means the happening of *Iki* (*Iki*, which has already been gathered together with hermeneutics, means graciousness, that is, the luminous "pure delight of beckoning stillness," which in beckoning to and fro is the lightening message of the unconcealment of the two-fold [44 ff.]. "*Koto*, then, would be the appropriate occurrence (*Ereignis*) of the lightening message of grace" (44). "*Ba*" means the petals that spring from *koto* (the happenings of *Iki*). Therefore, *"koto ba"* says "the petals that stem from *Koto*," or, the flowers that flourish out "of the lightening message of the graciousness that brings forth" (47). Simply put, *"koto ba"* says language is the flowering of flourishing *Iki*. That is, the Japanese has a thinking experience with language in which language shows itself to be the *flourishing of the graciousness that brings forth* (47).[11]

The inquirer has a similar experience. When he too learns to refrain from asserting a concept, he also finds a "more fitting word" than "language" to say what needs to be said: that word is "Saying" (*"die Sage"*). Properly listened to, "Saying" means: (1) letting appear and shine in the manner of hinting, by beckoning to and fro, (2) what shows in and shines in the beckoning to and fro, and (3) what is to appear and shine (47).

Here the thinkers do not creatively state the meanings of these words, much less invent them; rather, the Japanese speaker and the inquirer allow the still place to open where *"koto ba"* and "Saying" can be heard. Thus, the dialogue moves beyond its second level, where the thinkers thought aloud. When the thinkers grow silent in order to hear language, the dialogue passes beyond the speakers' meanings to a third level where language speaks to them. At this point the dialogue is no longer between the thinkers; finally there is a thoughtful experience of language where the thinkers move in a "dialogue from out of (*von*) the nature of language" (51).[12]

> Inquirer: . . . the kind of dialogue is determined by *that which* speaks to those who seemingly are the only speakers—men.
>
> Japanese: Wherever the nature of language were to speak (say) to mean as Saying, *it*, Saying, would bring about the real dialogue. (52)

But just here, where aesthetic talk of art and poetry leave off and where the thinkers cease to be creative virtuosos, the most poetic and artful language of the dialogue appears.[13] The language is festive: the dialogue moves by way of the "gaiety" of the "mutual interplay . . . holding sway" (46, 47). The scene of this wonderful language is a floral bower full of the scent of "leaves, including and especially the leaves of a blossom—petals. Think of cherry blossoms or plum blossoms" (45); it is full of "petals that stem from" the "holding sway over that which needs the shelter of all that flourishes and flowers" (47–48); "the intermingling scent of cherry blossom and plum blossom on the same branch" (53). Thus, the profoundest language in the dialogue (the saying of language itself) is also the most beautiful; in the event of language there occurs "that which in the event gives delight, itself, that which uniquely in each unrepeatable moment comes to radiance in the fullness of its grace" (45).

The dialogue, then, by moving beyond a metaphysical naming and even beyond willful human speaking, shows the words "*koto ba*" and "Saying" in a brief and wonderful burst which lets language go back to itself. Specifically, this level of the dialogue is itself an instance of what "*koto ba*" and "Saying" say: the third level occurs as a brief illumination which nonetheless endures. But, since the saying which takes place is indeed the same as the nature of language which it says, there is a dazzling coincidence: the dialogue on language is itself a flowering flourishing.

This is the climax of the dialogue. On the third level, the Japanese speaker and the inquirer hear that language is a saying or a flowering flourishing; at the same time, on the third level the saying of the nature of language flourishes.

But the dialogue does not end with this achievement.[14] Actually, the saying of language again leads to (re-)thinking language. That is, the third level of the dialogue again implies the second level. Accordingly, after the climax of the third level, the dialogue still approaches thinking at the second level.

The sequence of this final movement can be followed as the thinkers back off from the brief experience of the third level. While it appears that the Japanese speaker and Heidegger (just as Count Kuki earlier) "have come to be at home only now through our dialogue" in the beckoning hint of the special words, they retreat from the occurrence over the next two pages. Their thinking is not yet "at the wellspring" but still on its way (48). They have understood enough to be reluctant about plunging into a "discussion of the nature of Saying. That would call for a journey into the region where the essential being of Saying is at home"(49).

Because they do not, in fact, reside in this region (though they have visited it), the speakers return from the third level of the dialogue to think at the second level what they have just experienced: the dialogue from language. They now understand the necessity of letting the mystery of Saying be, so as not to miss its working by talking about it too loudly (50). They intend to avoid taking "up a position above language, instead of hearing from it," where the latter "would be called *from out of* language's reality, and be led *to* its reality: "a dialogue from language must be called for from out of language's reality. How can it do so, without first entering into a hearing that at once reaches that reality?"(51). In brief: from their hearing dialogue with and within language the thinkers are led back out to think "language's reality." (This movement seems circular. In fact, it seems to be an example of the hermeneutic circle or relation. But since the thinkers are now beyond both historical report and metaphysical conceptualization, they do not pursue Heidegger's earlier view or speak about the relation at hand by re-presenting that earlier notion. Instead, they attempt to think the relation they have just experienced.)

The remainder of the dialogue takes place at the second level: the thinkers clearly *move within* their own thinking again; the thought and the language proceed more directly, clearly, and smoothly. They think "Saying." "Saying" appears between them as what they take up to think, and in returning to thinking (at level two), they place themselves back within the thinking to which they already belong.

The dialogue ends with the thinkers still underway because even the extraordinary event of their dialogue with language does not "give us the right simply to shun trouble and the risk of speaking about language. Indeed not. We must incessantly strive for such speaking" (50).[15] "Indeed—so long as man has not yet been given the pure gift of the messenger's course that the message needs which grants to man the unconcealment of the two-fold," (53) they must seek it. It remains a "promise" (41) and faint echo to follow (53); it is *underway*, though just underway, in the whole of this dialogue on language.

| Japanese: | It seems to me as though even we, now, instead of speaking about language, had tried to take some steps along a course which entrusts itself to the nature of Saying. |
| Inquirer: | Which *promises*, dedicates itself to the nature of Saying. Let us be glad if it not only seems so but *is* so. (54) |

If, in the course of the dialogue, they do achieve originary thinking concerning the nature of saying and later think that experience (that is, return to level two), then the dialogue, in yet another way, brings thinkers and language together even while it says how the nature of language as granting involves its coming together with man. It does this by gathering: it gathers hermeneutics, *Iki, koto ba*, and Saying to say the nature of saying; it brings the thinkers together with language where their thoughts already belong within language's saying; finally, it again gathers the thinkers together at the second level of discussion and gathers their experience of the third level within this rethinking. The sequence exhibits a pattern. The dialogue moves from the thinking of language in level two to the saying of language itself in level three, where it reaches a climax, then, back to the final second level thinking of what happened in the third. Schematically we have: $2{\rightarrow}3{\rightarrow}2$, again a pattern of "to and fro," or "nesting within."[16] The two levels are given together, though each is shown as itself only in the process of gathering.

This is imaged in the yet more complex language of this aspect of the dialogue. The floral imagery of the third level unfolds to include humankind (and to incorporate and ground the human interaction of the second level) in a synoptic, controlling image: "play in a garden." We have already noted the garden imagery of the flowering shelter (the example of *koto ba*) and the wellspring; this also is the scene of song and saga (47): "so that in it there sings something that wells up from a single source" (8). In addition, there is *play*, which, at the third level, is not merely human, though it includes humanity. (Now human action is informed by the metaphors and imagery of level three so that it is changed stylistically and substantially from the willful activity associated with level one or what appeared earlier as deliberate human action in level two. Here there is neither ruthless pursuit or abandonment, nor yet the thinkers' self-controlled encounter as there might have been in the terms of the earlier levels. At the same time, this play is not without its dangers, since, for example, "language is more powerful than we" [31] and we are "used by what calls on man to preserve the two-fold" [32].) In the game of ring-around-the-rosey or hide-and-seek between humankind and the two-fold, they move together, coming neither too close nor straying too far apart. They have moved into a sphere of a free and allowing call, where a "veiled relation plays everywhere" which both opens and veils (53, cf. 44).

Here the Japanese speaker and the inquirer wait for the words which will surprise them. This scene of freedom (48, cf. "freeing hint" on 24) and of swinging (27) is also within the to-and-fro of calling—of "call calling from afar, calling still further onward" (16)—and in the sphere of confidence and trust.

The controlling image of the play-filled garden indicates how the third level informs the second level, how the event of language involves more than the merely human and yet echoes into human hearing and thinking. The scene is the final development of the opening grove and the intermediate house: clearly we are in the bower of language, where language speaks and sings. And just as clearly, the bower of language is the site of granting, that is, of the event of the gathering together of what already belongs together, the still concealed two-fold and humanity. The earlier sorts of language, which presented men in dialogue and discussion are transformed and informed by the style of the third level. We now hear about what comes out of the speaking of language—the gathering together of humanity with the two-fold. It is this belonging together of the two-fold and man in the already given flourishing of language that makes possible the consequent gathering of human beings in their own dialogue and discussion. Thus, the dialogue on language articulates the originary playful relation of respect which allows mystery and silence, where, for example, man as thinker allows language to hide, trusting that in its own way and time it will show itself to play—and that it will allow the free play for humanity, whom it needs and who needs to seek it. The goal of the game? Both could be themselves, they could show themselves to each other as they are, and they would belong to what needs and uses them; already belonging together, they could gather together.

In sum, the movement forward and backward of the third level of discussion involves a to-and-fro between man's thinking (the second level) and language's speaking (the third level). The speakers think together, which leads to their listening to language, and which again results in their thinking what was heard, represented thus: $(2 \rightarrow 3 \rightarrow 2)$. The intended and achieved result is the free swinging back and forth between the two levels of dialogue themselves (between the dialogue of the thinkers and between language and the listening thinkers toward whom it proceeds). The end, then, is not static; on the contrary, it is a source of movement because by gathering and holding together humankind and language in both these levels the dialogue ensures that thinking will always be underway. Thus, the play in the garden, which is the flourishing of the message, moves itself: it generates its own renewal. Origin and end renew each other.[17] Out of the second level of thinking, the third flowers; out of the flourishing of the third level of the dialogue, the second can become fruitful.

Since the dialogue on language itself says that ultimately the third level of dialogue necessarily concerns the movement back and forth between the thoughtful thinkers and the occurrence or flourishing of Saying, and since the dialogue on language itself actually moves back and forth between the second level (the thinkers thinking the two-fold) and the third (language's flourishing), the third level finally consummates the union of what is said and what is shown concerning thinking and language.

4. GRACIOUS GESTURE

To conclude, the dialogue, by weaving together three levels of discussion, says and shows more than any one of them, or any simple, sequential combination of them, could. Of course, since the whole dialogue is Heidegger's composition, it would be presumptuous to suppose that it really represents a saying of Saying or an event of unconcealment of the two-fold. Nonetheless, even if it is not an occurrence of the saying of Saying (level three), it can witness (at level one) the extent to which language already did hold Heidegger in its embrace and, as a human composition (that is, as a thought-ful saying by a thinker at level two) it can hint at that Saying, or aim to evoke what the experience of Saying would be like so that we may try to hear and think it. The dialogue, then, can give a hint not only of something promised, but of what is already so between language, humankind, and the two-fold.

Thus, the dialogue gestures toward the reader. The message it bears goes beyond the thinkers and, indeed, beyond the composer Heidegger[18] to beckon to the reader, as when the dialogue con-cludes: "Yet many a man could be drawn into the prologue to a messenger's course once he keeps himself ready for a dialogue concerning language" (54).[19]

In its movement along this pathway, insofar as this dialogue lets language appear together with thinking, the whole of "A Dialogue on Language" both says and shows that language is the happening of graciousness' (that is, is the granting of) beckoning hint or gesture. In this gesture, the dialogue gathers together humanity, language, and the two-fold, three sorts of speaking and thinking, the reader and composer, and much more. Furthermore, it does so in the style of gathering: in other words, it gathers itself, as saying and style together. *The dialogue* not only *says that language is the flourishing of graciousness' gathering-within,* that is, its *gesture; the dialogue itself is,* even if in the manner of a gathering hint, *the event of what it says: it is a flourishing of gracious gesture.*

CHAPTER THREE

Heidegger's Thinking and Language Concerning Thinking: What Is Called Thinking?

*W*hat Is Called Thinking? does not begin with the first sentence on the first page. By then the book already has begun, and we are underway with Heidegger. It starts instead with the title. The title announces the subject matter by raising a question. Or rather, it raises up the subject matter—thinking—as questionable. Presumably the book answers the question it raises by telling us about thinking, by gradually replacing the question with positive answers. The question yields to understanding, or it would seem, for the author raises the question with his title, then follows it with some two and a half hundred pages to resolve it. Why else would he do it? Why else would we trust him or want to read it at all?

But if the book answers a question, before the answer can make sense, the question must make sense, and to do that, it has to be clear. The question raised in the title, *What Is Called Thinking?*, is clear. But it is not simple.

Let's consider the question, What is called thinking?, then, with the original German, *Was heisst Denken?* in mind. What does it ask? What will Heidegger's answer be? Obviously, it asks about something which is called thinking; it asks, *What is it* that is called thinking? We know what it is that is called "chair" and what it is that is called or named "house." So the question is raised in regard to the term "thinking." To what does it refer? In German we can ask, *Wie heissen Sie?*—What is your name? (or, How are you called?)—and *Was heisst das?*—What is that called? One can answer, "I am named Bob; that is a chair and that a house." The question, then, inquires about something that is named and about the name for it. Here we are given the name, "thinking," and a question that asks for what the name belongs to. What does the term "thinking" name? Heidegger will *specify* what it is that is called or named "thinking."

That much is clear. But the question also asks something else. Again, imagine the question phrased in German, *Was heisst Denken?* Our pocket dictionary helps us hear what the German speaker asks, What names thinking? How odd. We might expect, *Who names thinking?* Then we could answer, "No one in particular" or, "The first people who used the word as listed in *Oxford English Dictionary* or *Grimm's Wörterbuch.*" But if we are given a moment to think, the "what" makes more sense. It would be the correct reference for language itself or a historical process. What names thinking? asks for the source or origin of the name "thinking." In its first form, the question asks about the object that the name "thinking" is attached to; in its second form, the question probes beyond that and asks for a subject—most likely an *impersonal* source—responsible for the naming. How does the object come to be named "thinking?"

The second version now appears as the more important; that is, it implies that the naming is not simply accidental, or even if it is, that it needs to be explained. An account must be given. A history must be filled in. No wonder that the book is longer than the first version of the question alone would seem to require. Further, the second version inquires into the authority behind the naming. How has it come about and on what grounds is this object called thinking? We need investigate not only the history of language and culture but the history of philosophy, since, as we might rightly suspect, philosophers and philosophical schools are responsible for naming something "thinking."

This insight helps to elaborate the question in its first version, too. If this question is a philosophical affair, then the earlier version asks not merely what is the object which is named "thinking" but also, and more deeply, what really is this object so-named? That is, we hear the traditional philosophical question, which moves beyond specifying existents to inquire into the essential nature of those existents. Thus, in its first version, the question asks what existent object or process is called "thinking," and more deeply, what is the essence of thinking: What is thinking, really? In its second version, the question asks about the history of the philosophical, cultural tradition that asks the first version of the question. In other words, it questions what has named this object or process called "thinking," presumably because the authoritative source of the naming understood its essence. How has the naming come about in our tradition? Both questions seem empirical and philosophical.

So far we have heard "what" as referring to both the object and the subject of naming ("what" is both a nominative and accusative interrogative pronoun). We have taken "called" to mean "named" and also "thinking" (*denken*) to be a gerund. But "call" also means evoke. We ask, What does justice evoke or call for?; What does the law call for? Here we ask what it is that justice or the law require; we ask what they call forth (from us). Heard this way, the question would ask, What does thinking call forth? Thinking then would be the subject of the sentence and would be doing the calling. The question would ask, Thinking calls (for), or requires, what? This sort of question would probe even deeper into doing the thinking. Here the author inquires beyond the first two versions; in fact, he investigates their assumptions and the real action of thinking. How do we think? What is evoked by thinking? What is required by thinking? Thus in its third form, the question asks, What is it that thinking calls for?

But our dictionary and grammar still tug at us. If "what" could be subject as well as object (we had to use "what" in both ways in the first and second versions) and if the third version again uses "what" to stand in for the object we are looking for, there must be a corresponding fourth version in which "what" again becomes the subject. If "what" is the subject of an active verb, "calls," we find ourselves asking, What calls (for) thinking? "Calling" would mean command, bid, or enjoin. For example, *Cassell's German Dictionary* gives as an example of the verb *heissen*, "*Er heisst ihn hereinkommen*"—"He bids him to come in." In this way, the question presses still further. It presses, for example, behind the third version to ask what moves in and through thinking. The third asks What it is that thinking bids us to do; the fourth asks, What calls for the thinking that we do, or for thinking in general. What is it that bids us to think? This fourth question also resembles the second, which asks for the source of the naming; the fourth asks about the source of the activity of thinking, What is it that calls for thinking?

We are in for more than we initially assumed. But we are in a better position to understand what Heidegger will say in the twenty-one lectures that lie behind the title *Was heisst Denken?* That is worth a little effort on our part. The question is still clear enough, but complex. The question raised by Heidegger, which we expect to be answered, is really a question with four variations: (1) What (as existent and essentially) is named "thinking"? (2) What so names thinking, that is, how is it that whatever it is becomes so named in our tradition? (3) What is it that thinking calls (for)?, and (4) What is it which calls for thinking?

As a teacher, Heidegger has the task of answering. And he does. In fact, he is careful to separate the four questions in the course of the lectures so we can be clear about what he says. Otherwise we might suppose he was contradicting himself or giving confusing answers to a simple question. But once we are aware that he is giving four answers to four questions, once we understand that the four sets of answers and four questions are variations on a single, complex question, we can follow what he tells us about thinking with relative ease. What then does the great teacher tell us about thinking?

1. WHAT HEIDEGGER SAYS CONCERNING THINKING

TRADITIONAL, REPRESENTATIONAL THINKING

First of all, "thinking" obviously does not refer to a thing, but to a process or an activity, as Heidegger makes clear: "What is called thinking? This time we would take the question in the sense listed first, and ask: What does the word 'thinking' say? Where there is thinking, there are thoughts. By thoughts we understand opinions, ideas, reflections, propositions, notions" (143–144. Also see 139).[1] In other words, thinking is the occurrence of thought, a process which distinguishes humankind from all other organisms. Hence, human beings are known as rational animals because of their capacity to think. Of course, this human activity clearly is related to others, such as perceiving, willing, and acting.

This ostensive definition clarifies the denotation of "thinking"; but, the connotation also is under question. Heidegger explains that the thinking process is to be understood as representation (*Vorstellung, vorstellen*), that is, as the forming of ideas:

> Is there anyone among us who does not know what it is to form an idea? When we form an idea of something—of a text if we are philologists, a work of art if we are art historians, a combustion process if we are chemists—we have a representational idea of those objects. Where do we have those ideas? We have them in our head. We have them in our consciousness. We have them in our soul. We have the ideas inside ourselves, these ideas of objects. (39)

Representation, then, is the process whereby we form an idea which grasps and holds an aspect of reality, which we have perceived, for example. Thinking is the ability to fix and retain what is to be thought in and by way of concepts.

Naturally enough, thinking also is remembering, for we not only form representational ideas but also summon them back, compare them, reflect on ideas we have had before, and so on. Memory as the power to recall ideas and as the human capacity to remember and retain is simply the ability to grasp the object of thought spread over time: retention is holding on to the objects of thought despite the flow of time. What is no longer perceived can yet be recovered and thought. Forgetting is the corresponding failure to recall.

In brief, thinking means the forming of ideas that represent what is thought. The interior, subjective process re-presents the object of thought. Where this is so, it is naturally important to form ideas correctly, so that the idea does conform to the object.

Of course, the issue has become complicated in the last several centuries with the debate over whether there is an independent, external reality in addition to our internal ideas. Certainly, at least since Descartes, the relation between subject/thought and object/object-of-thought has become especially problematic.

But without taking up this particular quarrel, the fundamental nature of thinking is clear enough. Thinking is not merely the helter-skelter forming of ideas; representation also involves judgment, that is, evaluation in order to form correct ideas. Here such correctness, understood as conformity, is equated with truth. Heidegger, then, does specify what it is that "thinking" names. Deliberately, he does not enter the dispute between "realists" and "idealists" or ancients and moderns but answers the question in a way which represents both the traditional view and that of modern, empirical philosophy and science. Yet, even if he stops, content with showing us the common ground of various viewpoints, not everything is answered. So Heidegger moves from the first version of the question to the second:

> It could be supposed that the forming of thoughts and the forming of ideas may well be one and the same thing. The prospect opens up on this possibility, that the traditional nature of thinking has received its shape from representation, that thoughts are a kind of representational idea. That is true. But at the same time it remains obscure how this shaping of the nature of traditional thinking takes place. The source of the event remains obscure. (44–45)

The answer to the second question is more elaborate than the answer to the first because it must trace the doctrine of thinking historically. In fact, the traditional doctrine of thinking is entitled "logic." This is because thinking on the forming of representative ideas can be either correct or incorrect. That is, thinking moves in the realm of truth and falsity. As a human occurrence whose processes can be observed by psychologists and theorists, thinking has long been studied as an activity following discernable norms and values. In other words, the forming of ideas which is named "thinking" is so named because that forming (at least when it is proper or correct) consists of movement according to the rules of logic. It is logic, then, which is responsible for the name of thinking.

But more than that, if the name is not arbitrary, the reason for it also is to be found in logic. Here we understand how logic as the traditional doctrine of thinking would provide the authority for the name and for understanding its essential nature as we do.

Heidegger elaborates: "Hence we must ask once more 'what is called thinking?'—and in this sense: what has been understood since ancient times by 'thinking'? Instruction on what to understand by 'thinking' is given by logic. 'Logic'—what is that?" (153)

Logic is concerned with thinking, but that means it is also concerned with language. If thinking is the internal forming of ideas which aims to correctly represent either external reality or former ideas, for example, then the relation between the thought and its object is of paramount concern. Since thinking aims at truth by having the right idea about the object of thought, thinking necessarily speaks. To grasp and fix an object by means of a concept is to posit a relation between the concept and object. It is to claim (correctly or incorrectly) that they correspond in some way. Thus, thinking is an internal assertion of that correspondence; the external assertion follows.

Accordingly, logic is the understanding concerned with *logos*, taken as the saying of something about something (a predicate is asserted about the subject of the statement where the two must be compatible).[2] That is, a proper relation must lie behind what can be said. Of course, anything can be uttered, even nonsense; but to be correct, subject and predicate must be properly related. Thus the rules of speech are not arbitrary. Further, the rules of speech are also the rules of thinking. For example, in a declaration, the terms related must not contradict each other.

We understand what it is that is called "thinking," then, according to what "is presented and handed on by a doctrine bearing the title 'logic' because thinking presents or affirms something as something, usually, but not primarily, in speech" (161–162).

However, the origin and authority of the naming and understanding are not merely found in an anonymous tradition. We know the decisive source of this doctrine, which began with the Greeks, who gave us *logos*, logic as "the name for the basic form of thinking, the proposition" (163). Logic and, thereby, our understanding of thinking, were fixed by Aristotle and Plato—in Plato's "Sophist" to cite one instance.

Since the time of the Greeks our understanding of thinking has changed, of course, for example, as we discovered subjects that demanded a new thought process in order to be mentally perceived. Here *logos* is transformed. To fully understand the historical development of logic and thinking through Greek idealism, to logic as dialectic, for example, is beyond the scope of Heidegger's intent here since he is only trying to answer the question of the origin of the naming of thinking by logic. This much is clear: man is the rational animal and thinking is the subjective process whereby he perceives or apprehends objects by reason and in which he forms ideas so as to represent mentally those objects and to form propositions about them.

But thinking is active in another way. It deliberately grasps what it thinks about, whether that is a present external object, or a previous idea or perception. It also leads to action, for instance, through technology, broadly conceived. That is to say, thinking also is willing. Or as Heidegger puts it, "The will is the sphere of representational ideas which basically pursue and set upon everything that comes and goes and exists" (93).

At this point in his lectures, Heidegger develops the answer to our two questions, What is that which is called thinking? and How and why does the tradition so name and understand it? by focusing on Nietzsche, whose own thinking process paradigmatically fixed what has been said so far. We are especially concerned with what he tells us about forming an idea, because that fundamental trait of traditional thinking leads to our current way of thinking.

The story of Nietzsche's thinking is the story of the rational animal. Nietzsche gives us an anthropological explanation, which sees man as "the beast endowed with reason" (61). Here reason is understood as super-sensual; that is, reason is the means by which man is able to pass beyond the animal-sensual. Thus, as Heidegger understood Nietzsche, "man himself is the metaphysical" (58). Nietzsche studies man's passage in regard to the sensual and nonsensual, which is actually the passage into man's full nature. Accordingly, he tells the story of man's passing beyond himself as he moves toward his future. This is, at the same time, the story of the manner of forming ideas, since that is what man does.

It seems obvious that thinking wants to think everything. Further, what is thought is present in and to the thinking that thinks it. Thinking, then, is the realm of the present, and thinking brings before it whatever it wishes out of past, present, and future alike. That is why the tradition understands its proper sphere as the timeless: existents come and go, but their essential characteristics are timeless; ideas are beyond the flow of time.

Because of this Nietzsche is concerned with the struggle of thinking against time. Furthermore, while thinking is the way man becomes who he can be, it is also a means of moral conduct. In *Thus Spoke Zarathustra*, Nietzsche tells the story of the self-overcoming man, which Heidegger quotes as follows: "The last man—the final and definitive type of man so far—fixes himself, and generally all that is, by a specific way of representing ideas" (62).

In his effort to measure and thus to form the world and himself, man finds only one barrier that finally stands up to his power and force. He learns to shape the face of the earth, to build a world to his liking, to form his own habits and control human activity. Though all this is subject to his will, will can only direct itself to what can be changed. Of course, it can, and does, direct itself everywhere; but, it can work its influence only on what is at hand now, or on what will be. Thus, it presides over the present and future. Try as it might, however, it seems powerless over what has slipped into the past. It can no longer act on what has already been. Frustrated by this stumbling block, willing suffers from what is revolting to it. But, because willing endures its contrary, revulsion arises in and from the will itself; this allows the 'it was' to burrow in and fester. Here, willing suffers from within itself. According to Nietzsche, as Heidegger interprets him, this revulsion is the essential nature of revenge (93).

Thus revenge (revenge against time and the suffering it causes), as Heidegger sees it, determines "the pursuit of thought, the formation of ideas of man so far"; correspondingly, "*that man be delivered from revenge*: that is the bridge" across to the superman (85).

Of course, all this involves a sophisticated understanding of time, an understanding governed by Aristotle's seminal thinking which holds that time "goes" in the sense that it passes away. This representational idea of time as the transitory, as the "successive flowing away of the 'now' out of the 'not yet now' into the 'no longer now'" characterizes western metaphysical thinking (97, 99).

Nietzsche's story of thinking, then, seems to deliver us from revenge against time by leading us across the bridge to the essential nature of man and thinking. The will is able to free itself, according to Heidegger, "from its revulsion against time, against time's mere past, when it steadily wills the going and coming back, of everything. The will is delivered from revulsion when it wills the constant recurrence of the same" (104). This is why Zarathustra teaches the eternal recurrence of the same and the doctrine of the overman at the same time. His story is the story of a change in thinking and of how representational thought thinks thinking in relation to time.

That which is called thinking is the forming of ideas in time, and thus willfully directs itself to overcome time. Thinking has come to be named and understood, in the tradition, in light of man's desire to be free from time: it is the forming of ideas in such a way that they are secure from time, so that they are independent. Thinking is the human activity at home in the timeless. Thus, what is called thinking needs to be understood by way of the traditional doctrine of thinking, logic.

Clearly, thinking is a, perhaps *the*, fundamental human activity. It is a psychological process, but not merely that. It is also a means to human freedom, to the development of our human nature. It is a part of our conduct. Hence, to become human means to learn how to think. Nor is this merely a statement about what it is necessary for a child to do in order to develop his potential humanity. Finally, it presents a further *question*. What must humans do to learn the thinking which will free them into their essential nature?

Asked in its third version, the question is, What does thinking call for? Heidegger says: "The third question inquires about us, it asks what resources we must rally in order to become capable of thinking" (157). In light of his answers to the first two versions, the answer follows straightforwardly. We need to learn how to form ideas correctly; we need to learn the art of representation. And insofar as the subject matter calls for it, we must also learn variations on the traditional forms of thinking; for example, we must become expert at dialectic and now logistics. Here we presume that, insofar as we are not thinking now, it is because of our inability, our neglect in these matters. What we need to do is to learn thinking so as to be (more) capable of it. Of course, this is a personal matter; each of us is responsible for setting aside other, distracting interests to focus our attention on this. But, more importantly, it is a cultural matter. As a civilization, we must learn to be capable of better representation. Logic will aid us in this, in the rules and methods of forming ideas, of judging, of asserting propositions. And we have available (especially with the aid of history of philosophy) several excellent paradigms of thinking.

One such model is Nietzsche. In his terms, as long as we still form ideas in the manner of the last man—"blinking," he calls it—we have not yet really thought. In order to become "overmen," men have to learn how to think. This, of course, involves the full human will and power, not merely a narrowly rational faculty. Nonetheless, it is still a question of developing our capacities in order to determine and fulfill our essential nature.

This already answers more than was asked. It tells us that our own, as yet undetermined, nature calls for thinking. That is, the first three questions and answers develop into a fourth which, according to Heidegger, "asks for the standard by which our nature, as a thinking nature, is to be measured" (157). Heidegger puts it this way, "The fourth question inquires about That which commands us to think, That which entrusts thinking to us" (157). It seems as if the answer is found in our potential humanity, in who we can become. That which calls for thinking would be human need. And what is needed is that which is useful to man, useful in the deepest sense of useful for man to become fully man. Here "use" is understood in terms of human utilization and production. The final need is human production, not of conveniences or even ordinary necessities, but of ourselves. The business of mortals would be making ourselves, as the third question and its answer indicate.

In Nietzsche's terms, this would be a matter of will. We will ourselves. Put this way, our willing would be that which calls on us to think so that we could finally become ourselves.

But Nietzsche and the tradition meant more by "will" than human will. This indicates a more elaborate answer to the fourth question. In fact, according to Heidegger, Nietzsche's remarks on thinking, willing, and time move in the sphere of metaphysics. This way of thinking is not so odd as it may first sound if we notice, in Heidegger's words, "that 'will' in the language of modern metaphysics, does not mean only human willing, but that 'will' and 'willing' are the name of the Being of beings as a whole" (95). This is so, for Schelling, Schopenhauer, Kant, Fichte, and Hegel, among others.

Thus, according to Heidegger, Nietzsche says what he does of man because of the way "being" is conceived.

> To modern metaphysics, the Being of beings appears as will. But inasmuch as man, because of his nature as the thinking animal and by virtue of forming ideas, is related to beings in their Being, is thereby related to Being, and is thus determined by Being—therefore man's being, in keeping with this relatedness of Being (which now means, of the will) to human nature, must emphatically appear as a willing. (91–92)

But if human willing (and thinking) seek revenge against time, and it now turns out that "will" fundamentally refers to Being, then time must be closely related to Being.

How can that be? Despite what Schelling says, for example, our western tradition holds that primal Being is eternal or independent of time. Heidegger explains that the tradition understands "in being" to mean being present. Accordingly, Being and Time are asked about at the same time; they are interpreted together in the metaphysical tradition: Being is being present.

If this is so, we have a more profound answer to our fourth question. What calls for thinking is not finally unfulfilled human nature, but that to which man is ultimately related: Being. Since man is dependent on or grounded in Being, it may not be surprising that what he has long, even more primally, thought about should be what calls for thinking. What thought ultimately thinks about, what makes man as thinker possible, is that which calls on man to think: Being. (Of course, this further informs us about the third question. We can now see that we need to learn how to think—to conceptually hold on to—Being as time and willing, too. In Nietzsche's terms, we must learn to will "will"; that is why he says we must learn to will the primal Being of beings, as the eternally recurrent willing of the eternal recurrence of the same.

The answer to the last question seems simple enough. That which calls on man to think is being—where everybody seems to understand the word in everyday usage. We say, for example, that there is a tree out in the yard. We say many things about it, but finally only one metaphysical thing: that it is; it is not so that it is not. Clearly, this is a strange and difficult thing to think; surely it calls for thinking.

Of course, it is not clear what the relation of a particular being to its Being is here, but we do know that western metaphysical thinking as described by Heidegger

> proceeds from beings to Being. Thinking ascends from the former to the latter. In keeping with the guiding questions, thinking transcends the particular being, in the direction of its Being, not in order to leave behind and abandon the particular being, but so that by this ascent, this transcendence, it may represent the particular being in that which it, *as* a being, is. (222–223)

Thus, "thinking" names the forming of representational ideas, understood according to the doctrine of logic, and what thinking calls for is our learning how to think the Being of beings. It must think that to which man is ultimately related: that which calls for thinking is the Being of beings.

ORIGINARY, RECOLLECTIVE THINKING

The answers make sense. They are the answers the metaphysical and scientific tradition has developed and feels at home with. And, they are correct. But they do not satisfy Heidegger. It is not that they don't or shouldn't satisfy us, but they don't satisfy

Heidegger. It is not that he finds them false or lacking in power or justification. Yet, for all that, he believes that they do not really answer the questions. These answers leave much unsaid and unanswered because they do not really ask what needs to be asked. That is, what is said finally leaves the subject matter unquestioned, and insofar as much is unasked, it is left unthought. Accordingly, what is needed is not further elaboration and refinement of the same answers and positions. Rather, a different sort of answer and position is called for, one which more deeply asks the questions.

That is what Heidegger claims. And that is why, along with the conventional answers, Heidegger gives an entire second set of answers, woven in with the first, but quite different. His own answers are carefully and deeply related to the conventional ones. Still, the look and sound of his own answers are strikingly different. What they say is quite something else.

Heidegger holds that for all their accomplishments and for all their knowledge, science, philosophy, and the other humanistic sciences do not really think about what is called "thinking." They talk about it as an object, with a good deal of sense and sophistication, but they do not really think it. In brief, he makes a startling, and seemingly arbitrary statement about what is most thought-provoking in our thought-provoking time: "*Most* thought-provoking is that we are still not thinking." (4)

What this means and what any alternative would be can only develop at the same time that we keep an eye on the conventional answers given above. As Heidegger says, "Especially we moderns can learn only if we always unlearn at the same time. Applied to the matter before us: we can learn thinking only if we radically unlearn what thinking has been traditionally. To do that, we must at the same time come to know it" (8). This is why he gave the correct, traditional answers.

But what is deficient in the sensible, conventional answers of the tradition? What sort of answers does Heidegger himself propose, for example, to the first question, What is it that is named "thinking"? Heidegger answers in a distinctive way, with a somewhat unorthodox family of words: "hidden," "memory," "gathering," "recall," "thank," "devotion," "heart," "bring forth," "let stand and lie," "keep," "guard," and "gift."

Heidegger claims that what must be thought about, for example, what it is that is named "thinking," withdraws from man; it has become hidden in the course of thinking, even as the tradition, with its logical and scientific doctrines, was specifying ever more clearly and distinctly what thinking was.[3] In order to answer our question, we must think what so far remains hidden.

Part of what has been hidden in that what is called "thinking" is memory. This seems absurd at first, since the first set of answers specified memory as an aspect of thinking. But Heidegger uses "memory" to mean something quite different than the mere ability to hold on to an idea or than the act of retaining a representation of something now past.

At first, of course, it does look as if memory were nothing more than a human mental capability. Now, Heidegger does not deny that memory is a psychological aspect of man, but only that it is exclusively or primarily such.

Heidegger thinks past this traditional position: "Memory is the gathering of recollection, thinking back. It safely keeps and keeps concealed within it that to which at each given time thought must be given before all else" (11 and 31); or again, memory is "the gathering of thinking that recalls. As soon as we give thought to this definition, we no longer stop with it or before it. We follow that to which the definition directs us. The gathering of recalling thought is not based on a human capacity, such as the capacity to remember and retain" (150).

Heidegger contends that we must recover this original meaning of "memory" that has been expelled in the last 2500 years; because of this, thought itself has need of memory. To think what it is that is named "thinking," Heidegger recalls that the Old English noun for thought is *thanc: thonc*, which today has taken the form of "thanks": it means a grateful thought. What does this mean, even granted that we may have lost the original meaning of "thought"? "The root or originary word says: the gathered, all-gathering thinking that recalls" (139). In contrast, thought, understood as a logical-rational representation, now has a reduced and restricted meaning:

> Both memory and thanks move and have their being in the *thanc*. "Memory" initially did not mean at all the power to recall. The word designates the whole disposition in the sense of a steadfast intimate concentration upon the things that essentially speak to us in every thoughtful meditation. Originally, "memory" means as much as devotion: a constant concentrated abiding with something. (140)

The contrast with representational thinking is striking, not merely because thinking is defined differently, but because the positions are based on such different presuppositions. The traditional view rests on the assumption (albeit one which is demonstrated) that thinking is an internal activity of and is the subject which is directed at an external object (even when a previous idea is thought about, it becomes an object of thought). Thinking aims to overcome the gulf between subjective process and object; yet, however adequate and correct the representation is, it rests on the difference and separation between the subject and object, the interior and exterior. For Heidegger, however, the matter is quite otherwise: Thinking is thanking:

> The *thanc* means man's inmost mind, the heart, the heart's core, that innermost essence of man which reaches outward most fully and to the outermost limits, and so decisively that, rightly considered, the idea of an inner and an outer word does not arise.
>
> The *thanc*, the heart's core, is the gathering of all that concerns us, all that we care for, all that touches us insofar as we are, as human beings. (144)

This recalling thinking is a giving thanks for what is given for thought. It disposes of what is to be thought. Again, "dispose" cannot be understood in our common sense of "get rid of," but according to the *thanc* (as it is still, and perhaps only, retained in the Alemannic dialect): "When the transaction of a matter is settled, or disposed of, we say in Alemannic dialect that it is 'thanked.' Disposing does not mean here sending off, but the reverse: it means to bring the matter forth and leave it where it belongs. This sort of disposing is called thanking" (146). Heidegger then asks us to consider a tree:

> We stand before a tree in bloom, for example—and the tree stands before us. The tree faces us. The tree and we meet one another, as the tree stands there and we stand face to face with it. As we are in this relation of one to the other and before the other, the tree and we *are*. This face-to-face meeting is not, then, one of these "ideas" buzzing about in our heads. (41)

Of course, scientifically we understand this. The example seems pointless, trivial. But for all the accuracy of representational knowing, Heidegger argues that it does not bring forth the blossoming tree in its radiance and fragrance nor leave it where it belongs: "But—to stay with our example—while science records the brain currents, what becomes of the tree in bloom? What becomes of the meadow? What becomes of the man—not of the brain, but of the man, who may die under our hands tomorrow and be lost to us, and who at one time came to our encounter?" (42). He argues forcibly that "we shall forfeit everything before we know it" if we hastily concede that the sciences determine the reality of the tree in bloom (43):

> When we think through what this is, that a tree in bloom presents itself to us so that we can come and stand face to face with it, the thing that matters first and foremost, and finally, is not to drop the tree in bloom, but for once let it stand where it stands. Why do we say "finally"? Because to this day, thought has never let the tree stand where it stands. (44)

But, it is not just the tree that needs to be thought and which helps us to see what is called "thinking." We also must set free Nietzsche's, Parmenides', and other thinkers' thoughts, as well as our own question, What is called "thinking"? However, in our scientific era, and with our representational definition of "thinking," we are not yet capable of doing this. The thinking, then, of which Heidegger speaks is not at all representational thinking. Whereas, in the latter, an "idea" (conceived as something formed in our minds) is that which is named by "thought," for the former, "idea" is not understood scientifically. He notes, "The word, 'idea' comes from the Greek *eido* which means to see, face, meet, be face-to-face" (41).

Thus, thinking as memory not only gathers, but lets what is gathered stand in its essential nature. Further, it "keeps and safeguards in the gathering" (208):

> All thinking that recalls what can be recalled in thought already lives in that gathering which beforehand has in its keeping and keeps hidden all that remains to be thought.
>
> The nature of that which keeps safe and keeps hidden lies in preserving, in conserving. The "keep" originally means the custody, the guard.
>
> Memory, in the sense of human thinking that recalls, dwells where everything that gives food for thought is kept in safety. . . . Keeping is the fundamental nature and essence of memory.
>
> Only that which keeps safely can preserve—preserve what is to-be-thought. The keeping preserves by giving harbor, and also protection from danger . . . from oblivion. (150–151)

In brief, Heidegger answers that that which is named "thinking," is, in an originary sense, *thanc* and memory: the gathering of recalling thought which brings forth and preserves.

Heidegger's own position is not simply different from the tradition; rather, it is meant to move beyond it through comparison. For example, he says our ordinary or traditional view of memory as merely a capacity to retain indicates that we prematurely end our inquiry with perceptual data. He systematically proposes a new or original meaning for a whole group of "concepts" in addition to memory: "recall," "need," "use," "gather," "thank," "dispose," "keep," "hear," and "idea," to begin a list.

Congruent with this, and implicit in the answer just given, Heidegger gives an alternative meaning to "language" and "history." For if in the ordinary answer, thinking is forming representational ideas and asserting a predicate about an object, whereas for Heidegger, thinking is nonrepresentational, then language too would be nonrepresentational. And if Heidegger is thinking of thinking in a way that gathers, recalls, and keeps it rather than forms concepts about it, then he is not treating the past as the object of scientific study, but in another way. (That is, if he were engaged in the history of philology, by definition he would hold that thinking is representation or would be thinking representationally).

What is it which is named "language"; or, better, what is that which usually is known as the outer, sensory aspect of thinking?

"Language," it seems, means two things at once. It obviously means one thing according to the traditional, representational view, which by now is found everywhere, even in our everyday, common speech, but it also means something else, as Heidegger explains:

> Language admits of two things: One, that it be reduced to a mere system of signs, uniformly available to everybody, and in this form be enforced as being; and two, that language at one great moment says one unique thing, for one time only, which remains inexhaustible because it is always originary, and thus beyond the reach of any kind of leveling. . . . Customary speech vascillates between these two possible ways in which language speaks. It gets caught halfway. (191–192)

Heidegger wants to free us from being caught between the two possibilities by separating them and by explaining their differences. In the ordinary, that is scientific, traditional view that developed out of metaphysics, language is understood as the means of expression. Of course, it expresses a great diversity of interior life (including perception of exterior objects), but basically it is the expression of thinking, which includes perception and willing. Here language is seen as what we use in speech; it is a tool that we employ according to our needs. Where we speak by using language, we, of course, use words. Words appear here as terms, that is, as the sensuous means for presenting a suprasensuous meaning. The sound of the terms is perceived by the senses, so we can communicate signification. Of course, because much of what we express is too important to disappear with the sounds that carry the sense, we have developed writing to fix the expression so we can retrieve it whenever we want. We generally call what we have written down "literature" (though we can distinguish philosophy, poetry, natural science, and so on within the cultural literature if we wish).

This makes sense. But, as in the case of the tree before which we stand, there is more to it than first appears. Like the tree that disappeared in scientific knowing, language disappears in the view that sees it as sound yoked to sense. In fact, as Heidegger puts it:

> When we hear directly what is spoken directly, we do not at first hear the words as terms, still less the terms as mere sound. In order to hear the pure resonance of a mere sound, we must first remove ourselves from the sphere where speech meets with understanding or lack of understanding. We must disregard all that, abstract from it. . . . The supposedly purely sensual aspect of the word-sound, conceived as a mere resonance, is an abstraction. (129–130)

Actually, language in its primary sense is not speech, or the means to speech, but something much more opulent than what can be captured in sound and script.

But language is not merely a more powerful human tool than we first believed. Heidegger holds that finally it is not a human implement. Just as thinking as a human capacity implies that language is employed when we utilize terms, Heidegger's view on thinking, as more than human activity, implies that thought speaks words. That is, the merely human already belongs within language.

> It is not we who play with words, but the nature of language plays with us. . . . For language plays with our speech—it likes to let our speech drift away into the more obvious meanings of words. It is as though man had to make an effort to live properly with language.
>
> Is it playing with words when we attempt to give heed to this game of language and to hear what language really says when it speaks? (118–119)

If language itself speaks, then we must listen to what it says so that we may understand what is said, and, in turn, speak ourselves. This must be done over and over again.

If this is so, we have to be concerned not so much with using terms, as with "what words tell us" (136), for example, to hear what Old English or Greek words say: Here what is needed is a way to let those words tell us what *they* have to say; this requires changing our position so we can hear words in their own realm. Heidegger's answer to what language is, then, implies that language and history belong together. To think language, or what it is that is called "language" and what language says, involves going into the past. We have already seen Heidegger do this. But isn't that to do historical and philological science, that is, to think thinking and language representationally? After all, to ask what the word "thinking," for example, designates, requires that we go back into the history of the word.

We know what the words "past" and "history" mean. The past is that time which has gone by the present and is no more; as defined earlier, the past is the "it was." Events form history the way tiny, individual organisms form a coral reef. History also names the branch of scientific inquiry that aims at knowledge about the past, about history. For example, we can try to know the past of a language, or the whole of a language, and the process of its development through the judgments of history, or other specialized historical sciences such as philology.

Of course, the flow of time and events is prior to historical representation; events in time form the object of scientific observation and judgment. In short, time flows into the past and history accumulates before it can be known.

We often think of local history—the history of our family or town, the history of a group of settlers, the history of a particular word, or the history of a striking event. But history adds up: all the specific events build up into a total history. In its grandest sense, history is the sum of all past occurrences in all their rippling effects, in all their relationships; the scientific specialization called "history" thus studies only parts of the whole by virtue of methodological and practical considerations. We have a clear idea, then, of what history is. We conceive history as universal history which we can study by comparing various aspects with each other and the whole.

This is why we need to find out what the words "language" and "thinking" mean in order to know *what* it is which has been and now is named "language" and "thinking" and *why*. Only then can we correctly form an idea of them. Heidegger elaborates:

> In order to reach the realm of speech from which the words "thought" and "thinking" speak, we must become involved with the history of language. That history has been made accessible by the scientific study of languages. But attention to what words tell us is supposedly the decisive step and directive on that way of thinking which is known by the name philosophy. And can philosophy be based on the explication of terms, that is, on historical insights? . . . Philosophy cannot be based on history—neither on the science of history nor on any other science. . . . All sciences are grounded in philosophy, but not *vice versa*. Knowledge of history, like all knowledge of matters of fact, is only conditionally certain, not unconditionally. . . . But philosophy is that super-historical knowledge which, ever since Descartes, claims unconditional certainty for its tenets. (131–132)

It appears, then, that the question, What is it that is called "thinking" (or "language" or "history") cannot be known both philosophically and historically. The former is an ahistorical knowledge, and the latter is strictly historical (think, perhaps, of historicism). How then could inquiring after thinking by way of the words do anything except muddle our prospects and involve contradiction?

Actually, Heidegger inquires into what it is that is called "thinking" and "language" neither ahistorically nor in the manner of historicism. The same holds for his inquiry into what is called "history." That is, just as Heidegger gave alternative answers to what is called "thinking" and "language," so he holds that history is not to be thought representationally. In contrast to historical study, which inquires into the causal chain of events beginning with the beginning, Heidegger's nonrepresentational thought aims to discover what keeps itself concealed in the beginning—origin.

Beginning is not the same as origin. Where the former merely (though powerfully) marks the start of a series of events and remains in the past, the latter is prior to any start and enables beginning; it gives to us what happens and continues to speak to us;

it endows and endures as long as it is held by memory—the thought that gathers.

In fact, Heidegger holds, source and origin cannot be found by representational "historical" knowing. Though he does not dispute that they have their own correctness, Heidegger juxtaposes (a) the representational idea of "history" as naming the accumulation of past events and the scientific knowledge of this objective data, with (b) the thought of "origin" as naming a continuing wellspring or source.

History can report more and more correctly. But, Heidegger argues, we can ascertain historically and with minute detail what a thinker said about metaphysics, and yet not at all understand what the thinker really thought so that we merely report the thoughts rather than thinking them through ourselves (cf. chapter 2 above). What any thinker thought finally is beyond scholarship; only originary thinking itself can find it and hope to keep it in mind and memory. But the same is true for understanding what thinking, language, and history are. For example, scientific knowing (which includes traditional metaphysics as well as the other natural and cultural sciences) can correctly report on its past, but cannot come to understand either its own origin or the nature of history. Heidegger maintains:

> It cannot do so, scientifically. By way of history, a man will never find out what history is; no more than a mathematician can show by way of mathematics—by means of his science, that is, and ultimately by mathematical formulae—what mathematics is. The essence of their sphere—history, art, poetry, language, nature, man, God—remains inaccessible to the sciences. . . . The essence of the spheres I have named is the concern of thinking. As the sciences *qua* sciences have no access to this concern, it must be said they are not thinking. (33)

This is not to demean science but to describe it so as to set it free from impossible demands and misunderstanding. The knowledge of science is in no way denied; indeed, sciences are properly called sciences, that is, fields of knowledge, because, compared to thinking, they do have a vast accumulation of knowledge. Yet they cannot be freed to be what they are, nor can we understand thinking, until we see the limits of science and that thinking too must be called on.

As a consequence, Heidegger inquires into his subject matter by means of originary thought. An originary understanding and relation of language, history, and thinking appears, for example, when Heidegger takes Parmenides' saying as an instance of how language may say something originary and therefore inexhaustible (as we have just seen). Because Parmenides' saying "does not presuppose what is called thinking, but first indicates the fundamental traits of what subsequently defines itself as thinking" (209), understanding his saying is in no way a problem of the historical or philological interpretation of a text. Or, as another example, in order to understand language, Heidegger avoids seeking historical knowledge about terms and speech (that would be representational thinking about language—representationally conceived); instead, he attempts to recall or gather again the original sense of words and their originary saying. By thinking originary words such as *thanc*, he attempts to indicate, or at least follow a clue toward, "the realm of speech from whose unspoken sphere those words initially speak" (141).

Such originary thinking involves a radically different and more profound understanding not only of the nature of language, history, and meaning, but also of thinking itself (in contrast to the traditional representational view which holds that they are merely human processes or products where direct activity results in artifacts, which pass into the reservoir of the past). That is, whereas according to representational thought, thinking is relegated to the realm of the merely human and is reduced to nothing more than willful mental activity, Heidegger contends that thinking is the gathering back of the originary and the gathering back into the originary. That is why for Heidegger "thinking" names memory: "The gathering of thinking back into what must be thought is what we call memory. We do not understand this word any longer in its common meaning. Instead, we are following the directive of the ancient word (*thanc*). And we take it by no means only in the sense of written history" (143).

But, if Heidegger proposes that memory, understood as *thanc* and originary gathering, is an alternative, originary answer to the question What is it that is named "thinking?" (And, if along with this, he proposes parallel, originary answers to the questions, What is named "language," "history," and so on), then the second question, How has this been so named? also would be answered differently. The second question necessarily appears here because *even though he has not yet fully explained his answers to the first question*, he needs to show the basis for what he says before they can be filled in. Indeed, by contrasting the history of a term and the originary saying of a word, Heidegger already has been considering the first question in the mode of the second, or at least has turned it in that direction. How is it that in our tradition what has been named "thinking" has been so named?

> When we raise the second question, what do we understand by thinking according to the prevailing doctrine, it looks at first as though we were merely seeking historical information about what view of the nature of thinking had come to predominate and is still in force. But if we ask the second question *qua* second question . . . this question is no longer historical—in the sense of narrative history—though it is an historic question. But it is not historic in the sense that it represents some occurrence as a chain of events in the course of which various things are brought about. (164; see also 167)

Here, asked originarily, the second question not only asks how "thinking" names memory, or the gathering recall, but also how it has come to be that "thinking" traditionally names the activity of forming representational ideas—how representation has been known and named by logic. We have already seen the second question answered from the ordinary perspective of representational thought: "But at the same time it remains obscure how this shaping of the nature of traditional thinking takes place. The source of the event remains obscure. . . . Let us be honest with ourselves: the essential nature of thinking, the essential origin of thinking, the essential possibilities of thinking that are comprehended in that origin—they are all strange to us" (45). We need to answer the second question anew then. It asks for the *origin* both of thinking understood as memory and for that of logic, which understands and names the forming of representational ideas.

Heidegger attempts to go back to the origin of thinking as memory, which is also, perhaps, the same origin as that of thinking as determined by logic. To do this, he takes up a saying of Parmenides, which presumably speaks of the origin, or, at least, points to it. In its usual translation, the saying is: "One should both say and think that Being is." But we will not hear what is said here if we merely take "saying" and "thinking" in their modern representational meaning, as Heidegger has begun to show. They too must be reinterpreted, just as "language," "history," and "memory" were. We have to move beyond the correct dictionary translations of the Greek verbs *legein* and *noein*. Surely it is correct that *legein* means "to state" and *noein* "to think"; but what does that mean? Because Parmenides speaks for the first time, at the beginning of Western thinking, concerning what is called "thinking," we cannot use later concretions to interpret what is said in a still unsettled way.

Because breaking through our usual fixed translations requires originary language, and because it is Heidegger's language which is originary, rather than any paraphrase or restatement of it, Heidegger's accomplishment must be allowed to present itself in its own words. Heidegger's originary language must be allowed to stand more than may be customary, if we are to hear it.

Legein usually means stating; but, since Heidegger has already shown that we need to go beyond the conception of stating as a speech activity to understand language as also, and perhaps primally, meaning saying, so too *legein* is connected with saying.[4]

> Let us at last speak out and say what "stating" means! Let us at last give thought to *why* and in what way the Greeks designate "stating" with the word *legein*. For *legein* does in no way mean "to speak." The meaning of *legein* does not necessarily refer to language and what happens in language. The verb *legein* is the same word as the Latin *legere* and our own word *lay*. When someone lays before us a request, we do not mean that he produces papers on the desk before us, but that he speaks of the request. When someone tells of an event, he lays it out for us. When we exert ourselves, we lay to. To lay before,

lay out, lay to—all this laying is the Greek *legein*. To the Greeks, this word does not at any time mean something like "stating," as though the meaning came out of a blank, a void, but the other way around: the Greeks understand stating in the light of laying out, laying before, laying to, and *for this reason* call that "laying" *legein*. The meaning of the word *logos* is determined accordingly. (198–199)

Heidegger argues then that we will be able to understand what is called "thinking" and "stating" only if we take them up into *legein*, where the latter is now understood according to Parmenides' saying. As Heidegger puts it: "Laying, *legein*, concerns what lies there. To lay is to let lie before us. When we say something about some thing, we make it lie there before us, which means at the same time we make it appear. This making-to-appear and letting-lie-before-us is, in Greek thought, the essence of *legein* and *logos*." (202).

Similarly, we must not translate *noein* mechanically as "thinking," especially where "thinking" is thoughtlessly taken in its contemporary sense.

> In *noein* what is perceived concerns us in such a way that we take it up specifically, and do something with it. But where do we take what is to be perceived? How do we take it up? We take it to heart. What is taken to heart, however, is left to be exactly as it is. This taking-to-heart does not make over what it takes. Taking-to-heart is: to keep at heart.
>
> *Noein* is taking something to heart. The noun to the verb *noein*, which is *noos*, *nous*, originally means almost exactly what we have explained earlier as the basic meaning of *thanc*, devotion, memory. (203)

In brief, what is called "thinking" has its origin in (and is so-called because of) the early Greek conjunction of *legein* and *noein* as it is found in Parmenides' saying. In short, Heidegger translates *legein* as letting-lie-before-us and *noein* as taking-to-heart. He goes on to explain four essential aspects of his originary translation (208 ff.).

In the first place, Parmenides' saying goes, "It is necessary to let-lie-before-us and take-to-heart." Heidegger's translation helps show how and why *legein* comes before *noein*: *legein* comes first and has precedence because we can take to heart only what lies before us. Further, and more fundamentally, what *noein* takes to heart is gathered and thereby kept safe in the gathering which is *legein*. Thus, *legein* surpasses *noein*.

Secondly, the two are not merely coordinated in series; rather, each enters into the other. On the one hand,

> *legein*, the letting-lie-before-us, unfolds of its own accord into the *noein*. . . . We have already taken to heart what lies before us. *Legein* is tacitly disposed to *noein*.
>
> Conversely, *noein* always remains a *legein*. When we take to heart what lies before us, we take it as it is lying. By taking to heart and mind, we gather and focus ourselves on what lies before us, and gather what we have taken to heart. Whence do we gather it? Where else but to itself, so that it may become manifest such as it of itself lies before us. The language of the saying is indeed exceedingly careful. . . . the letting-lie-before-us and the taking-to-heart enter upon and into one another in a give-and-take. (208–209)

Thirdly, the translation does more than render a more fitting meaning of the two words; according to Heidegger, it allows Parmenides' saying to become audible because it does not presuppose what is called "thinking," but points to the essential characteristics of what only later develops as thinking. What is caled "thinking" is initially announced with the saying of the two words.

In the fourth place, finding here a first hint of the essential traits of thinking, we see that *legein* determines *noein*. This means both that "*noein* unfolds out of *legein*" (that is, taking to heart is not any kind of grasping what lies before us, but is in the manner of letting come what lies before us) and "*noein* is kept within *legein*" (that is, the heart, into which things are taken, itself belongs within the gathering where that which lies before us is kept safely).

This complex answer to our second question returns us to our first question. If what is called "thinking," in Heidegger's account, is so-called because of an originary relation between *legein* and *noein*, then we can understand thinking as memory in a deeper way. *Legein* and *noein* inform thinking as the gathering recalling (recall how he explains taking-to-heart in regard to *thanc*, devotion, and

memory). The conjunction of *legein* and *noein* also further distinguishes thinking from the representational forming of ideas (understood as a grasp, assault, manipulation, or apprehension of what is
before us, (cf. chapter 2 above) and shows thinking's essential
nature. Positively, what it is that is called "thinking" is memory,
that is, the gathering back so as to keep and protect that which is
given. It is so called because it is taking to heart and keeping at
heart what already lies before us as a gift to be left unchanged. As
Heidegger describes it: "The *noein* perceives beforehand by taking
to mind and heart. The heart is the wardship guarding what lies
before us, though this wardship itself needs that guarding which is
accomplished in the *legein* as gathering" (207).

Heidegger's alternative second answer does more than merely
elaborate his originary answer and sharpen the difference between
it and the common answer. It also incorporates the ordinary
answers to both the first and second questions. That is, his interpretation of the originary *legein* and *noein* re-answers those questions
in a fuller way: it explains why what is called "thinking" in the
tradition is so called and gives an account of how this has come
about. The common answers themselves are seen as partial and
derivative, though in no way merely arbitrary, in light of their
origin. If what is commonly named "thinking" is so named because
of the understanding which we call "logic," the doctrine of logic (of
logos) is itself so named and understood because of a specific
understanding of *legein* and *noein*.

How is it, then, that what is called "logic" and thereby what
traditionally is named "thinking," are so called? Heidegger holds
that *legein* and *noein* are seen as the definitive characteristics of
thinking's essence only in the completion of Greek thought which
occurs in the works of Plato and Aristotle. But an understanding of
these characteristics emerges out of the prior conjunction of *legein*
and *noein*. That is, as noted, *legein* "means to state, to repeat, to tell"
(198). Yet, we will misunderstand this if we understand stating by
way of the representational view of language, where it means
speaking in the sense of organic activity.

According to Heidegger, the Greek view is opposite the modern
one: whereas today we would hold that stating involves meaning

that is created mentally and then physically expressed, the Greeks understood stating in the light of letting-lie-before-us what lays there:

> Laying, *legein*, concerns what lies there. To lay is to let lie before us. When we say something about something, we make it lie there before us, which means at the same time we make it appear. This making-to-appear and letting-lie-before-us is, in Greek thought, the essence of *legein* and *logos*.
>
> The essential nature of stating is not determined by the phonetic character of words and signs. The essential nature of language is illuminated by the relatedness of what lies there before us to this letting-lie-before-us. (202, cf. 205)

Thus, to the Greeks, the essential character of language is found in telling understood as laying. Again, laying is not to be taken as primarily the human activity; rather, what counts in our laying is that "what must be laid lies there, and henceforth belongs to what *already* lies before us. And what lies before us is primary, especially when it lies there *before* all the laying and setting that are *man's* work, when it lies there prior to all that man lays out, lays down, or lays in ruin" (205). Because telling turns out to be a laying, where laying means both that which *is* and then the statement of it, telling is called *legein*. As Heidegger explains this, *legein* does not by itself adequately define thinking—nor does *noein* alone; nor, yet, do even the two together in just any way. Of course, later, the originary belonging together is lost sight of; thinking becomes understood as proposition (from its character as the *legein* of the *logos*) and also as apprehension by reason (from its character as noein). That is, what belongs together in Parmenides' saying later was taken to be merely coupled together and then separated. Heidegger briefly indicates how aspects of this original unity, by way of later, partial stresses and varying combinations, unfolded into what has become the Western European tradition. For example, once *legein* becomes understood only as proposition and *noein* as merely reason, they are recombined into what the Romans name *ratio*.

> Thinking appears as what is rational. *Ratio* comes from the verb *reor*. *Reor* means to take something for something—*noein*; and this is at the

same time to state something as something—*legein*. *Ratio* becomes reason. Reason is the subject matter of logic. . . . But the original nature of *legein* and *noein* disappears in *ratio*. As *ratio* assumes dominion, all relations are turned around. (210)

The story can be traced through medieval and modern philosophy, through the Enlightenment to the present day. For example, according to Heidegger, without *logos* at the root of Western logic, there would be no Christian doctrine of the trinity or concept of the second person of that trinity, no Enlightenment (Kant's main work, the *Critique of Pure Reason*, proceeds by way of logic and dialectic.), no theory or practice of dialectical materialism, no logistics or technology.

Thus, what subsequently is called "thinking"—the activity of forming representational ideas—is so called because the doctrine of thinking—logic—understands thinking as *legein, logos* in the specific "sense of proposition, that is, of judgement. Judging is thought to be the activity of the understanding in the broad sense of reason. The perception of reason traces back to *noein*" (229).

Accordingly, thinking thought by way of the originary letting-lie-before-us and taking-to-heart is distinguished from logic. Put another way, the sort of thinking and saying (or language) associated with logic is not originary, but, Heidegger's own special concern is to locate thinking in relation to such originary language. Thought back to origin, without taking myth and logic to be separate and opposed the way they have been since Plato, "myth means the telling word. For the Greeks, to tell is to lay bare and make appear—both the appearance and that which has its essence in the appearance, its epiphany" (10). Poesy shares the same source and ground, which is why poesy at its most genuine is a thinking back, or recollection.[5] That is, Heidegger finds that the essence of the thinking he is explaining as memory and by way of *legein* and *noein* is close to *mythos* and poetry, properly understood. For example, and in contrast to the common view, he says, "Thought and poesy, each in its own unmistakable fashion, *are* the essential telling. . . Thought and poesy never just use language to express themselves with its help, rather, thought and poesy are in themselves the originary, the essential, and therefore also the final speech that language speaks through the mouth of man" (128).

If thought and poesy speak words, whereas science employs terms to gain knowledge, Heidegger places thinking and poetry close together and holds both apart from science. He argues that the relations (both proper differences and similarities) have been lost sight of. In one way this has happened because originary *legein* and *noein*, once seen together, have been reduced to mean mere speaking and thinking as they are understood according to logic. Specifically, for example, the richer originary understanding is lost to us moderns because we have developed the concept of literature, which levels differences between thinking, poesy, myth, and history. As already seen, in our representational manner we no longer hold onto the originary sense that Heidegger discusses. Accordingly, Heidegger claims that the works of Homer, Sappho, Pindar, and Sophocles are not merely literature because there is a distinction between language as saying and laying and language seen as the means of expression. Understood in light of the latter view—that of logic—literature is what is written down, copied, and distributed for an audience and thus becomes the object of interest and taste.

It appears that Heidegger is merely distinguishing the written and spoken forms of language. For example, he says that Socrates let himself be placed in the draft of thinking which is why he is the West's purest thinker and why he wrote nothing. In contrast, Nietzsche could not resist writing. His piercing written scream is heard, for example, in *Thus Spoke Zarathustra*. Around his writing a whole literature has grown up, which as Heidegger points out, has not yet really found him. "It is as though Nietzsche had foreseen this too; it is not for nothing that he has Zarathustra say: 'They all talk about me . . . but nobody gives me a thought'" (53, cf. 169).

But what Heidegger says of Nietzsche indicates that spoken language is not merely contrasted with written language. Indeed, that view really proceeds from the representational theory of language where speaking and writing are two different ways of using language as the means of expression. There we really can speak of oral or written literature. Actually, the real contrast is between language understood as saying and laying and language understood as speech or a tool: "literature" is a concept developed within the latter understanding. Thus, Nietzsche's real thought and saying is buried when it is seen (or transformed) into mere speech, that is, into language as objective means for subjective expression and which, for example as script, then distracts us from thought and keeps us busy with the ever new. What counts, then, for Socrates, Nietzsche, or any other great thinker are the thinking and saying which give voice to "what language tells, what it speaks and what it keeps silent" (206, cf. 16).

Thus, when thinking and language are no longer seen by way of *noein* and *legein*, memory that recalls and holds and saying as laying disappear; logical representation and the written/spoken expression of the concepts determines what comes after: "Thinking has entered into literature; and literature has decided the fate of Western science which, by way of the *doctrina* of the Middle Ages, became the *scientia* of modern times" (18). Even though Heidegger acknowledges that we still have an inadequate understanding of the nature of literature, we now see something helpful:

> Through literature, and in literature as their medium, poesy and thought and science are assimilated to one another. If thinking is set over against science, it looks by scientific standards as if it were miscarried poesy. If, on the other hand, thinking knowingly avoids the vicinity of poesy, it ready appears as the super-science that would be more scientific than all the sciences put together. (135)

This is all so because of the essential relation of thought and language to science, which is under the sway of scientific objectification that itself establishes and maintains the object-materiality in every specific area. That is, all this depends on the elaboration of the traditional representational view. As Heidegger suggests, "We do not notice the scientific-literary objectifications of that which is, simply because we are immersed in it. For that same reason, the relation of thinking to poesy and to science remains today utterly confused and in essence concealed, particularly since thinking itself is least familiar with the origin of its own essential nature" (136).

In light of this, Heidegger's own position attempts to recall origin and to overcome the ordinary view: "But precisely because thinking does not make poetry, but is a primal telling and speaking of language, it must stay close to poesy" (135).

Accordingly, the question, What is called thinking? is closely related to the question, What is called poetry? They both have to do with language as saying and laying and with remembering thinking that gathers and holds at heart what lies before us. They are alike and belong together; but that does not mean that they are identical. For example, "Parmenides' language is the language of a thinking; it is that thinking itself. Therefore, it also speaks differently from the still older poetry of Homer" (186). Again, then, when we become involved in questioning the nature of poetry and science, it also becomes clear that any proper answer depends on thinking through our basic question, What is called thinking?

In sum, Heidegger answers the second question (How is it that what is called thinking is so named?) in a way that incorporates and accounts for the origin of the common answers of the traditional view; in addition, his answer positively fills in what "thinking" and "saying" mean. That is, his own answer to the first question, what it is that is called thinking, is also fleshed out by "letting-lie-before-us and taking-to-heart."

But even this masterful achievement does not settle the matter; rather, it opens it up further: "our more careful attention to what is named in the word 'thinking' brings us directly from the first question to the decisive fourth" (142). We need to understand the belonging together of *legein* and *noein*. "The conjunction of *legein* and *noein*, however, is such that it does not rest upon itself. Letting-lie-before-us and taking-to-heart in themselves point toward something that touches and only thereby fully defines them" (210). In Parmenides' saying they already lie-before-us; but, how is it that they so lie there (and in such a way that later the two terms each signify what philosophy comes to understand by thinking)? If we attempt to hear what thinking essentially is summoned to, we arrive again at the fourth question (the third also will reappear, but later): what is it that calls for laying and letting-lie-before-us and for taking-to-heart?

Legein and *noein* must be thought in conjunction; however, that conjunction is governed, according to Parmenides' saying, by *chre* (correctly translated as "needful"): "Needful: the letting-lie-before-us so (the) taking-to-heart too" (214). How is it that what are called thinking and saying and their very origin are laid before us in Parmenides' saying as "needful"?

The word "needful" derives from "hand" and "handling." What I handle, I use or have use for. Ordinarily we understand "using" as something we do; that is, like "thinking" and "remembering," "using" seems to us to refer to a human activity. What else would it mean? Heidegger transforms "using," just as he did other words, from the realm of mere human production to an originary sense:

> "Using" does not mean the mere utilizing, using up, exploiting. Utilization is the only degenerate and debauched form of use. When we handle a thing, for example, our hand must fit itself to the thing. Use implies fitting response . . . use is determined and defined by leaving the used thing in its essential nature . . . only proper use brings the thing to its essential nature and keeps it there. So understood, use itself is the summons which demands that a thing be admitted to its own essence and nature, and that the use keep to it. To use something is to let it enter into its essential nature, to keep it safe in its essence. (187)

Use, then, not only has to do with letting-lie-before-us, but with calling and keeping. Calling, of course, in its ordinary meaning, has to do with sound; we sound a call and hear the sound —Nietzsche's cry, for example, is a call, that is, a sound which expresses an appeal. It is also the case that to call is to name. The name is given to the thing by way of coordination. That is, between the object to be named and the name (the sound/term) we conceive a correct, or at least serviceable, relation. In ordinary speech we attach meaning to sounds, to terms, for the purpose of communication. This basic naming allows us to call for this or that so that we are able to put it to use. Indeed, we use the activity of calling to do all this.

Heidegger, however, distinguishes and elaborates a more primal meaning of calling. More than merely making a sound, or even uttering a cry—using a call to call—"the call, by contrast, is a reaching, even if it is neither heard nor answered" (124). For example, we call to someone to come and join us for dinner. Calling means summoning; it reaches out and invites. What is called for in a situation is what is summoned there, what is needed if it is to lie there in its essential nature. Because it is a reaching out and an invitation, "to call" means to move or to get something underway. As an example of a gentle, nonaggressive setting in motion, Heidegger cites the way the *Gospel* speaks of Christ calling on a crowd gathering around him: "And that the old word 'to call' means not so much command as letting reach, that therefore the 'call' has an assonance of helpfulness and complaisance, is shown by the fact that the same word in Sanskrit still means something like invite" (117). This sense of calling clarifies a deeper relation between calling and naming. However, according to Heidegger's position, "to call is not originally to name, but the other way around: naming is a kind of calling, in the original sense . . . every name is a kind of call. Every call implies an approach, and thus, of course, the possibility of giving a name" (123).

But this means that the question, What is it which is called/named thinking? derives from and points back to a more primal meaning where "to call" means "to commend, entrust, give into safe-keeping, keep safely, . . . to call into arrival and presence, to address commendingly" (119, cf. 120). Thus, when we understand the question, What is called thinking? in its fourth sense, where it asks about what calls upon us to think, we are closest to the inmost significance of "to call."

> As soon as we understand the word "to call" in its original root significance, we hear the question "What is called thinking?" in a different way. We then hear the question: What is That which calls on us to think, in the sense that it originally directs us to thinking and thereby entrusts to us our own essential nature as such—which is insofar as it thinks? (124)

Asking "What is that calls on us to think?" inquires after the origin of the call.

That which calls us to think in this way presumably can do so only insofar as the calling itself, on its own, needs thought. What calls on us to think . . . needs thinking because what calls us wants itself to be thought about according to its nature. What calls on us to think, demands for us that it be tended, cared for, husbanded it its own essential nature, by thought. (121, cf. 125)

Heidegger, then, rethinks "calling" and "naming" in the same way as he rethought "thinking," "language," and "use." The originary meaning includes the merely human meaning—which now prevails because the richer meaning is no longer remembered. In regard to the fourth question, we now understand that what calls us to think is not merely something anthropomorphic; further, inquiring into "to call" involves us in the question of the need of what calls on us to think, that is, in use that is more than human use. Rather than conceiving of use by way of human busy-ness and rather than seeking mere contrast with contemporary utilization, we need to think the proper use which itself illuminates our mortal lives.

Use and call, then, belong together: "So understood, use itself is the summons which demands that a thing be admitted to its own essence and nature, and that the use keep to it. To use something is to let it enter into its essential nature, to keep it safe in its essence" (187).

Accordingly, Heidegger holds that in Parmenides' saying "we may assume without fear of being arbitrary that the 'using' mentioned here is spoken in a high, perhaps the highest, sense. We therefore translate *chre* with 'It is useful'" (187). How is it useful? "'To use' means to let a thing be what it is and how it is. To let it be this way requires that the used thing be cared for in its essential nature—we do so by responding to the demands which the used thing makes manifest in the given instance" (191, cf. 192).

In brief, to understand what it is that is called thinking and how it is so called, it is necessary to inquire into what calls on us to think. But it turned out that it is not merely useful for us, for our purposes; it is useful in a more profound sense—useful to what calls for the thinking. That is why Parmenides says, "Useful is: the letting-lie-before-us so (the) taking-to-heart too."

But what, if not merely or primarily man, calls for thinking? That is, what is it to which letting-lie-before-us and taking-to-heart are useful? Are taking-to-heart and letting-lie-before-us useful to what calls for thinking? What finally determines the nature of thinking? Heidegger maintains, "What else but that to which *legein* and *noein* refer? And that is identified in the word immediately following. The word is *eon*. *Eon* is translated as 'being'." (214, see also 215).

Heidegger has already considered the common metaphysical answer to this fourth question. Taken as a human activity, what calls for thinking is human nature; that is, what we are yet to become is in need of thinking in order to fulfill its essential nature. Further, traditional metaphysics tells us that Being calls for thinking. Here, since Being is understood in regard to what is needful to it, Being appears as Willing. The concern with need that surpasses and metaphysically grounds human will would be Being's need, and its concern with what is needful would name that which needs and therefore calls for thinking: Willing.

Heidegger attempts to think the origin of all this by inquiring into the past, by asking for that call which first summoned *legein* and *noein* to their nature and which later echoed in the rule of logic as the essence of thinking. The answer seems to be given in the last words of Parmenides' saying, "One should both say and think that Being is." "Being is" seems to say *that* being is and *what* it is (its essential nature): being is and "part of the fundamental character of being is that it is: Being" (172). It seems as if everyone knows this: we say that this or that is constantly. The tree is; it is large; it is an apple tree; there is a bird in the tree. It seems obvious that we are so close to what is, that it is so easy to note that being is, that we can easily dispose of the saying and the answer.

But Heidegger wants us to do more than acknowledge that we *perceive* beings, to do more than notice that '"being is."' In the same fashion that he asks, "What really is that which the tradition commonly calls 'thinking', 'memory', and 'language'?" he now asks, "What is called being?"

Granted that "everyman" has something in mind with each use of the word "being," Heidegger contends that there is wild confusion in the use of the term, a confusion that is handled practically by reducing "being" to mean what can be indicated as being before us and which we perceive. Here, however, these terms are empty shells and sounds.

"Being" and "to be" appear, naturally enough, as the objects of reference for *legein* and *noein*. But then why should *legein* and *noein* refer to being? Because it is inevitably what we speak of and think of? Because without it, we could not speak and think of anything at all? On the other hand, Heidegger would ask, "Being can be, can it not, without there being men who take it to heart?" (218, cf. 43). It appears that the difference between the first and second option is a difference in view about which is the subject and which is the object. Does thinking call for being or being call for thinking?

Heidegger points out that *eon* ("being") has two different meanings because it is a participle. Because "being" has both nominal and verbal meaning Heidegger maintains that "'being' means something in being and the act of being" (220).

In fact, "being" is the participle of participles: because of it we can say and think all others. The duality which it designates, then, is the *paradigmatic duality*. "In keeping with that dual nature, a being has its being in Being, and Being persists as the Being of being" (221). Logic, since Plato and Aristotle and through the ancient grammarians, thinks and speaks of this, as Heidegger reminds us:

> When we say "Being," it means "Being of beings." When we say "beings," it means "beings in respect of Being". We are always speaking *within* the duality. The duality is always a prior datum, for Parmenides as much as Nietzsche. The duality has developed beforehand the sphere within which the relation of beings to Being becomes capable of being mentally represented. That relation can be interpreted and explained in various ways. (227)

For example, Plato's theory that a being participates in its idea presupposes just this duality of being and Being.

Thus, Western metaphysical thinking, with and after Plato and Aristotle, moves toward Being from beings, as thinking transcends particular beings in order to represent them. That is, the realm of metaphysics is based on the duality of individual beings and Being, and the history of metaphysics is the history of the elaboration and variation of positions on the relation of being to Being.

Heidegger believes that this uncovers a fundamental assumption behind the tradition of metaphysics, an assumption which was not explicitly thought out:

> The *distinction*—the duality of the two—must be given beforehand, in such a way that this duality does not as such receive specific attention. The same is true for all transcendence. When we pass from beings to Being, our passage passes through the duality of the two. But the passage never first creates the duality. The duality is already in use. It is the thing most used, and thus most usual, in all our stating our ideas, in all we do. (228)

Heidegger insists, "however, *no* further inquiry and thought is given to the duality *itself*, of beings and Being, neither to the nature of the duality nor to that nature's origin" (224). But this is not accidental. Indeed, traditional thinking (understood as the forming of ideas about the object of thought) cannot—necessarily—think either the duality or its own foundation in that duality, for conceived as an object, the duality neither held nor allowed to let-lie-as-it-is, nor can the representational science, for all its historical and philosophical knowledge, understand its own origin. Thus, if in the manner of forming conceptual ideas, "we stop for a moment and attempt, directly and precisely and without subterfuge, to represent in our minds what the terms 'being' and 'to be' state, we find that *such an examination has nothing to hold onto*. All our ideas slip away and dissolve in vagueness" (225).

Accordingly, it is the task of originary thinking to think the duality and the origin of metaphysics in that duality. That is why Parmenides' saying says what it does: "Useful is the letting-lie-before-us, so (the) taking-to-heart, too: beings in being." In order for there to be the history of metaphysics and for that history to be understood (and, thereby, what representationally has been called thinking), and in order for us finally to think thinking and origin properly—that is, to think both the first set of traditional, representational answers and Heidegger's own answers—Heidegger maintains that, "the duality of individual beings and Being must first lie before us openly, be taken to heart and there kept safely" (223).

This advances immeasurably beyond the way the tradition commonly asked—and accordingly answered—the fourth question: "Does the call which calls us into thinking issue from being, or from Being, or from both, or from neither?" (218). Heidegger's recalling thinking would have us inquire instead into the duality as duality.

Heidegger's account of the duality (the Being of beings) as the unthought origin of Western metaphysics further clarifies why and how the tradition answers the fourth question as it does. For example, in its spokesman, Nietzsche, what appears to be an anthropological answer finally is a metaphysical answer because the doctrine of the superman is the way Nietzsche presents his basic metaphysical doctrine, the doctrine of the Being of beings. Thus Heidegger's masterful interpretation of Nietzsche speaks of will, revenge, the superman, the eternal recurrence of the same because they all respond to what calls for thinking:

> Who is Zarathustra? He is the teacher of the eternal recurrence of the same. The metaphysics of the Being of beings, in the sense of the eternal recurrence of the same, is the ground and foundation of the book *Thus Spoke Zarathustra* . . . Zarathustra teaches the doctrine of the superman because he is the teacher of the external recurrence of the same. Zarathustra teaches both doctrines 'at once' (XII, 401), because in their essence they belong together. Why do they belong together? Not because they are these particular doctrines, but because in both doctrines there is thought at the same time that which belongs together from the beginning and thus inevitably must be thought together—the Being of beings and its relatedness to the nature of man. (106)

Thus, the originary answer to the fourth question shows the origin of Western metaphysical thinking to lie in the duality!

But Nietzsche is not one thinker among many to be studied arbitrarily because of personal interest. Rather, Heidegger insists, "All the themes of Western thought, though all of them transmuted, fatefully gather together in Nietzsche's thinking. This is why they refuse to be historically computed and answered for" (51). No historical answer, then, but only an originary answer to the fourth question, suffices. That is, what Heidegger points to as the duality is what calls for thinking—and the duality appears in the modern era as willing.

Previously Heidegger had shown how "willing-being" answered the fourth question; now he refines that so we see it is not simply Being which calls, but what was unthought before: the Being of beings. "The word 'willing' here designates the Being of beings as a whole" (91). Without explicitly realizing it, talk of "willing" and "being" was really talk of the duality—now uncovered as the origin of Western metaphysical doctrine.

It would seem, then, that Heidegger provides his answer to the question, What is That which calls for thinking? even if the answer understandably cannot be worked out here in full detail: That which calls for thinking is the duality, the Being of beings.

However, even if this names what it is that calls for thinking, do we understand the answer? Even if we find the Being of beings expressed at the very beginning of Western thinking—in the statements of Parmenides and Heraclitus—do we think it, or merely notice it, or follow its progress historically? If we do not know what "being" or "to be" mean, or if we merely substitute other terms for these, Heidegger warns us that we cannot hear what, for example, Parmenides' saying says:

> What is missing is that we did not try to say those words over in the same way as we did the words *chre* and *legein* and *noein*. (226)

We ask, what calls for thinking?

But this is not an historical inquiry into the various views of thinking which have been formed in the course of its history. Rather, our question is: what is That which directs and disposes us toward the basic characteristics of what in time develops into Western European thinking? What is it that calls, and to whose call something responds in such a way that it is then called thinking, in the sense of the *legein* of *logos*, as the *noein* of reason? That which calls is what *legein* and *noein* refer to because it relates them to itself, and that means uses them. It is what the saying in its final words calls. (232)

What does *eon emmenai* mean, thought in Greek? (229)

Heidegger admits that since he cannot provide all the preparations necessary for uncovering what *eon* says, his answer necessarily will appear arbitrary. He answers accordingly, assuming we will be able to hear his answer "in a questioning mode: the word *eon* indicates what is present, and *emmenai, ennai* mean 'to be present'" (233). What is present is present to us and is with us as it abides in the encounter.

The Being of beings means, then, the presencing of what is present.[6] But according to Heidegger, Parmenides and Heraclitus do not primarily or first consider being present and enduring as mere duration. Rather, "what is present has risen from unconcealment. It takes its origin from such a rise in its being present" (236). Thus, what lies before us, for example, a tree, lies before us with other things that are present. Then he adds:

> And presence itself? Presence itself is precisely the presence *of* what is present. Presence does demand unconcealment, and is a rising from unconcealment—though not generally but in such a way that presence is the entry into a duration of unconcealment. The Greeks experience such duration as a luminous appearance in the sense of illuminated, radiant self-manifestation. (237)

Here we have the climax of Parmenides' saying and Heidegger's answers to the four questions. The presence of what is present is That which calls for thinking and claims *legein* and *noein* "for itself, in respect of itself" (239)!

This central insight explains the subsequent development of Western thought, which works out the nature of logic, thinking, being, Being, and time, though, importantly, the determining presence of what is present is lost track of as the traits of presence are set aside in favor of other traits of the Being of beings.

Thus, the primal unspoken duality still works in Kant, Hegel, and Nietzsche. From Aristotle through Nietzsche, being and time are thought together because "in being" is conceived as "being present." Hence, asking about "Being and time" raises questions about what is unthought in the history of metaphysics. At one and the same time, metaphysics attempts to think of "Being as an eternity and independence of all time" but also conceives of "Being itself as being present, even as the enduring presence," that is as defined—as ruled by—a specific view of time (102–103).

That is why Nietzsche, at the culmination of metaphysics, struggles with this question of the Being of beings (the presence of what is present) as he does, in terms of reverence. Because, the Will (Being) raging against time (understood as passing away) is at the very core of Western metaphysics, Neitzsche, the final spokesman for the tradition, thinks of the will's freedom as the deliverance from the revulsion against time. This freedom would come in willing the constant recurrence of the same, that is, in will, as primal being, willing its own eternity.

Here, we find that Heidegger's answer to the fourth question, What is That which calls for thinking? is the ground for all the other answers which he gives in *What is Called Thinking?* As he puts it, "In *eon emmenai* is concealed the call that calls into the thinking of the West" (240). The presence of what is present sets Western thinking on the road that leads the tradition to say that it is the Being of beings, finally understood as Will, *that* calls for thinking; in turn, this accounts for how what is called thinking is so called—the doctrine of logic explains how thinking holds out against time; finally, because of the traditional view of the laws and procedures of logic, it is the formation of representational ideas—concepts grasping the objects of thought from the flow of time—that is named thinking.

But these traditional philosophical answers are incorporated into the fuller understanding of Heidegger's originary answers. Thought originally, that is, recalled in memorializing thinking, the presence of what is present, understood as the duality, is That which calls for thinking. That is why letting-lie-before-us and taking-to-heart too, conjoined as useful to the presence of what is present, are the source of the naming of what is called thinking. That is why, finally, the first question was answered as it was.

> What is called thinking? At the end we return to the question we asked at first when we found out what our word "thinking" originally means. *Thanc* means memory, thinking that recalls, thanks.
>
> But in the meantime we have learned to see that the essential nature of thinking is determined by what there is to be thought about: the presence of what is present, the Being of beings. (244)

With this final answer, which ripples into and moves all the other answers, the book ends.

But these answers to the question, What is called thinking? have further implications: as humans we must respond to what is (to be) thought; specifically, we must respond as thinkers. That is why the question, What is called thinking? asks, in its third mode, What does thinking call for? Earlier, we passed over this third question when moving from the second question to the fourth. Now we need to hear Heidegger's answer to the third question. If the presence of what is present is that which calls for thinking, what does the presence of what is present call for? What does it require of us if we are to think? Granted, the fourth question and its answer is, as Heidegger tells us, the decisive one:

> It sets the standard. For this fourth question itself asks for the standard by which our nature, as a thinking nature, is to be measured. The third manner of asking is closest to the fourth. The fourth question inquires about That which commands us to think, That which entrusts thinking to us. The third question inquires about us, it asks us what resources we must rally in order to be capable of thinking. (157)

Since we are called to respond to what calls for thinking, it is apparent that, finally, we are not called on merely to form ideas correctly, according to the rules and precepts of logic. That is not to say that we can think incorrectly, falsely, or carelessly, or that we can form ideas willy-nilly or abandon logic for pseudomysticism.

The tradition does correctly teach what we must do in order to think correctly, according to the canons of logic. Nonetheless, the tradition cannot answer how we are to think nonconceptually. What is required, then, is not simply a matter of honing our scientific skills. In brief, when we hear that it is useful for us to think, it is not "as though we were dealing merely with an invitation to be attentive whenever we form ideas, as though the saying, expressed in terms of the usual translation, intended to say: it is necessary that we think" (214). This is why, for all the scientific knowledge and skill we have, Heidegger asserts that we are not yet thinking.

In the first place, then, we must leave off thinking in the ordinary representational manner; this means abandoning our attempt to function as subjects who grasp the objects of thought by way of concepts because that puts us over against what we are trying to think. But, to be an opponent is not the same as to think. Instead of a confrontation with Parmenides, Nietzsche, or science itself, thinking seeks to encounter them. That is, we are called on to abandon the stance of detached, objective thought which begins in doubt and skepticism, and, instead, to begin to think by becoming involved with the nature of thinking, with what thinking thinks. To have a correct grasp of what is being reported or talked about is not yet to be involved in that which is being said (cf. chapter 2 above). "However," Heidegger says, "every dialogue becomes halting and fruitless if it confines itself obdurately to nothing but what is directly said—rather than that the speakers in the dialogue involve each other in *that* realm and abode about which they are speaking, and lead each other to it. Such involvement is the soul of dialogue. It leads the speakers into the unspoken" (178).

And how do we begin? Not by retreating to a certain vantage point, to an indubitable bit of data, but by getting underway. To do so we must open ourselves to what will come by questioning.

In this movement and questioning we must pass beyond the desire for certainty and correctness and according to Heidegger accept *risk*: "This implies: we must submit, deliver ourselves specifically to the calling that calls on us to think after the manner of the *logos*. As long as we ourselves do not set out from where we are, that is, as long as we do not open ourselves to the call and, with this question, get underway toward the call—just so long we shall remain blind to the mission and destiny of our nature" (165).

We must, then, respond to what thinking thinks; this is what is said in the sayings of Parmenides and Nietzsche; indeed, it is what is said in the saying of That which calls on us to think. What is thought and said is the Being of beings. Thus, Heidegger tells us, before all else we need to pay heed to the Being of beings and learn to render service by giving it thought. That is, we are called on to think That which calls for thinking by giving itself to us as a gift: the presence of what is present. Consider the ways in which the presence of what is present could call on us to think: it could direct, demand, or instruct us to think. Actually, it sets us in motion toward it: it invites us. It entrusts itself to our safekeeping.

If we are to respond to the call which calls on us, we must first hear it. Accordingly, we are asked to listen. For example, we must listen to the four questions and to the sayings of the thinkers and of language itself. But even here we are finally called on to listen to the Being of beings. The whole book *What Is Called Thinking?* is an attempt to so listen; we are called on to participate.[7] We are required, then, to respond to what is said.

But, saying has been seen to be a laying and what is said to be what lies before us. Thus, hearing saying would be letting-lie-before-us what-lies-before-us. Further, since what lies-before-us is what we find to take to heart, what calls for thinking—the presence of what is present—calls on us to both let-it-lie-before-us and to-take-it-to-heart, too. We easily treat particular beings this way; but, when we are enjoined to think, the duality first must lie before us in order to be taken to heart and safeguarded. That is what thinking requires. "No one knows what is called 'thinking' in the sense of the third question until he is capable of *legein te noein te*" (231).

Letting-lie-before-us and taking-to-heart, too, what the thinkers say and That which calls for thinking requires that we be capable of reverence and care. Here we are called to put aside all self-importance and desire for control. In fact, being called on to think in this way amounts to being called on to become human.

That which calls for thinking calls us into our essential nature. That is why the third question is so important to us.

> That which directs us to think, gives us directions in such a way that we first become capable of thinking, and thus *are* as thinkers, only by virtue of its directive. (115)

> We ourselves are in the text and texture of the question. The question "What calls on us to think?" has already drawn us into the substance of the inquiry. We ourselves are, in the strict sense of the word, put into the question by the question. (116)

That is why experiencing, or being called on to think, strikes us as a lightning bolt and shakes us to our depths.

Of course, in light of all that has been said, we can appreciate that what thinking calls for is not primarily anything human and certainly is not mere representational thinking. To become capable of thinking we must come to understand that thinking is not merely the result of *our* reaching out or responding, but also is the gift of the presence of what is present—what gives itself as that which is most thought-provoking.

> What is most thought-provoking gives food for thought in the original sense that it gives us over, delivers us to thought. This gift, which gives to us what is most thought-provoking, is the true endowment that keeps itself concealed in our essential nature.

> When we ask, then, "What is it that calls on us to think?" we are looking both to what it is that gives to us the gift of this endowment, and to ourselves, whose nature lies in being gifted with this endowment. We *are capable* of thinking only insofar as we *are* endowed with what is most thought-provoking, gifted with what ever and always wants to be thought about. (126)

We can understand, then, why Parmenides' saying, seen from the point of view of what is of use to the duality says: "Useful is the letting-lie-before-us, so (the) taking-to-heart, too: the presence of what is present." But, from the point of view of man in his need to think—to respond to what calls him—we can understand why "useful" *includes* what we call "need" in the usual translation: truly, for us, "needful is the letting-lie-before-us, so (the) taking-to-heart, too: the presence of what is present."

Since That which calls for thinking gives both itself and our nature, we are most thankful for the gift and are devoted to preserving it. That is, what thinking calls for is the *thanc*. Thinking thinks by thinking That which calls for thinking.

> The *"thanc,"* as original memory, is already pervaded by that thinking back which devotes what it thinks to that which is to be thought—it is pervaded by thanks. . . . We receive many gifts, of many kinds. But the highest and really most lasting gift, given to us is always our essential nature, with which we are gifted in such a way that we are what we are only through it. That is why we owe thanks for this endowment, first and unceasingly.
>
> But the thing given to us, in the sense of this dowry, is thinking. As thinking, it is pledged to what is there to be thought. . . .
>
> How can we give thanks for this endowment, the gift of being able to think what is most thought-provoking, more fittingly than by giving thought to the most thought-provoking? The supreme thanks, then, would be thinking? . . .
>
> When we think what is most thought-provoking we think properly. When we, in thinking, are gathered and concentrated on the most thought-provoking, then we dwell where all recalling thought is gathered.
>
> The gathering of thinking back into what must be thought is what we call the memory. (142–143)

That is what is called thinking.

2. THE STYLE OF THE THINKING AND SAYING

Even if we catch a glimpse of what is called thinking when Heidegger asks and begins to answer the four questions, it is obvious that thinking is not something already accomplished; rather, it must be learned. That is the aim of the book and of our attempt to understand what it says: to learn what is called thinking and, transitively, to learn to think. If thinking is the thankful, recalling memory of That which calls for thinking, how does Heidegger let-lie-before-us and take-to-heart, too, the presence of what is present? How, also can we?

Because Heidegger is concerned with this, in addition to asking and answering the four questions so that we might learn something about the matter and how to go about it, he takes care to show us how he thinks and how we might learn to think. That is, in addition to what he *says about* what is called thinking, he *shows* us thinking.

Heidegger himself calls on us to attend to the style of his thinking when he writes, "If we are to remain underway we must first of all and constantly give attention to the way. The movement, step by step, is what is essential here (170)." The movement, then, is not extraneous to the thinking. Quite the contrary, what we heard about in the first part of this chapter (the double set of answers to the four questions) was itself an abstraction from what thinking is. We are so used to the abstraction, which we often call "content" or "ideas," that we forget it is derived from a prior unitary experience or reality and *assume* the content is what, and all that counts in writing. We assume the content *is* the thinking. It might seem that now we are implying the opposite: that the movement, structure, or form is the thinking. But form, too, is an abstraction from the whole. In fact, while it is true that the form of Heidegger's thinking also is that thinking, it is more important to see how the form and the content are both abstractions, made by representational thinking, which need to be thought through. Both can be seen in their original unity, which is the originary thinking itself. Or, put another way, the thinking can be recovered by attending to the way of the thinking, because *the way Heidegger's thought moves coincides with what he thinks*. The two, though distinguishable, are not, in fact, separate. Heidegger himself clarifies this in an essay entitled *Sprache und Heimat* (*Saying and Home*) where he does not interpret originary poetry as a matter of form and content, that is, not as a representationally understood statement of content. Rather, he contends, originary saying has the character of saying as showing (cf. "A Dialogue on Language," above).[8]

Notice that *how* Heidegger thinks obviously corresponds to

some of the characteristics discussed in the first section. We were told that thinking is recollective: thinking is the remembering which is the originary; it is the gathering of what-lies-before-us and the taking-it-to-heart, too. This is just what Heidegger *does*. In this book he is far beyond any merely idiosyncratic or subjectivistic reminiscence (as the representational conception of memory might have it); here he recalls the subject matter itself.

He proceeds, for example, by calling up original thinking. Witness that he brings Nietzsche's and Parmenides' thought before us. There is no doubt that this careful and reverent attention to their thinking is a taking-to-heart. I am not able here (or, really, not able at all) to render that masterful accomplishment, but the reader of *What Is Called Thinking?* knows how Nietzsche's thought comes alive as Heidegger unfolds it from its own center. By the time he shows us how "Zarathustra teaches the doctrine of the super-man because he is the teacher of the eternal recurrence of the same" (106), we have experienced his recollective thinking.

And he does more. That is, his efforts are not simply aimed at telling us about the Being of beings; rather, he struggles to bring the duality before us. Insofar as he is successful, his thinking is recollective because the origin of thinking is recalled. What calls on us to think is evoked through the recollection of Nietzsche's think-ing (Nietzsche's Zarathustra teaches both these doctrines because they belong together, and they belong together because in both doctrines the Being of beings is thought) and through the recollec-tion of Parmenides' saying (the presence of what is present is what guides the saying and the command to think). In brief, Heidegger does remember the originary. Because he proceeds according to the originary sense and directive of thinking, *the way his thinking goes is an example of what thinking is.*

For such a careful writer as Heidegger, it would not be sur-prising if, in addition to the large movement of his taking-to-heart, the very vocabulary of the procedure which lets-lie-before-us would correspond to what has been told to us about recollective thinking. Even a cursory glance indicates that this is so: the most significant words (as well as the metaphors, symbols, and images) of *What Is Called Thinking?* are, for example, "remembering," "gathering," "belonging," "calling," "recalling," "thanking," "hearing," "keeping," "needing," "using," "gift," "naming," "lay and lie before," "reverence," "preserving," and "saying." This familiar vocabulary contrasts with the language of representational thinking which is distinctively aggressive (for example, subjects "grasp," "control," "manipulate objects, and so on).

This kind of language certainly is striking. At first it may seem unorthodox and, perhaps, arbitrary. Indeed, it is unorthodox—deliberately so. Heidegger proceeds by first raising the traditional "standard" and comfortable way of thinking about thinking in order to display it as *one way* of thinking. That is, he makes it problematic for us by the way he talks. His unorthodox vocabulary, simply by being unorthodox, forces us to see another possibility. Further, his consistent use of this vocabulary elaborates the originary character of originary thinking.

In fact, this way of talking strives to be opposite to the arbitrary and willful use of strange terms.[9] Indeed, such a vocabulary would be required by the subject matter itself. Thinking as recollection, and ultimately, the presence of what is present, cannot speak in the terms of representational thinking or of Being understood metaphysically, though the lingering influence of Being is hard to break free from. The language of the tradition, which appears nonarbitrary (and it is not arbitrary) because it is long familiar, blocks access to, or causes us to forget, what thinking and the duality are and have to say. That is, the special vocabulary which Heidegger employs is not *his* language, but that through which language itself may speak to us anew.

Consider the tone of what Heidegger says. It is not a tone full of self. The modern subjectivistic self, for example, confronts the world as a foreign object, with which it struggles and which it attempts to master. Indeed, it confronts itself in the same way. Here Nietzsche is the representative of modern man, concerned with overcoming not only nature and time, but man himself. We see this in the figure of the self-overcoming man. Nietzsche's words (for example, "the wasteland grows," "deliverance," "blinking," "revulsion," "decomposition," "punishment," "lying," "suffering," and "despisable") surely elaborate the vocabulary of the will—even of Willing itself—in mortal combat with the forces to which it finds itself subjected and, finally, in combat with itself (its own desires, needs and prospect). Because we prefer not to hear or think what is described here, thinking "therefore must at times become a scream. . . . But Nietzsche has to scream" (49).

Nietzsche's language is the language of power, and, above all else, the struggle for power. Of course, it is interesting. Such talk is stimulating, even titilating and seductive. It arouses us; it evokes the sphere of action and of power. Who would not be stirred by the prospect of such willfullness: "Arising from them, here and there, all Epicurean god, the superman, he who transfigures existence: *Caesar with the soul of Christ*" (69).

In contrast, the calm saying of Parmenides and the homely, quiet vocabulary of Heidegger seem dull. In fact, they seem so tame in comparison with Nietzsche's that they risk boring the reader. Though I will say more about this sort of language later, it is enough here to notice how strikingly different it is, and how interesting it is in its own way. If we can set aside our ordinary attraction to what is most stimulating, we find that the tone that Parmenides and Heidegger use is also attractive in its gentle and unobtrusive way. But it is interesting not because of anything related to will and power, but because it opens the prospect of the opposite: humility before something beyond all will and power. That is, the quiet talk sounds the tone of a restrained grandeur. Words like "gathering," "belonging," "heeding," "keeping," "gift," "grateful reverence," and "presence" are hypnotic in their way, for they call to us, too. Through them we hear the inherent lure of the subject matter, that which speaks to us in Parmenides' saying. The tone here is both solemn and gay; it is the heartwarming call of thinking and, finally, of the duality—the presence of what is present.

Clearly, this new tone underlies not only the vocabulary, symbolism, and imagery of Heidegger's thinking, but his procedure as well. Rather than move smoothly by way of sharpening and extending the grasp of concepts, Heidegger proceeds slowly. Because we have gradually become accustomed (over the past twenty-five centuries) to the ideas which now must be thought anew, we must take care not to underestimate that long habituation in a hasty attempt to be done with the task quickly. Accordingly, Heidegger "roughens" the way by considering small, seemingly unrelated aspects of the subject, by retracing steps, by going over and over the same material, by giving hints, by suggesting correspondences without fully elaborating them, and by sketching relationships. But in doing so, he gradually—and in his own way, systematically—probes deeper and deeper into what is thought. He goes about thinking by gradually uncovering what thinking is and what calls for thinking.

For example, according to the representational view, "thinking" signifies a certain mental activity or process and "logic" signifies the doctrine of thinking. The matter seems so straightforward that it scarcely raises attention. But we do not hear what is assumed. We expect that an exploration of signification will take place in *What Is Called Thinking?* and that any correction in what "thinking" or "logic" signify or in their relationship will proceed according to the canons of traditional scholarship, for example, according to those of logic, philology, and history. Further, we assume that any result will be presented according to the rules of these discursive sciences. Naturally, then, it seems that Heidegger's alternative treatment of "the new meaning of the question, What does call for thinking? has been obtained here by arbitrarily forcing on the question a signification totally different from the one that all the world would attach to it on hearing and reading it" (116).

But Heidegger wants to show that the question is not primarily one of signification at all, much less merely of correct signification. Accordingly, he does not finally proceed by way of discursive signification. Of course, he does tell us about thinking, as the first section of this analysis showed, but what he tells us is not what he is fundamentally *doing*. And even where he does tell us of thinking, he does not state a doctrine about thinking, or conceptually prove anything about thinking. Rather, as his tone and procedure show, he is gathering, recalling, and holding before us what should be taken to heart; that is, he is busy thinking before our very eyes. Insofar as all this is so, even if it is only sketched here, Heidegger says and does the same thing. Or, he thinks in and by what he does.

But this is true in a much deeper way than the obvious correspondences just considered can indicate. What he ultimately does is very intricate and precise. Because the relationship between what he does and his own two sets of answers to the four questions is both complex and profound it needs to be elaborated.

To begin, recall the contrast between the answers of the traditional representational metaphysical position and those of recollective, originary thinking. The two sets of answers were seen to be not merely different, though they are that, but related in a curious way. It turned out that the former are derived from, and in a necessary way "reduced" from the latter. That, and how, this is so could only be seen when thinking passes over from the former to the latter. That is, only when thinking manages to find its way to the ground of originary thinking can it see itself for what it is and understand the essence of representational thought (the essence of science and technology, for example). The difference between the two, as well as their relation—finally, the essence of thinking—appears only insofar as thinking succeeds on its way to become thinking. This means passing over from one sort of thinking to the originary sphere of the other sort. This is what Heidegger tells us.

At the same time, Heidegger *does* this: the passing over occurs in *What Is Called Thinking?* We have already seen how he does this again and again. He leaps from the traditional representational concepts of thinking, memory, history, language, usefulness, and being, for example, to their originary sense. Again and again he jumps from the ordinary conception to the new one—or better, past concepts altogether. First he elaborates the one side, then he leaps into what initially appears to be a chasm, but which turns out afterward to have been safe ground—ground already and long prepared to receive our leap in thought and to keep us safe. We could say that what goes on in *What Is Called Thinking?* is just this sort of jumping from one position to the other. In the end, both positions are left standing, but the jump has been effected. Because he jumps and does not merely talk, Heidegger says, "Our explanation has itself constantly been talking about thinking"; yet he also maintains, "We reflect not only on the source of the calling, but with equal resolution on *what* it calls on us to do" (127). His talking about thinking is necessary, then, but the complex answers to the four questions given in the lecture take "us to places which we must explore to reach the point where only the leap will help further. The leap alone takes us into the neighborhood where thinking resides" (12, cf. 7, 8, 21).

Because thinking involves such jumping, man bridges the chasm. The bridge may be as etheral as the individual leap in one thought or as substantial as a well established way of passing across from one place to another—what we normally understand by "bridge." Verb turns to noun; process and event become objectified; originary thinking reduces to conceptualization. It is to overcome these comfortable, thoughtless representational bridges that Heidegger thinks as he does. His shocking words, for example, point out the gulf, and demonstrate that the gulf "that lies between thinking and the sciences, lies there unbridgeably. There is no bridge here—only the leap. Hence there is nothing but mischief in all the makeshift ties and asses' bridges by which men today would set up a comfortable commerce between thinking and the sciences" (8).

Several important things are happening here, all at once. First, Heidegger is calling our attention to what is going on unnoticed. We have become so used to crossing the bridges thrown up by the long tradition that we are no longer aware of what we are doing. That means we are no longer aware of the gulfs we are crossing: it is as if the chasms were gone and the two territories were joined together like a gap in the earth closed by an earthquake. Heidegger points out the gulf for what it is, and thereby allows the bridging to lie before us as it is, as strange and wonderful. (Though our comfortable thoughtless crossing is disturbed, our task and achievement shows itself as important.)

As an example of his technique of jumping, consider the way Heidegger jumps from traditional representational thinking over to originary thinking in lecture seven of Part II of the book, where he separates the usual and originary translations of Parmenides' saying and then crosses the bridge back to the essential meaning. He begins by noting the word structure of the usual translation. Usually the translation inserts the connecting words "both" and "that" to order the other words. By connecting and thus coordinating them as it does, the translation synthesizes them. This sort of translation comes about because of the way we study language and sentence structure—in terms of syntax.

In contrast, Heidegger proposes that we attend to the word structure of Parmenides' saying by inserting three colons which separate the saying into four separate lines so that it reads: "Needful: the saying also thinking too: being: to be." From the vantage point of our usual syntactic understanding and translation we call this word order paratactic, "the words follow each other without connection. They are lined up side by side" (183). Normally this is understood as a deficiency because such language is seen as either a mutation from, or as not yet developed into, syntactic structures. For example, paratactic structure seems to characterize the language of primitive peoples and, within our own syntactic languages, certain stages of development which occur when children learn to speak.

This distinction of the usual syntactic translation from Heidegger's proposed paratactic rendering seems to fit in perfectly with our common view of the early Greek thinkers or pre-Socratics, among whom we count Parmenides. In fact, however, the distinction allows a further separation between our ordinary and the originary view and moves us closer to what is problematic about the saying, rather than allowing us comfortably to "understand" it and ignore what we do not understand.

Think what the usual view implies. The usual view of language as having paratactic or syntactic structure, for example, as corresponds to the common view of history. These sentence structures and the people who use them are ordered in time, for normally the paratactic preceeds the syntactic just as childhood goes before adulthood and as Parmenides was prior to Socrates and Plato. But, Heidegger notes, this posits a measure for Parmenides: to call him a pre-Socratic or pre-Platonic "is not just a chronological designation but a downgrading. For Plato is considered the greatest thinker" (184). This designation is possible because of a judgment we have come to make, and this judgment depends on the criteria we have accepted. Plato is considered the West's greatest thinker because the philosophies derived from his work have most powerfully influenced Western thinking. But is this a proper standard? Can we measure the greatness of anyone's thinking by the extent and duration of its influence? The opposite standard—that the earliest is the best—assumes that the later thinking is confused or in decline. Then, in a romantic view, perhaps, we would adulate the earliest thinkers and language and attempt to philosophize as the pre-Socratics did. Of course, such an inverse view is no better; it shares the same assumptions as the first one.

Heidegger's proposed alternative translation, then, clearly sets up the traditional understanding not only of the translation, but of language, history, Parmenides, and philosophy as one position, as an initial starting point from which Heidegger moves away. In contrast to the usual view, he lays out the originary position, and raising the problematic (the realm of thinking we do not yet inhabit) as an opposite shore, jumps over to it.

Counterpoised to the syntactic structuring, which attempts to specify the meaning of the saying by coordinating words, the paratactic structure offers colons. Heidegger asserts, "The saying *speaks* where there are no words, in the field between the words which the colons indicate" (186). Later, when he has moved away by way of *legein* and *noein* to *eon* by even further leaps, he says, "*Eon* speaks . . . before all else in every conjunction of words, and thus particularly in those junctures of the language which are not specifically put in words. *Eon* speaks throughout language, and maintains for it the possibility to tell, to state" (233).

Opposing the evaluation which the ordinary view has adapted, Heidegger himself dissents, and also reminds us that the relative judgment of Parmenides and Plato is the result of the influence of Platonism and not the understanding of Plato himself. That is, going against the common view, Heidegger has passed over to an originary position, closer to Plato's own—for Plato himself held to his own origins in a way that Platonism does not.

Later, Heidegger again lays out the same alternative sites of thinking and moves back to the originary in what he says of Aristotle. He holds that whereas Aristotelianism falsified the problematic in the desire to find clear-cut answers, Aristotle himself persisted in the questioning attitude. Of course, the generation of systems, by or among followers, is understandable because we need a way to secure and hold things together to provide order and allow for thought. We gain this reassurance by the systematic formation of ideas through concepts. As a result, system-building takes control of thinking.

Rejecting the view that attempts to grasp and assess a thinker or a thought in terms of what came earlier or later, Heidegger questions a thinker by starting from that thinker's own thinking. But this is not an attempt to understand the thinker in his own terms; that is impossible because no one fully understands himself. Rather, it is an attempt "to take up a thinker's quest and to pursue it to the core of his thought's problematic" (185). He does this by jumping into originary thinking.

Thus, traditional conceptual thinking is one position and that of Parmenides, Plato, and Aristotle the other, as the following sentence dramatically claims: "But all of the great thinking of the Greek thinkers, including Aristotle, thinks nonconceptually" (212). Heidegger both separates the two alternatives and clearly leaps across in his originary attempts to hear and interpret, for example, the problematic of Parmenides' saying.

When we see that his proposed alternative translation is part of his jump, and therefore includes the point of departure and arrival, we can understand why Heidegger first took up Nietzsche and then Parmenides. They are the opposite ends of the bridging: "Concept and system alike are alien to Greek thinking. Greek thinking, therefore, remains of a fundamentally different kind from the more modern ways of thinking of Kierkegaard and Nietzsche who, to be sure, think in opposition to the system but for that very reason remain the system's captives" (213).

We can briefly notice Heidegger's juxtaposition of Nietzsche and Parmenides and thereby the two ways of thinking by looking at how he presents their language. Nietzsche's language is assertive, full of self and will; Parmenides' saying simply *stands there* on its own, as it were. Nietzsche's words are full of the speaker's meaning, which includes, of course, his rhetorical force or intention to

move us; in Parmenides' saying something long hidden and unspoken calls through the saying and speaks to us—it speaks even to
Parmenides himself. Nietzsche's words aim to move us into the
sphere of power and action (Heidegger begins this book by noting
that we want to do and act [3, 4]); Parmenides' words call on us to
think. Clearly both Nietzsche and Parmenides and both modern
and Greek thought must appear here in order for Heidegger to have
sites for his jump; clearly too, his originary thinking attempts the
jump right here in these sections.

The moves within the jump are clear. Heidegger (1) considers
legein and *noein*; (2) indicates how modern, representational-conceptual thought obfuscates our translation and our understanding of
these words; (3) treats Greek thinking as nonconceptual; and (4)
again raises the problematic when, for example, he shows how the
"conjunction of *legein* and *noein* . . . does not rest upon itself" (210)
and therefore attempts to hear Aristotle's enduring question, What
might particular beings in their Being be? Not only does this make
a leap from representational to originary thinking, but from *legein*
and *noein* to *eon*.

I noted before that several things are going on at once in
Heidegger's "bridging." In addition to letting the gulf lie before us
and, consequently, the leap, too, (which he shows us by attempting
it), he is performing a leap in regard to "bridging" itself. That is,
here he is jumping from the ordinary conceptual meaning of
"bridge" to an originary one: his treatment of "bridging" is an
occasion of leaping (or bridging, originally understood). Ordinarily
we think that a bridge merely allows passage between two independent objects already opposed to each other. The objects stand as
they are, the subject throws a bridge across so that he may cross
over. Obviously, we start in one place and go over to another.
Apparently, nothing much changes; things remain as they were,
except now the subject can come and go as he pleases and more
comfortably. This seems to be the common representation of
"bridge" and "bridging."

There is a great danger here, though at first it is hard to
see—even for so great a thinker as Nietzsche, according to Heidegger. What is familiar "always remains the real danger zone,

because the familiar carries an air of harmlessness and ease, which causes us to pass lightly over what really deserves to be questioned" (154). "And what is most thought provoking—especially when it is man's highest concern—may well be also what is most dangerous" (31). Here Heidegger is raising the central issue of these lectures. He is letting the gulf we must cross lie before us: how are we to understand the leap, passage, and bridge if not in the traditional representational way? How are we to understand the site which the passing leaves and the site to which the passage goes? What is the relation between the two sites and the passage? (In fact, what are relatedness and connection at all?)

Before we see Heidegger's extraordinary answers to these questions, note how the subject matter calls for a treatment of both the act of jumping (thinking) and its scene. To treat the leap/bridge, Heidegger must be concerned with the whole picture, and the elaboration of this image involves place. It might not be an exaggeration to say that the whole range of concerns in *What Is Called Thinking?* could be found by exploring Heidegger's treatment of *place*.

To begin, Heidegger speaks of the place which thinking seeks: "Toward what sphere of the spoken word do (words) direct us? A thought—where is it, where does it go? . . . In order to perceive a clue, we must first be listening ahead into the sphere from which the clue comes" (138). Heidegger's attempts to move from the realm of speech to the unspoken sphere from which words like "thinking" and "memory" originate. As thinkers, then, we are at one place and think toward another. The place thinking seeks will become clearer if we first see where we are.

For several thousand years we have been in the "sphere of metaphysics" (223). For example, "metaphysics in the widest sense . . . is the sphere where we from the start place Nietzsche's thinking on revenge, and on deliverance from revenge" (90): this is the "space of freedom from revenge" (88), Zarathustra's concern with passage, and "the words about the growing wasteland" (90). Furthermore, Heidegger adds, "Once we reach that heartland, we are in the realm from which the words were spoken: 'The wasteland grows' . . . then a long perspective is bound to open up on the nature and essence of representational ideas. We shall have an open view of the area in which thinking so far is moving—even Nietzsche's own thinking" (94).

Even as we see that we are within the metaphysical-representational realm, it also becomes increasingly clear that we are not at home here. For example, even the terms most central to the tradition, "being" and "to be," "strike us as alien substances in the language" (216). This is not accidental; rather, it is a symptom of how useless we take them to be, "and what is useless belongs no place. Thus it is out of place wherever it appears" (205).

Yet, what seems to belong nowhere actually does have its place. Heidegger places the metaphysical sphere and its attendant homelessness where it belongs—within the originary. When Parmenides insists that it is useful to think and say "being," he is indicating place. Thus Heidegger insists that in order to hear what the Greek words say "we must transplant our hearing to where the telling statement of the Greek language has its domain" (228, cf. 202). "Greek thinking, even before its beginnings, is at home with the prevalence of *eon* as the presence of what is present" (235). And all thinking since Parmenides remains here. For example, Kant's thinking, for all its differences, "moves nonetheless in the same . . . sphere as the thinking of the Greek thinkers" (243).

Representational thought, then, belongs within originary thought—in both we also dwell within language. We can overcome our homelessness by moving from representational thought and representational language to the originary. We will "never come to abide anywhere," for example, if we metaphysically think of language as sound with sense attached later; here we "remove ourselves from the sphere where speech meets with understanding or lack of understanding" (129). Really "as hearers, we abide in the sphere of what is spoken" (130). As another example, Heidegger tells us that we need to understand "call" in its "native realm"; "but, it is unhabitual not because our spoken speech has never yet been at home in it, but rather because *we* are no longer at home with this telling word, because we no longer really live in it" (118). It is as though man had to make an effort to live properly with the language. It is as though such a dwelling were especially prone to succumb to the danger of commonness. (119)

The question becomes then, Can we learn to dwell in our proper place? This does not mean looking for a place to become thoughtless: the questions will remain, for they require "that we settle down and live within" them (137); "we are here taking a way of *questioning*, on which the problematic alone is accepted as the unique habitat and *locus* of thinking" (185). Our very stay on earth is problematic. Heidegger also reminds us that according to Hölderlin's hymn "The Ister River," "There is no stay here for mortals, in the sense of dwelling at home" (190) unless we are made welcome. He then explains that, like Parmenides, Holderlin speaks of "use" to indicate the opening of our place:

> "It is useful" says here: there is an essential community between rock and shaft, between furrow and earth, within that realm of being which opens up when the earth becomes habitation. The home and dwelling of mortals has its natural site. But its situation is not determined first by the pathless places on earth. It is marked out and opened by something of another order. From there, the dwelling of mortals receives its measure. (191)

Insofar as we are able, or become able, to inhabit a world, "our sojourn in this world rests upon thinking" (165). (It also rests upon poetry, though it is a task beyond *What Is Called Thinking?* to secure "for poesy the freedom of its natural habitat. Besides, poesy must first itself determine and reach that habitat" (134).

Our place, then, is in thinking and saying: "thinking would dwell within memory—memory understood in the sense of its originary expression" (147) which means "a constant concentrated abiding with something"(140). "When we, in thinking, are gathered and concentrated on the most thought-provoking, then we dwell where all recalling thought is gathered" (143). Questions in dialogue "involve each other in *that* realm and abode about which they are speaking, and lead each other to it" (178). This is the sphere of the unspoken and most thought-provoking, which calls for thinking and calls us welcomed to our dwelling on this earth. "The call . . . is a reaching, even if it is neither heard nor answered. Calling offers an abode" (124). "The call sets our nature free, so decisively that only the calling which calls on us to think establishes the free scope of freedom in which free human nature may abide" (133).

Thus, we arrive at the *place of places*. In answer to the first inquiry into place, we can say that the sphere toward which we are directed is the sphere of what calls for thinking. If our place is within thinking and saying, and if we are on their questioning way from the metaphysical to the originary realm, we finally can come to dwell in our proper place only when we understand that all this belongs within the duality. The presence of what is present is the sphere containing all others. That the duality calls us means it calls us into arrival and presence and "thus lets our nature reach thought, arrive in thinking" (118). "But in order that metaphysical thinking may first of all discern its own sphere, and attempt its first steps in that sphere, 'It is useful to let-lie-before-us and so the taking-to-the-heart also: beings in being.' The duality of individual beings and Being must first lie before us openly" (223) before we can dispose of it, that is, leave it where it belongs (146). This is how Plato can speak of the *locus*, the site, the place of Being and beings (227).

In all this specification of place, Heidegger is both locating and relating the aspects of what is called thinking in a concrete way and is pointing to the principle of their unity. We have the spheres of man and being, of representational and originary thinking and saying. It appears that the answers Heidegger gave to the four questions were in fact a detailed elaboration of what would be said about and from each of these particular realms. But if the concrete means of presentation and what we abstract as his answers are the same, we would expect a source for this coherence. Here we are asking not only for the scene of his jumping from representational to originary thinking, nor only for the realms of which he specifically speaks, but for the *central principle of organization behind what he says and how he says it*. The central organizational principle is that which holds the belonging-together and also lets the cluster of plural meanings come forward; this principle may be explicit or implicit, abstract or concrete.[10] It enables a unity which is different from the logical unity of representational thinking.

Notice that inquiry after the central principle of organization does not ask for what the subject (author, Heidegger) consciously had in mind when writing, nor for an objectified, detachable form. Rather, it looks for how it is that the work is a Saying that first brings to light what is said. In the essay *"Sprache und Heimat"* mentioned above, Heidegger argues that originary saying has the character of *Bilden*.[11] Now, if we understand this word representationally, it would mean that "saying" is a picturing or imaging. Here *Bild* would be given its modern representational translation which derives, for instance, from the Latin *imago*. But this understanding is itself the metaphysically interpreted grasp of imaging after and toward what is imaged, that is, of *Bild* as representing. In contrast, understood according to Heidegger, Saying as *Bilden* belongs to *Gebild*. Originarily thought, *Gebild* means *pilon*, in the Old High German, or "push" and "impulse"; that is, a first-letting-come-forth (*her-vor-bringer*). In the *Gebild*—the articulating or delineating—of originary saying, things first come to language.

To ask for the *Gebild* of a saying, then, is to ask how the saying goes in, or is unfolded, which suggests rounded out. (In German, one says *Er ist gebildet*, meaning "he is well rounded, brilliantly educated, and cultured"). But the usual English renderings of *Gebild* smack too much of the representational; for example, even Hofstadter's rendering of a poem by Heidegger resorts to "image formed": "Only image formed keeps the vision/Yet image formed rests in the poem."[12] Since originally *Gebild* means the unified exfoliating manner of saying, I will use the word *figura* to translate *Gebild* nonrepresentationally (instead of the unwieldy "central organizing principle which holds together and lets come forward").

We might assume that the *figura* or central delineation of *What Is Called Thinking?* is "man thinking Being and Being grounding man." From such a seminal idea we could understand thinking as the activity which aims at Being and which comes closer as it more and more carefully follows the rules of logic; we could also see that Being, as the basis for being and man, calls for this reciprocal thinking. But this would be misleading: it implies that man and Being are given independently of one another and that one would be prior. That is, man and thought might be the starting point, from which one would proceed toward Being. Being, then, would be understood from the human viewpoint and in human terms. Or the opposite: Being, as independent and prior to man, would ground man; here, the "necessity" of man and his relation to Being would be problematical.[13] But this schema is misleading. For example, in the case of Nietzsche's thought and talk of passage from one site to another, this would indicate that one might "propose an attempt to reinterpret, transform and dissolve Nietzsche's metaphysics into a doctrine of human nature, into an existential anthropology." But the movement is neither from man toward Being nor Being toward man, nor yet both added together, as the following passage suggests:

> Every philosophical—that is, thoughtful—doctrine of man's essential nature is *in itself alone* a doctrine of Being of beings. Every doctrine of Being is *in itself alone* a doctrine of man's essential nature. But neither doctrine can be obtained by merely turning the other one around. . . . We ask what the relation is between man's nature and the Being of beings. But—as soon as I thoughtfully say "man's nature", I have already said relatedness to Being. Likewise, as soon as I say thoughtfully: Being of beings, the relatedness to man's nature has been named. Each of the two members of the relation between man's nature and Being already implies the relation itself. To speak to the heart of the matter: there is no such thing here as members of the relation, nor the relation itself. Accordingly, the situation we have named between man's nature and the Being of beings allows no dialectical maneuvers in which one member of the relation is played off against the other. . . .
>
> *No* way of thought, not even the way of metaphysical thought, begins with man's essential nature and goes on from there to Being, nor in reverse from Being and then back to man. Rather, every way of thinking *takes its way* already *within* the total relation of Being and man's nature, or else it is not thinking at all. The oldest axioms of Western thought, of which we shall hear more, already state this fact. (79–80, cf. 86, 89, 100)

That is, we cannot simply start by thinking of man or being and go toward Being; nor can we proceed the other way around. Rather, in both the doctrine of man and Being "there is thought at the same time that which belongs together from the beginning and thus inevitably must be thought together—the Being of beings and its relatedness to the nature of man" (106): "the relation between Being and human nature carries all things, in that it brings Being's appearance as well as man's essential nature to fruition, therefore the relation must find expression at the very beginning of Western metaphysics" (107).

This shows us the heart of Heidegger's thought! His styled saying (from which we abstract in part, and perhaps unthoughtfully, for our own purposes) presents the "giving all at once of what belongs together: Being, being, man, thinking, and saying." This lies behind what Heidegger says about thinking, saying, calling, being, Being, man, relatedness, belonging, gift, gathering, bridge, passage, jumping, traditional and originary positions, and the four questions themselves. For example, what appears to be nonsensical talk about "calling" when seen from the viewpoint of the one directional scheme (man moving toward Being or its opposite, Being moving toward man) becomes clear as an affirmation of the complex master *figura*, where all the aspects must be held at once. The "call" calls within the whole: "The calling makes us think what is most thought-provoking. The call endows us with thinking as the dowry of our nature. Through the call, then, man is in a way already informed of what the word 'thinking' means" (132). Further, Heidegger says, "In order to perceive a clue, we must first be listening ahead into the sphere from which the clue comes" (138). All thinking and saying are always within *the whole, given beforehand*.

But it is not merely Being and man which are already related; rather, being and Being are already given together in and by the duality. As Heidegger puts it, "We are always speaking *within* the duality . . . the duality has developed beforehand the sphere within which the relation of beings to Being becomes capable of being mentally represented" (227). Thus we have "thinking and saying belonging within and moving to and fro between Being and being. Let us note well—*eon emmanai*, the presence of what is present, and not what is present as such and not Being as such, nor both added in a synthesis, but: their duality, emerging from their unity kept hidden, keeps the call" (242). If man is a being, and if the duality is always given all at once, we would have "thinking and saying belonging within and moving to and fro between Being and human being." Man is gathered into the duality.

Further, as just seen, thinking and saying are gathered in here too (227). It might seem as if thinking and saying were two independent activities which somehow became joined together:

> The conjunction of *legein* and *noein*, however is such that it does not rest upon itself. Letting-lie-before-us and taking-to-heart in themselves point toward something that touches and only thereby fully defines them. Therefore the essential nature of thinking can not be adequately defined either by *legein*, taken alone, or by *noein*, taken alone, or again by both together taken as conjunction. (210)

They are given only together with the presence of what is present: "Only thus can thinking be awakened and called upon to take to heart the present, in respect of its presence" (235). When Parmenides says, "For it is the same think to think and to be," Heidegger explains: *Eon*, the presence of what is present, accordingly keeps and guards *noein* within itself as what belongs to it. From *eon*, the presence of what is present, there speaks the duality of the two. There speaks from it the call that calls us into the essential nature of thinking, and admits thinking into its own nature and there keeps and guards it" (242).

In brief, Heidegger's unified saying concerns the "giving all at once and belonging together of the presence of what is present, the human, and thinking and saying (where, within the duality, thinking and saying move to and fro between the duality and the human)." With such dense language, it becomes clear why any teacher, much less poet, would seek a way to hold on to this thought. As a mnemonic and heuristic aid, and not as an attempt to represent, we could try to show it in a sketch. Again, the *figura* made

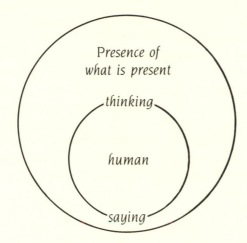

concrete in a sketch only is meant to aid originary—retrieving —thinking this is the same as a teacher's sketch on a blackboard to help students see, remember, and think what he says. The delineation shows the "giving all at once and belonging together" of what is sketched; the sketch shows "the belonging in and moving to and fro within" and also hints at the human jumping over to the duality by way of thinking and saying. Consider a concrete figure: Letting-lie-before-us and taking-to-heart-too would be the ways man belongs to and within the presence of what is present; they would be ways of passage within the duality.[14]

Thinking and saying appear, according to such a figure, as neither activities emanating from man toward Being, nor *vice versa*. Rather, thinking and saying are ways man and the duality belong together. Because this *figura*, merely hinted at in the sketch, or something like it, is understood as primal, Heidegger can speak of the partial aspects as he does and say, "Being calls," "language speaks," or "we think." These partial "truths" are true, or disclose themselves, only when understood as particular manifestations of the whole, abiding situation.

Because this organizational principle indicates that man and the duality are both given at once, Heidegger consistently rejects the common view, which credits man with creating, for example, language or thinking. If that were so, we would need the rejected, subjectivistic-willful model: man as the starting point "moving toward . . ." For example, Heidegger says that the light cast on thinking here "is not introduced by the lamp of reflection," rather, thinking is brought into its own light (28); "Nietzsche neither made nor chose his way himself, no more than any other thinker ever did. He is sent on his way" (46); "we must note that the saying is not offered by Parmenides as the expression of a demand *he* makes. Rather, the saying is addressed to Parmenides himself" (175). Parmenides responds to the saying and call; that is, he moves within the relation indicated by the *figura*. He inhabits his place within the duality and allows himself to be kept safely there; but "man only inhabits the keeping of what gives him food for thought—he does not create the keeping" (151).

To suppose we create concepts which thereby constitute reality or its meaning and a world order is sheer caprice according to Heidegger. Sea, mountain, and tree lie before us; each is "released into the freedom of its station, and is not the effect of our doing and thus dependent on us" (201). "It lies there *before* all the laying and setting that are *man's* work" (205), "and this letting lie, would it not be that laying which is the stage for all other laying that man performs" (206). *Eon* speaks of this, but "what it says *speaks* in our speech long before thinking gives attention and a name of our own to it. When thinking is expressed, this unspoken something is merely clothed in a word, it is not an invention but a discovery, discovered in the presence of the present already expressed in language" (235). Just as what lies before us can be freed by the telling word, so can we by the call which calls on us to think. But because "call" is understood in light of the *figura*, "freedom, therefore, is never something merely human, nor merely divine; still less is freedom the mere reflection of their belonging together" (133).

Accordingly, when we are called on to think, we are not asked to use our ingenuity (122) or understand what is useful for ourselves (again, that would be derived from "man given first and moving toward . . ." Use is nothing that we first create and perform; it is a response which leaves the "used thing in its essential nature" and so "brings the thing to its essential nature and keeps it there. . . . Proper use is rarely manifest, and in general is not the business of mortals" (187). "Using, thought of in this way, is no longer, is never the effect of man's willing" (196). Thus, man is part of the whole, but not the willful source. In light of the *figura*, Heidegger can summarize thus: "the essence of technology stems from the presence of what is present, that is, from the Being of beings—something of which man never is the master, of which he can at best be the servant" (235).

But, if we are to neither understand meaning as proceeding outward from man's activity nor substitute the opposite objectivist view for the subjectivist, how are we to understand the relation between man and the duality? Relation does not mean what the common view might suppose—the conjunction of what already exists independently. That would be relation understood scientifically, which would be derivative from the originary meaning. What is related is from the start already engaged and, at least tacitly, mutually disposed, even if that engagement is not yet brought into the open. Thus, Heidegger speaks of thinking as remaining related to what must be thought even when we are not capable of really thinking, and of a relatedness of man to history: "This means: insofar as we *are* at all, we are already in a relatedness to what gives food for thought" (36). That is to say, what is given in the *figura* already obtains. Relation is the event of that whole. There prevails "a peculiar relation regarding that which is, a relation that reaches beyond man" (84): "the thinkers thinking would thus be the relatedness to the Being of beings" (86): so is saying (202). That which calls is what *legein* and *noein* refer to because it relates them to itself, and that means uses them (232); at the same time, this is "what touches us in the sense that it defines and determines our nature" (144).

This is why our nature is revealed to us in the relationship: what calls for thinking "first entrusts thought and thinking to us as what determines our nature" (125). Heidegger further explains:

This is also why, in the question "What calls for thinking?" we ourselves are in the text and texture of the question. The question

"What calls on us to think?" has already drawn us into the substance of the inquiry. We ourselves are, in the strict sense of the
word, put into question by the question. (116)

Again, the matter is not one-sided. That which calls on us to
think in this way presumably can do so only insofar as the calling
itself, on its own, needs thought. What calls on us to think, and thus
commands, that is, brings our essential nature into the keeping of
thought, needs thinking because what calls us wants itself to be
thought about according to its nature. What calls on us to think,
demands for itself that it be tended, cared for, husbanded in its own
essential nature, by thought. (121)

Thus, *relatedness* is the event of each aspect coming into its essential
nature: we either have nothing or what the whole *figura* delineates,
which we have sketched as follows:

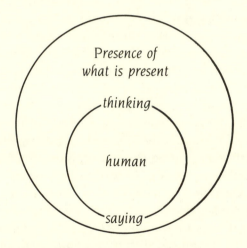

But what sort of relation is this? Heidegger consistently says
that what is related originally "is the same." This is not to say that
what is so related is identical, though this would be the normal
understanding according to the laws of logic with its tendency
toward uniformity. Logically, what is the same is thought as
univocal, according to the law of identity, as Leibniz and others
saw. That is why we ordinarily interchange "identical" and "the
same."

However, this traditional and still current way of understanding "the same" is, as we now should expect, not what it originally meant nor how Heidegger uses it. For example, he says, "What is stated poetically, and what is stated in thought, are never identical; but there are times when they are the same—those times when the gulf separating poesy and thinking is a clean and decisive cleft" (20); the task of the thinker is to "think this One as the Same; and to tell of this same in a fitting manner. . . . The limitlessness of the Same is the sharpest limit set to thinking" (50). For other examples, we can look to these lines: "This, too, we must still learn, to read a book as Nietzsche's *Thus Spoke Zarathustra* in the same rigorous manner as one of Aristotle's treatises; the same manner, be it noted, not the identical manner" (71); "Thus Plato's definition of the nature of thought is not identical with that of Leibniz, though it is the same. They belong together in that both reveal *one* basic nature, which appears in different ways" (165); "To lay and to tell relate in the same mode to the same, in the mode of a letting appear. Telling turns out to be a laying, and is called *legein*" (207). Or consider Parmenides' saying, where Heidegger explains that, as different forms of the same word, *eon* and *emmenai* "designate, so it seems, the same thing. . . . According to the wording, the same thing is now said twice—and thus nothing at all is said. That is, unless the same word *eon* says different things in the first and the second place. And so it does" (219): it means the presence of what is present.

Parmenides also says explicitly in fragment 8, 34 ff., "For it is the same thing to think and to be" (240). And what does *to auto*, correctly translated as "the same," mean? If "the same" does not mean identical, it resists our collapsing what is the same into uniformity. What is the same is both said to be together, and yet is held apart. This is important. It connects "the same" and "place": what is the same is close: "closeness, however, is something essentially different from the vacuous leveling of differences." For example, "the essential closeness of poesy and thinking is so far from excluding their difference that, on the contrary, it establishes that difference in an abysmal manner. This is something we moderns have trouble understanding" (134). Heidegger holds that *to auto* must be thought originally by way of something like "for not apart from . . . but rather only together with": accordingly, *to auto* ("the same") "means what belongs together" (241).

Relation, then, *is an already belonging*. That is why Heidegger speaks of Nietzsche's doctrine of the superman and the eternal recurrence of the same as belonging together in their essence: they belong together (*zusammengehören, zusammengehörigkeit*) "because in both doctrines there is thought at the same time that which belongs together from the beginning and thus inevitably must be thought together—the Being of beings and its relatedness to the nature of man" (106). The four questions "belong together," too (114), and so does what Parmenides' saying says: perhaps not "everything that belongs to thinking belongs to us" (158); "all mortal doing belongs within the realm in which the *chre* makes its appeal" (196); "what must be laid lies there, and henceforth belongs to what *already* lies before us" (205); thinking as thanking and disposing bring a matter forth and "leave it where it belongs" (146); what *eon* and *emmanai* indicate "belongs together" (219); "*noein qua noein* belongs together with *einai* and thus belongs to *einai* itself" (240); "*eon*, the presence of what is present, accordingly keeps and guards *noein* within itself as what belongs to it (242). We notice how belonging and place naturally come together in light of the *figura*: belonging is typically *belonging within* the realm of the duality or with thinking and saying (see, for example, 80, 174, 181, 192).

But Heidegger also elaborates the manner of this belonging (219) and its source when he says, for example, "in giving thanks, the heart in thought recalls where it remains gathered and concentrated, because that is where it belongs" (145). That is, *belonging occurs because what belongs together* (as the same) *is already gathered together*. In fact, "gathering" (*versammeln, Versammlung*) is one of Heidegger's most primal words here, though he does not succeed in saying it as fully as he might or as he does in other originary works. Nonetheless, like all other key words, this cannot be taken as a term in its common sense. Gathering is not merely the activity of collecting independent existents.[15] Recall how gathering characterizes thinking itself and man: "his essential nature consists in memory, the gathering of thought" (31).

But Heidegger does not just think thinking and man's belonging to the duality by way of gathering; *he performs gathering* here in *What Is Called Thinking?* This is what he does by recalling the originary sense of words and the very origin of thinking—the duality; this is what he accomplishes by bringing "man," "thinking," "saying," and the "duality" together, (and further, he gathers us into all this, too, or tries to, by showing us thinking). *He gathers.*

But, returning to how gathering operates in the book, we find it is the central event behind all others, but that it is not merely a human activity. "The gathering of recalling thought is not based on a human capacity, such as the capacity to remember and retain. All thinking that recalls what can be recalled in thought already lives in that gathering which beforehand has in its keeping and keeps hidden all that remains to be thought"(150). For example, "all the themes of Western thought, though all of them transmuted, fatefully gather together in Nietzsche's thinking" (51); in Hölderlin's hymns "is announced . . . a still unspoken gathering of the whole of Western fate" (69–70). Saying as well as thinking, then, is a gathering: "poetic statement gathers into a poem"(162). Further, *legein* is prior to *noein* because *legein* "gathers, and keeps and safeguards in the gathering, whatever *noein* takes to heart. . . . Conversely, *noein* always remains a *legein*. . . . By taking to heart and mind, we gather and focus ourselves on what lies before us, and gather what we have taken to heart. Whence do we gather it? Where else but to itself, so that it may become manifest such as it of itself lies before us"(208–209).

Thinking and saying, then, are both gathering; they gather us together with what should be said and thought. In a way, we are the site of that gathering of all that concern us. It is possible that the thing which touches us and is in touch with us if we achieve our humanity . . . is concentrated, gathered *toward* us beforehand. In a certain manner, though not exclusively, we ourselves are that gathering. The gathering of what is next to us here never means an after-the-fact collection of what basically exists, but the tidings that overtake all our doings, the tidings of what we are committed to beforehand by being human beings. For in giving thanks, the heart in thought recalls where it remains gathered and concentrated, because that is where it belongs. (144–145)

But, if thinking, saying, and humans are all gatherings, they are so only as gathered to what calls them: "In every calling a call has already gathered" (124), Heidegger says. "When we ask, then, 'What is it that calls on us to think?' we are looking both to what it is that gives to us the gift of this endowment, and to ourselves, whose nature lies in being gifted with this endowment" (126). The Being of beings gathers us. "The participle *eon*, being, is not just one more participle among countless others; *eon, ens,* being is the participle which gathers all other possible participles into itself" (221). Presence gathers; it gathers in continuance and rest. "Rest, in the presence of what is present, is a gathering. It gathers the rising to the coming-to-the-fore, with the hidden suddenness of an ever-possible absenting into concealedness" (237).

Nota bene: gathering is the primal occurrence: the presence of what is present, man, thinking, and saying belong together as gathered, as gathering.[16] This is what calls for thinking and saying; "*noein* is kept with *legein*. The heart into which it takes things belongs to the gathering where what lies before us is safeguarded and kept as such" (211, cf. 207). And what lies before us when we do think? According to Heidegger, "When we, in thinking, are gathered and concentrated on the most thought-provoking then we dwell where all recalling thought is gathered" (143). Where do we dwell here? What lies before us as our dwelling place is not merely the duality—the presence of what is present—but all that is gathered. And what is gathered and belongs in the gathering is what the *figura* lays before us.

Thus this *figura* is the central organizational principle of what Heidegger says (for example, it accounts for his answers to the four questions and, in its partial and degenerate forms accounts for what the tradition says), for the way he says what he does (it accounts for the homely vocabulary, for images and metaphors, and for the development of place, relation, belonging, and gathering), and for what he actually does (his gathering common meaning back into originary meanings, his gathering of thinking, saying, man, and the duality in the book, and his gathering us together with all that is already gathered). In retrospect, we can see that, in fact, the *figura* does more than merely "organize" content; it *gathers and holds together the whole of the work—the book as thoughtful-saying.*

Consider an extended example where Heidegger is *doing* something special. From first to last, *What Is Called Thinking?* is concerned with this bridging and leaping which we must learn. In light of the whole book, we see that even the first lecture elaborates the leaping and bridging in terms of the *figura.* Heidegger notes early on that we cannot move to thinking or to what must be thought by the sure and easy process of scientific research (an example of representational bridging); rather, we must leap over the gulf between the sciences and thinking in order to think (18). What of the gulf? How is it that we cross from one side to the other? Heidegger indicates that the poet, rather than the scientist, originarily says what gulf and leap are. Accordingly, Heidegger inquires into Hölderlin's words, which show what is most thought-provoking and which, in turn, is what we attempt to think. The poet's words, then, may summon us on a way of thought.

In a draft for one of his hymns, Hölderlin says, "We are a sign that is not read." But what does this mean? How is it connected to gulfs and leaps? The explanation lies in the hymn's next two lines:

> We feel no pain, we almost have
> Lost our tongue in foreign lands.

The pain (which we do not feel) is pain from the rift with what is.[17] This gulf is in fact hidden from us; it is forgotten. We feel no pain. This is elaborated by what follows, . . . "we almost have/Lost our tongue in foreign lands." Here "foreign lands" says the same as "rift" and "gulf." Apparently, foreign lands are those in which we do not belong, lands in which there is a gulf between us and where we do belong. But what is foreign here, or strange, is not merely caused by man and his doings; it also caused by what is turned away from man. While it is strange and thought-provoking that we still are not thinking, this estrangement is connected with concealment. Thus, it is not merely that we do not belong in those lands that are strange, but that our belonging is almost forgotten or, even worse, that and how we have become foreigners is concealed and no longer even recalled. This is why the poet does *not* say, "we have lost our tongue in foreign lands"; instead, he says, ". . . we *almost* have/Lost our tongue in foreign lands." (My emphasis.) Put another way, it is not that nothing can be said or understood; rather, what can be said or understood seems lost, or almost lost. Accordingly, Hölderlin begins by saying "We are a sign that is not read." We hear "is not read" together with "feel no pain" and "lost our tongue in foreign lands"; but, we also must hear "we are a sign" together with the "almost." That is, we *still* are a sign. Because of this, it is necessary to read the sign and to recall—to language— what it means. This also is why thinking is memory, the gathering of recollection, which is close to poesy. If the sign is to be recalled and read (our tongue not lost), the pain would also be recalled (not forgotten). We may feel the pain then. But, if we are to speak, what will we speak of? If we are to be a sign, if we are to become and remain pointers, to what will we point?

Representational thinking would have an answer here. As Nietzsche points out, because we seem to suffer from the past, we seemingly must speak of overcoming such suffering and point to some deliverance from the "it was." Metaphorically, we must overcome the gulf between past and future, between what is beyond will and within its realm, by bridging the gulf between them. That is, we put up a bridge that overcomes, indeed, abolishes the gulf. The gulf, and with it its pain, is eliminated by the bridge. Here, constructing and using the bridge is the same as filling in the gulf with bulldozers.

Hölderlin, however, gives quite a different answer. In fact, he indicates that the representational answer does not abolish the pain or rift, but merely ignores or forgets it: the sign is not read. This is to say that we must allow the strange to remain strange rather than hurry to eliminate or ignore any possible source of uneasiness. We must learn to let the rift be. Only when the rift and its pain endure can we endure them. In enduring them, we point to them. Where all this is so, we indeed could become ourselves (as signs) and, perhaps, even could be read. Here we would regain our tongues and really would not be in foreign lands. Instead, we would be where we belong. That is, we would dwell within the duality, we would point to our already belonging within it (we would even draw toward and point to what withdraws from us, or, perhaps first, into the withdrawal).

Hölderlin and Heidegger both are interested in how to say and think this. (That Heidegger's interest operates *within* what the *figura* points to explains what real interest is: "Interest, *interesse*, means to be among and in the midst of things, to be at the center of a thing and to stay with it." (5).[18] And both Hölderlin and Heidegger say the same: we must learn to think and say, that is, to remember, to gather together what lies there even if it becomes concealed, forgotten, and mute. Indeed, precisely what the *figura* points to has been concealed, unthought, and unspoken in the forgetful, partial views of traditional, representational thinking and in the withdrawing of what withdraws from us. And in light of the *figura*, then, we also can understand how Nietzsche's thought of bridge and passage already is within the domain of the duality (see 78–80, 106–107 and above 97 ff.).

In the first lecture, then, Heidegger and Hölderlin point to the thinking and saying which allows the rift to be, which endures the pain of such a rift, and which thereby attempts to recall what the *figura* hints at. Such thinking is originary bridging.[19] Here at the beginning of the book, Heidegger is attempting to overcome bridging as it is representationally understood and thereby is pointing to and speaking of leaping within the duality, though we may not have been aware of it on a first reading of the first lecture, as Heidegger notes (12).

We have seen that in the first lecture Heidegger's and Hölderlin's leaping and originary building along with the partial bridging derived from representational thinking move within the *figura* (or what the *figura* points to) and thereby let the lecture lie before us. But this is merely one example of what goes on everywhere in the entire lecture series. That is, the entire book presents originary (and derivative, representational) leaping and bridging this way. Because of this, *all passage*, that is, *all thinking*, saying, and acting can be understood in light of the *figura*. Indeed, the whole *figura*, or what it points to, is presupposed. For example, according to Western European metaphysical thinking, thinking proceeds (ascends) from man or being to Being; but, precisely here, all that belongs together and is gathered together—the duality, which includes man and his relationship to the duality—is given beforehand, even if it is unthought. Further, Heidegger says, "The same is true for all transcendence. When we pass from beings to Being, our passage passes through the duality of the two. But the passage never first creates the duality. The duality is already in use" (227–228). All that belongs together already is gathered and continues to gather.

In light of the *figura* we also can see how the two sets of answers to the four questions, and especially the traditional view, are a "partial" rendering of what needs to be said and thought. Any anthropomorphic position (delineated as man → Being) or any "absolutely objective" one (delineated as Being → being, man, history) is only a facet of the master figure. Moreover, it is a forgetting of the whole, of the whole story and the whole of what is to be thought. In such partial, forgetful accounts what is called thinking is not recalled, held, or kept because the whole of what gathers is not gathered and thereby kept safe.

This is why Heidegger constantly speaks of pointers (and markers, tracks, and so on) the way he does. Man is a pointer (9, 51, 85, 148–150), the ways which thinking and saying take point (12, 46, 88, 139, 141, 178, 186, 225), and the four questions point (103, 114) because all those point to the unspoken origin of thinking, that is, to the whole. They all partially indicate and finally, together, delineate the *figura* and what it more complexly shows. By following these partial, fragmentary pointers, we ourselves point in the right direction and may discover what withdraws and is forgotten even while it continues to draw us and to call for recollective thinking: the whole gathering.

> As we are drawing toward what withdraws, we ourselves are pointers pointing toward it. We are who we are by pointing in that direction. . . .
>
> To the extent that man *is* drawing that way, he *points* toward what withdraws. *As* he is pointing that way, man *is* the pointer. Man here

is not first of all man, and then also occasionally someone who points. No: drawn into what withdraws, drawing toward it and thus pointing into the withdrawal, man first *is* man. His essential nature lies in being such a pointer. (9)

This clarifies why Heidegger speaks of clues: in order to say and think the whole that already belongs together, we must piece it together. Thinking is the gathering of clues in order to approach the originary gathering (138, 150). To cite one example of what Heidegger says is enough to see that what appears as nonsensical to the common view, with its logic of man moving toward Being or Being moving toward man, is actually another articulation of the complex figure in one of its possible variations, which once again, we sketch as follows:

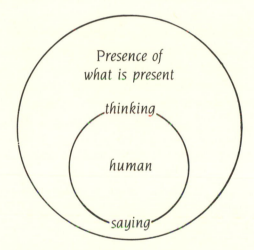

In terms of hearing and saying, Heidegger draws out the figure thus: "In order to perceive a clue, we must first be listening ahead into the sphere from which the clue comes" (138, cf. 142). The clue runs back and forth, and we pass along it.

We also can see that Heidegger's development of the four questions is a weaving. That is, by going back and forth between them he is gathering together saying and what is laid before us in saying, thinking, and what calls for thinking—man and duality. The outcome of this weaving and gathering is the *figura*, which, like Penelope's weaving, is gathered and unraveled over the course of time. As it unravels, we must continually attempt to recover—to recall—it. That is, Heidegger's technique of raising, re-raising, and connecting the four questions is a case of showing us thinking because thinking is the faithful, persistent gathering of what belongs together. It is by laying before us and taking these questions to heart that Heidegger both moves toward what calls for thinking and also provides us with an example of thinking. The four questions, and especially the second and fourth together (respectively, How is it that what is called thinking is so called? and What is That which calls for thinking?), not only set him on his way; finally, they are the way itself.

Consider one instance in which Heidegger does what he says thinking is (that is, what the whole involves). He lays *legein* and *noein* out before us and he also clearly takes it to heart. In the course of this letting-it-lie-before-us and taking-to-heart-too, he gathers *legein*, *noein*, and human being into the duality (see, for example, 182–244, 209, and what has just been said above about gathering).

Thus, by letting the four questions lie before us and by taking them to heart, Heidegger both says and thinks what is called thinking. In thinking what is given to him, and us, as a gift to be thought, Heidegger thinks and says "the calling" within the duality according to the *figura*. "In reality, the calling stems from the place to which the calls goes out. The calling is informed by an original outreach toward. . . . In every calling, a call has already gathered. The calling is not a call that has gone by, but one that has gone out and as such is still calling and inviting" (124, cf. 116–128). Because the call moves between the duality and man, who belongs to the duality, "calling offers an abode" (124).

Insofar as Heidegger is able to dwell in this abode, his dwelling in the calling is his keeping of what calls for thinking. His saying and thinking (really Parmenides') "once again gathers, and keeps and safeguards in the gathering whatever *noein* takes to heart" (208), and "taking to heart is: to keep at heart" (203). But, of course, it is not merely Heidegger himself who does the keeping:

> All thinking that recalls what can be recalled in thought already lives in that gathering which beforehand has in its keeping and keeps hidden all that remains to be thought. . . . Memory, in the sense of

human thinking that recalls, dwells where everything that gives food for thought is kept in safety. We shall call it the "keeping". . . . Keeping alone *gives* freely what-is-to-be-thought, what is most thought provoking, it frees *as a gift*. But the keeping is not something that is apart from and outside of what is most thought provoking. The keeping itself is the most thought provoking thing, itself is its mode of giving. (150–151)

Later he adds, "The presence of what is present, accordingly keeps and guards *noein* within itself as what belongs to it" (242). Thus, it is useful to say and think the duality; the duality uses man. Always, fitting use allows something to come into its own nature and to be safeguarded in that essence. Heidegger does his part to recall, preserve, and guard what calls for thinking by holding safe what is to be thought. We see this in what he says, but also in what he does. The overall movement of his thought recollects, lets-lie-before-us, and takes-to-heart-too, and thereby gathers what already belongs together. One principle way he does this is to safeguard what calls for thinking by holding it for thought in the central organizational principle which *What Is Called Thinking?* delineates, that is, in the *figura*, which itself holds the gathering which occurs in Heidegger's thought and the gathering which Heidegger's thought is part of. The *figura*, then, figures and keeps what is called thinking, Heidegger's thinking, what calls for thinking, and insofar as this thinking is heuristic, what it is that thinking calls for from us.[20]

Where this is so, the thinking and the style of thinking coincide. To attend to the way a thinker thinks is not to do anything other than to try to follow the thinking itself. That is why Heidegger examines Nietzsche's thought. Nietzsche's thinking of the eternal recurrence of the same, the superman, and the revenge against passing away is metaphysical; at the same time that the metaphysical thought of willing the eternal recurrence of the same "carries and determines the inner movement of the work *Thus Spoke Zarathustra*, the work moves in the style of a steadily increasing hesitation and *ritardando*. That style is not a literary device; it is nothing less than the thinker's relatedness to the Being of beings, which must find expression" (107).

Of course, it is not only Nietzsche who, in thinking the relation between Being and human nature, manifests that relation in his thinking. This has been so since the beginning of Western thought. In Parmenides' thought, too, where he "would set his words down with thought and deliberation" (197), the style is the same as the thinking itself. That is why we needed to follow his saying "word by word," and even see what it says "in the field between the words": "Parmenides' language is the language of a thinking; it is that thinking itself" (186). We have also seen that this is also true for Heidegger. The way of his thinking is the same as what he thinks; the movement of his thought by way of the *figura*—indeed, all that we might call the style of his thinking—is the thinking itself.

All this bears directly on our understanding of what is called thinking. Reading about and listening to how Heidegger thinks about thinking is nothing other than attempting to learn what thinking is. And following the style of Western thinkers such as Parmenides, Nietzsche, and Heidegger also is an attempt to understand how it is that what is called thinking has become so called; that is, it is an attempt to understand our tradition's relation to the duality, where the duality has determined "the style of all Western-European philosophy" (224).

This has a further implication. If Heidegger's way of thinking is itself an example of thinking, and if we want to learn thinking, then we can learn thinking by following the example of the thinker. Here, we would understand Heidegger as a teacher who tries to teach us to think, or to learn to think, by the example of his own thinking. By following the way he thinks, we might learn to think ourselves. This is what the book means on its second level.

We already have noted the exemplary character of his originary thought which takes-to-heart and lets-lie-before-us thinking itself. But to interpret Heidegger's thinking as a model for learning how to think moves us beyond understanding what his thinking is. It moves us to consider the effect his thinking is intended to have upon us. Put another way, it asks about Heidegger's teaching, *What Is Called Thinking?* in the mode of the third question. How is it that Heidegger, in this book, *teaches us to do* what we are called on to do in order to think?

3. THE TEACHING AND LEARNING OF THINKING

Since Heidegger's style and thinking are the same, by reading his book and attending to its style we become involved in thinking itself. That is, Heidegger both says that thought is a gathering or recollecting thinking and actually goes about such a recalling gathering. But he does not only gather human being, the duality, thinking, and saying together and, finally, himself. Indeed, if he did nothing more it would be a great accomplishment; but Heidegger also gathers the reader in, too. *What Is Called Thinking?* operates so as to effect thinking in the reader. It does this in several stages, finally operating heuristically in a direct sense. In the first section of this chapter, we saw how what Heidegger said about the four questions involved what thinking calls for. What thinking required of us was to learn originary, recollective thought which gathers in memory. In the second section of this chapter, we saw that Heidegger thought this way in his book. We saw that the style of his thought was both an occurrence of what is called thinking and an example of what thinking calls for. (And since it incorporated what he said in the first part, the first part belongs within such thinking too.)

Clearly, though, Heidegger does not merely go about his task privately and then also allow us to eavesdrop as it were. He engages the reader as a fellow thinker, as someone who also is involved in the task of learning thinking. That is, finally, he deliberately gets us to learn thinking by teaching us how to think. Of course, this is complex; we learn not only from straightforward successes, but also from mistakes and failures, from dead ends and false shortcuts, just as he does.[21]

Heidegger intends for us to take him as a model for our conduct in thinking. This does not mean we should mimic him or that he is a wonderfully and always successful thinker, but that we can learn how to think by seeing how he attempts going about it. Just as Parmenides pointed the way for Heidegger and helped him learn how to think more adequately what called for thought, so Heidegger points the way for us with all sorts of signals, clues, and hints (some more subtle than others) in order that we can follow him by making our own way. In addition to the first two levels where we hear what Heidegger says about what is called thinking and on a second level where we see how he goes about it, *What Is Called Thinking?* is also on a third level the event (or opportunity for the event) of the teaching and learning of thinking.[22] In short, beyond saying what originary, recollective thinking is and doing it himself, he attempts to provide us with the directives and skills we need to do it, too.

That is why he begins the book as he does: "We come to know that it means to think (*"was Denken heisst"*) when we ourselves try to think. If the attempt is to be successful, we must be ready to learn thinking. As soon as we allow ourselves to become involved in such learning, we have admitted that we are not yet capable of thinking" (2). Of course, we all think some way or to some degree; we are involved already in thinking and belong to it (and have for a long time), "and yet man is not capable of really thinking as long as that which must be thought about, withdraws" (7). While we cannot wrestle back that which turns from man even while it calls to him, we can become more capable of thinking.

Of course, Heidegger is not so bold as to claim that he really is capable of the thinking that is called for; he says he, too, is a learner: "Not one of us here would presume to claim that he is even remotely capable of such thinking, or even a prelude to it. At the very most, we shall succeed in preparing for it" (146). Similarly, he writes, "We are still not thinking, none of us, including me who speaks to you, me first of all" (14) and "This is why we are here attempting to learn thinking. We are all on the way together, and are not reproving each other" (14). Still, because he may be a more learned learner, he can also be our teacher:

> Teaching is more difficult than learning because what teaching calls for is this: to let learn. The real teacher, in fact, lets nothing else be learned than—learning. . . . The teacher is ahead of his apprentices in this alone, that he has still far more to learn than they—he has to learn to let them learn. The teacher must be capable of being more teachable than the apprentices. (15)

We should know by now that becoming capable of thinking, learning to think, does not mean merely developing our ability to perform some mental activities more correctly or quickly, nor increasing our interest in representing some object of thought. Rather, if thinking is a grateful and responsive relationship to what calls for thinking (the gift which we incline toward), it is nothing willful at all, but a learning to dispose ourselves to what is addressed to us.

Here that is the fourfold question, What is called thinking? and the duality which gives itself to us as food for thought. That is, we begin to learn by properly giving ourselves over to what calls for thinking, and we do that by learning to hear its call and what the questions ask. Thus, this book attempts precisely the project of learning to listen closely to the question, What is called thinking? in its fourfold sense.

Learning thinking is an action, an action which begins where saying what thinking is leaves off. If we are to understand thinking as an action which truly is part of who we are (not merely as attached to us) and, therefore, as inseparable from what we understand, we can approach it by way of an old word—"habit." "Habit" is a helpful word in regard to the learning of thinking because the thinking we are trying to become capable of has a double meaning. On the one hand, *we think*, even if this does not indicate that thinking is merely a mental activity; on the other hand, *we live within thought* because thinking is one way we are related to the presence of what is present and by means of which it gives itself to us. And "habit" presents us with this double sense. On the one hand, it indicates significant, deliberate action (as opposed to trivial activity). Here, "habit" means the mode in which one lives, and thereby character and a personal way of acting. On the other hand, as Chaucer used it, for example, "habit" is a verb which means to dwell in or to inhabit. But what habit and thinking as action point to is not clear, according to Heidegger.[23]

Part of the problem, then, in our still not thinking is that we do not understand habit and habitation. Indeed, far from its originary sense, we normally suppose habit is not at all action, but mere activity; indeed, that it is precisely thoughtless activity such as nervously smoking. But this diminished sense of habit and the sorts of activity which it indicates are just what we must overcome if we are to learn thinking.

How is it, then, that we are thinking—obviously—and that our culture has been doing so for a long time and that we are not yet thinking? The answer lies within the contrast of traditional, representational thinking and the thinking which it is not yet, or no longer—originary, recollecting thinking. Learning thinking involves the passage from the former to the latter. Therefore, what is thinking, traditionally understood, which we must unlearn in order to learn thinking, or at least, listening? Heidegger answers thus: "you will make close listening essentially easier for yourselves if you will rid yourselves in time of a habit which I shall call 'one-track thinking'" (26).

Single-track thinking is attractive—especially to the will which always wills forward and brooks no impasse, where the essence of technology has dominion and time rolls past. The speed and ease appeal. One-track thinking enables us to be done with issues, with our business, quickly. But this sort of thinking is dangerous because it speeds past what must be thought, just as does the easy use of labels. For example, we label Nietzsche's thought "existential," "nihilistic," or "pessimistic," we label Aristotle a "realist," and we are done with them. But, here we have not thought about them. One-track thinking, then, prevents thinking. "And that such matters have remained unthought is indeed first of all due to the fact that the will to action, which here means the will to make and be effective, has overrun and crushed thought" (25).[24]

But what is one-track thinking that it can do this? Though one-track thinking is not merely one-sided thinking, it levels everything to one level. We see this in the drive of the sciences toward the univocal, in technology's tendency to the homogeneous, and in the spread of the uniform in what is popular (for example, in popular entertainment, food, opinion, and so on).

Merely one-sided views (here thinking means as much—or as little—as having a view), which treat everything "with equal uniformity and mindlessness," lead to one-track thinking: "For it is only on the place of the one-sided view that one-track thinking takes its start. It reduces everything to a univocity of concepts and specifications the precision of which not only corresponds to, but has the same essential origin as, the precision of technological progress" (34). Scientific knowing, that is, the traditional forming of concepts, has its power in its univocal tendency: representational thinking succeeds insofar as it is, successfully and essentially, one-track thinking which produces and also feeds on absolute univocity.[25]

One-track thinking can only be overcome when it is seen for what it is and when its criteria do not spread and apply uniformly to judge all thinking—especially the thinking we need to learn, which, in fact, shows the measure for the derivative, partial one-track thinking.

Heidegger teaches us to recognize the shortcomings of this, our common way of thinking, and to learn to start to really listen by a simple procedure. Over and over again, he prompts us *to hear all that is said* and to discover what we missed when we did not hear everything. That is, he shows us how we are failing to think and how to try to improve. There is no need to list all the occasions and ways in which he does this; typically, he *signals* us to pay attention by using such phrases as "by no means only," "nor merely," "never exclusively," the reason is "no only, and not primarily," "if we simply took the view," and "not only . . . but also."

Such signals alerts us that we may be going so fast that we hear only part of what is being said. For example, when Heidegger says that we are not yet thinking, we immediately assume that thinking is a process and that he obviously is mistaken, or that he means that it is our fault because we have neglected something. But he then explicitly points out that he did not mean merely that; he also meant that what must be thought has turned away from man. In short, we go so far and so quickly down one track that we miss the complex thought. We also fail to hear even what he says about us:

> Let us listen more closely! The assertion says, what is most thought provoking is that we are still not thinking. The assertion says neither

that we are no longer thinking, nor does it say roundly that we are not thinking at all. The words "still not," spoken thoughtfully, suggest that we are already on our way toward thinking, presumably from a great distance, not only on our way toward thinking as a conduct some day to be practiced, but on our way *within* thinking, on the way of thinking. (30)

Another example is when Heidegger says that Socrates is the purest thinker of the West: "This is why he wrote nothing. For anyone who begins to write out of thoughtfulness must inevitably be like those people who run to seek refuge from any draft too strong for them. An as yet hidden history still keeps the secret why all great Western thinkers after Socrates, with all their greatness, had to be such fugitives" (17). Later he adds:

> In the preceding lecture it was said that Socrates was the purest thinker of the West, while those who followed had to run for shelter. There comes the horrified retort: "But what about Plato, Augustine, Thomas Aquinas, Leibniz, Kant, Nietzsche? Dare we reduce these thinkers so much in comparison with Socrates?" But our questioner has failed to hear what was also said: all great Western thinkers after Socrates "with all their greatness." Someone, then, could still be the purest thinker without being one of the greatest. That would give us here much to think about. For that reason, the remark about Socrates began with the words: "An as yet hidden history still keeps the secret why all great thinkers after Socrates, with all their greatness. . ."
>
> We hear something of Socrates, the purest thinker—we fail to hear the rest, and then along the one track of something half-heard we travel on right into being horrified at such one-sidedly dogmatic statements. Things are similar with the conclusion of the second lecture. There we said that our way remains outside that mere reflection which makes thinking its object. How can anyone make such a statement after he has for two hours spoken of nothing else but thinking? However, to reflect on thinking, and to trace thinking in thought, are perhaps not altogether the same. We must give thought to what reflection means. (26–27)

Here Heidegger is teaching as explicitly as possible. His signals and explanations are perhaps like red flags; but, he has to begin to get our attention (recall that "Nietzsche, most quiet and shiest of men, knew of this necessity"; "a man who teaches must at times grow noisy. In fact, he may have to scream and scream, although the aim is to make his students learn so quiet a thing as thinking" (48).

We soon learn to pay attention to any signal that indicates more is being said than we may hear at first. For instance, when he speaks of thinking and the *hand* as the basis of the cabinetmaker's craft, he knows we might object that even the most rural cabinetmaker today uses machines, and uses the occasion to instruct us:

> The point is correct. But in this case, and in this form, it has not yet been thought out. The objection falls flat, because it has heard only half of what the discussion has to say about handicraft. We chose the cabinetmaker's craft as our example, assuming it would not occur to anybody that this choice indicated any expectation that the state of our planet could in the foreseeable future, or indeed ever, be changed back into a rustic idyll. The cabinetmaker's craft was proposed as an example for our thinking because the common usage of the word "craft" is restricted to human activities of that sort. However—it was specifically noted that what maintains and sustains even this handicraft is not the mere manipulation of tools, but the relatedness to wood. But where in the manipulations of the industrial worker is there any relatedness to such things as the shapes slumbering within wood? This is the question you were meant to run up against, though not stop there. For as long as we raise questions only in this way, we are still questioning from the standpoint of the familiar and previously customary handicraft. (23)

As we learn through these examples, we become more alert for the signals, and alert for subtler signals. When we read "it sounds" or "it seems" or "we obviously must," we begin to slow down and question what we are reading and what we are thinking.

Heidegger continues teaching this technique throughout the book, getting us first to hear and then to think about crucial words that are easily overlooked, like verbs, for example, and what the structure implies, as in Parmenides' saying. Sometimes he is very explicit, pointing out that he is stressing what would be overlooked; elsewhere he says nothing, leaving us to discover it on our own. In short, especially with signals, but even without them, he teaches us.

We learn to listen, to try to hear all that is said, implied, or left unsaid, to think through what is given for thought, including the text's and our assumptions (especially the most hidden ones), and we learn to stop trying to think too quickly.

In all of this, we are learning to overcome one-track thinking, Heidegger prepares us to open our ears to hear multiple meanings: "What is called thinking? The question sounds definite. It sounds unequivocal. But even a slight reflection shows it to have more than one meaning. No sooner do we ask the question than we begin to vacillate. Indeed, the ambiguity of the question foils every attempt to push toward the answer without some further preparation" (113). At first it might seem that such an ambiguity is a defect. Whatever has several possible meanings would have them because of a looseness, because of a lack of the univocal meaning the sciences more perfectly exhibit. But as Heidegger explains, this is not so:

> This multiplicity of possible interpretations does not discredit the strictness of the thought content. For all true thought remains open to more than one interpretation—and this by reason of its nature. Nor is this multiplicity of possible interpretations merely the result of a still unachieved formal-logical univocity which we properly ought to strive for but did not attain. Rather, multiplicity of meanings is the element in which all thought must move in order to be strict thought. . . . Therefore, we always must seek out thinking, and its burden of thought, in the element of its multiple meanings, else everything will remain closed to us. (71)

To insist that the works of Nietzsche, Aristotle, or Plato can be understood by applying a "universal schema" forces the works into the categories we have formed, rather than letting them lie before us as they are. As it is itself, each great text has its own character; by its nature each is polysemous. Accordingly, any account (that is, *logos*—where, indeed, *logos* itself has an undeniable multiplicity of meanings) we give of its meaning must be the result of reverence and devotion to the text, not the product of our willfulness. While this is so of great books in which the thinker's thought is laid down, it finally is because of the nature of thought and what calls for thought (which is the whole point of the second level of meaning of *What Is Called Thinking?* as described in section two of this chapter). Every great thinker has seen "that everything that lies before us is ambiguous" (201).

Multiple meaning, then, is the rich sphere within which thinking thrives. Even though it would seem—to common sense thinking, which wants simple, manageable results—that this would lead to chaos, in reading a text, for example, multiple meaning is not identical with jumbled, vague meaning. The multiple meaning of which Heidegger is speaking has its own order, though it is not the order of univocal thought.

By saying this, Heidegger indicates how we might go about reading and interpreting. The first step is to recognize multiple meaning: we cannot understand what we fail to hear. Heidegger describes the process as a *movement* from the common and apparently natural and obvious to the strange or weird. (Indeed, he shows that the tendency to one-track thinking itself is weird.) We need to learn to pass from where we believe ourselves to be comfortable over to the uncanny (*unheimlich*). At times, Nietzsche shouted in order to wake readers up from common ideas and views, at other times, he worked indirectly and quietly. Heidegger, in turn, attempts to wake us up to Nietzsche:

> We could leave sound common sense to its own devices if its obstinacy did not again and again crop up *within ourselves*, even when we make every effort to abandon the commonplace, the obvious as the standard of thinking. . . . For notwithstanding many exaggerations and dark allusions, everything Nietzsche offers to our thought looks largely as if it were perfectly obvious—including even the book *Thus Spoke Zarathustra*, including even his doctrine of the superman. But that is pure illusion. (78)

Here is the first great obstacle, then: what we miss or ignore because it seems obvious. For thinking, the obvious always remains the real danger zone, because the familiar carries an air of harmlessness and ease, which causes us to pass lightly over what really deserves to be questioned. (154)

To get us to stop and pay attention, and thereby pass over

from what seems natural to what seems strange, the teacher has to resort to *strategies*. As we said, Nietzsche alternatively shouted and spoke quietly (sometimes he even spoke of the opposite of what seemed his subject matter). Heidegger says that, in general, these strategies involve exaggeration. For someone asleep in the last row, broad gestures and extreme words may be required. This manner of encounter is deliberate.

> Basically, there are only two possibilities: either to go to their encounter, or to go counter to them. If we want to go to the encounter of a thinker's thought, we must magnify still further what is great in him. Then we will enter into what is unthought in his thought. If we wish only to go counter to a thinker's thought, this wish must minimize beforehand what is great in him. We then shift his thought into the commonplace of our know-it-all presumption. (77)

Another example, is Parmenides' saying. How odd that it should insist that "one should both say and think that Being is." "Being is" seems self-evident, even totally vacuous. But Heidegger shows that it is not (and we suppose Parmenides would have done the same). He moves us from noticing "only the monotony of the sentence 'being is'" to hearing how "what the sentence says in truth is something altogether different" (180). That is, he helps us to find what is astonishing. He does this by showing that what is said about *legein, noein,* and *eon,* for example, is curious. "How curious that stating is to be a laying" (200); "if we continue to be careful, we shall instead find something curious. It will strike us as strange—and that impression must in no way be softened" (211); "then *legein,* as a laying and a letting-lie, would be something uncanny in the midst of all the current canniness of human existence" (206). He does the same elsewhere, with the verb "to call":

> But if we are to hear the question in a sense which asks for what it is that directs us to think, we find ourselves suddenly compelled to accept the verb "to call" in a signification that is strange to us, or at least no longer familiar. . . . And why do we prefer the customary meaning, even unknowingly? Presumably because the unaccustomed and apparently uncustomary signification of the word "to call" is its proper tone: the one that is innate to the word, and thus

remains the only one—for from its native realm stem all the other. (117–118)

We have already seen how Heidegger does this. Indeed, his entire movement of thinking from the common representational way of thinking to originary thinking is exactly this passage from single-track to multiple meaning, from the obvious to the strange—when we assume that our concepts grasp what originary terms mean, we are not yet thinking. (We will return later to see how he accomplishes this "raising the unaccustomed" by the way he translates.)

We learn, then, to pass over to the unfamiliar. We learn to take up residence in an alien place, where the "harmonious and artless progress of natural speech" is disturbed by words like "being" and "to be": "Ultimately, there is a chill around these terms. We do not quite know where the chill comes from—whether it comes from what they indicate, or from the frozen, spectral manner in which they haunt all philosophical discourse and writing. All this will cause misery to a man who is honest with himself" (217, cf. 225). We must learn to dwell in this uncanny place where we apparently are not at home in what is said and thought (118, and section 2 above). This is the land of originary, multiple meaning.

If we understand this, parts of the book which seem odd, which run against common sense, which are posed in an obviously disturbing way, or which seem to fly in the face of what we expect show themselves to be *strategies* that Heidegger employs both to waken us to issues and to teach us how to go about the same thing ourselves. That is, he is teaching us that learning thinking requires us to make problematical what must be thought. And he is showing us how to do this. For example, he brings Parmenides' saying forceably before us by stressing the structure, by inserting colons he magnifies the *manner* in which the saying goes:

How would it be if we took this occasion to be astonished that seemingly so obvious a saying is pronounced with such emphasis in a thinker's works? How would it be if we were astonished about it, and let our astonishment make us aware that perhaps something problematical, something worthy of questioning, is involved here?

> We just now stressed the structure of the saying, only in order to get closer to the area of its problematic. . . . The problematic alone is accepted as the unique habitat and *locus* of thinking. (182–183, 185)

Further, the more successfully we learn to hear the wealth of what is said, the more we learn to question it; that is, it becomes increasingly problematical. But that means that the problematic must not only be raised, but maintained, even cultivated. (For example, Heidegger notes that people become agitated because he keeps on raising the question of logic. Because of this cultivation of the problematic, the questioning and answering of genuine thinking are not those of one-track thinking. The latter asks in order to pose problems, and answers in order to dispose, to eliminate or solve, the question.[26] But here the questions remain; indeed, they more truly become questions. Consider the question, What is called thinking? Heidegger's answer to the question

> maintains the question in its problematic. When we follow the calling, we do not free ourselves of what is being asked. The question cannot be settled, now or ever. If we proceed to the encounter of what is here in question, the calling, the question becomes in fact only more problematical. When we are questioning within this problematic, we are thinking. . . .
>
> To answer the question "What is called thinking?" is itself always to keep asking, so as to remain underway. (168–169)

Accordingly, we can understand the lecture series and our possible frustration at what it does *not* do insofar as we learn what Heidegger is teaching us about how to think: "The title of this lecture course is a question. The question runs: What is called thinking? As a course of lectures, we expect it to answer the question. As the course proceeds, then, it would make the title disappear bit by bit. But the title of our lecture course remains— because it is intended as it sounds. It remains the title of the entire course. That course remains one single question" (214–215). Of course, in teaching us to raise a problematic by moving from the unthought and common to the questionable and strange, Heidegger is showing us how to let something lie before us and how to take it to heart too.

Once we find the problematic with its multiple meaning and begin to let it be questionable, the next step is to clarify the meanings without reducing them. Specifically, we must clarify the ambiguity which conceals and allows several possible ways of dealing with it. We learn how to deal with each specific case of multiple meaning by not only finding the meanings themselves, but why and how they are just those meanings. While it is true that many words have multiple meanings accidentally, some of the language itself and the careful thinkings of the thinkers are truly, essentially polysemous. For example, "the multiple meanings of the word *eon*, however, are neither accidental nor vague. Rather, the word has two meanings in a specific and definite sense" (219, cf. 221). Or, as we have seen, the question, What is called thinking? has four meanings in a precise way. This means that we must understand the meanings, each in themselves and as they belong together.

We have to find the unity behind them. What disturbs us, then, from our one-track thinking about what is called thinking "lies less in the multiplicity of its possible meanings than in the single meaning toward which all four ways point" (114). This is what calls for thought; this is why each thinker needs one thought only.

That is, we begin to see that there is a unity behind the many questions. Yet because of the unity, the multiplicity remains as it is. Accordingly, though originary thinking learns to live in complex, multiple meaning, it also finds that what it thinks originally also is simple. Of course, "simple" does not mean "allows of a quick, easy solution"; rather, it means "belongs together as aspects of the same." For example:

> It takes us a while to accept the multiplicity of meanings of the question "What is called thinking?" The question is fourfold. But it stems from a oneness, a simplicity. Accordingly it does not break up into a chance multiplicity. Simplicity introduces measure and structure, and also initial power and endurance, into the four modes in which the question may be asked. (132, see also 152)

The simple is what is most easily and often overlooked "because it is simple—too simple for the easy fluency of common notions" (239).

Thus, what began as learning to hear multiple meaning ends in learning to (try to) find the simple. The teacher may have had to "shout" at us in the beginning; but, insofar as we learn to think, we end in a still reverence. Nietzsche understood this. One technique is necessary to wake us up; quite another is required to say what needs to be said after the alarm has sounded. Thus, noise may be needed at first, though continued noise results only in a din; quiet and gentle conversation is necessary for us to hear thinking, though the quiet would never be possible unless the common views and understanding were shaken and overcome by an initial noise. This enables us to see why Nietzsche spoke as he did, at times crying out, at times whispering "the silent words" and "thoughts that come on doves' feet"—or even remaining silent altogether (73).

Heidegger makes a similar move in his book. First, he rouses us from our representational slumber by discussing Nietzsche. It is easy to spur us with Nietzsche's energetic talk of power, revenge, will, and the superman. Then, once we begin to wake, Heidegger calms us by turning from the stimulating Nietzsche to Aristotle, and, finally, to the quiet realm of the unspoken. That is part of the reason why he says, "It is advisable, therefore, that you postpone reading Nietzsche for the time being, and first study Aristotle for ten to fifteen years" (73). By turning to Aristotle, and later to Parmenides, Heidegger teaches us to hear what is quietly important, which is presented modestly rather than dramatically, and to try to hear the originary, still source of saying and thinking.

When we learn from the arrangement of the book to move from the exciting to the unpretentious, we come to be at home in what appeared strange. The teacher induces us to leave our customary sphere to discern that we belong where at first it appeared that we didn't. This is what Heidegger himself has done in the lecture series and what he implicitly and explicitly teaches us to do. An example of the implicit or quiet teaching is the way Heidegger tends to move us from nouns to verbs. Over and over he begins by thinking about a word and its meaning in regard to things. For example, in the course of thinking about "bridge" it soon becomes clear that the noun depends on verb or verbal sense. It is the action of bridging that is fundamental. He follows the same procedure for "hold" and "keep," and for "present," "pointer," and "track." Over and over, things yield to prior action, subjects and objects give way to movement. Each case finally uncovers the strange and points to the simple.

This action essentially belongs to thinking. Whereas one-track thinking is in a hurry for a result (since activity is commonly mistaken for action), Heidegger teaches that originary thinking is a true action. That is, the sorts of steps which he teaches are the doing of thinking.

Because thinking is underway, Heidegger constantly speaks of "*way*." To learn thinking "we must get underway" with it; even though we are not yet thinking properly, we nonetheless already are underway thinking (see, for example, 8, 25, 45–46, 75). The way of, or toward, thinking is long and anything but a smooth progress; we must leap and jump (12). On our way we may be aided by the ways other thinkers have gone: Nietzsche's words provide a "marker on the way" (46), for example. But the ways of other thinkers are not anything idiosyncratic or "creative." No thinker, according to Heidegger, ever made or chose his way himself; "he is sent on his way" (46). Because of this, the ways of other thinkers give evidence of origin and of what is beyond what is said—where "way" means "the tone from which and to which what is said is attuned" (37).

Accordingly, it is important for us to attend to other thinkers' ways and to the way the question asks, What is called thinking? That is, we attempt to find a "way of access to the tradition of thinking generally. The best and basically only manner to find out is to go that way" (75). Yet, at the same time, we are underway on our own specific way, not merely on some general or universal way (8, 44). As a result, we must properly pass along the ways of others only "at the proper junctures along our way" (21) and "to the extent to which our own way requires it" (60).

On our way from common, representational thinking to recollective, originary thinking, we learn what thinking calls for and what calls for thinking only when we hear in the originary sense. For example, here Heidegger teaches us to hear "call" by moving us into the midst of its unaccustomed multiple meanings: "When we hear that question, the meaning of 'call' in the sense of 'instruct, demand, allow to reach, get on the way, convey, provide with a way' does not immediately occur to us. We are not so much at home with these meanings of the word that we hear them at first, let along first of all" (117).

In these lectures, Heidegger is teaching us by calling us in precisely this sense: he demands, allows, and instructs by providing a way for us to get on the way. He makes his way in answer to the call which calls us; in turn, he calls us to the way by telling the originary story of "calling," "use," and "thank," for example.

Briefly note what happens as Heidegger speaks of "thank." He begins by exploring the relation of "thought" to "thank" by way of the Old English *thank* or *thonc* and its surviving contemporary forms. In the process, he moves beyond the history of words to think what "thinking" and "thank" mean; that is, he unfolds a way of hearing what the originary word says. Further, what Heidegger says and does points to the thought-provoking sphere of the unspoken. Thus, the unfolding of the story of "thank" aims at a richer, inexhaustible originary realm, beyond the impoverished common one. In pointing to and listening ahead into the sphere of the unspoken, he helps prepare the way for thinking. He is responding to the directives of the clues which come from that sphere, and to the forerunners to those clues. In this thinking and story-telling, the originary connections between what belongs together "will dawn on us" (145). In brief, by telling us the things which he does, Heidegger is helping us make our way. In his very speaking of "way" he is acting; here his saying is a doing.

Thus, a thinker both makes a way for himself, and also shows us how to do so for ourselves. In the first place, what the thinker, for example, Nietzsche, says and how he says it, "the tale that these words tells, does not just throw light on the stretch of the way and its surroundings. The tale itself traces and clears the way" (46, cf. 28). Subsequent thinkers must also try to become clear about such ways, to reach the heartland of earlier thinkers because no way of thinking is given, or pre-made, like a highway. Each thinker must make his way anew, even if it is over the same ground. But because thinkers go the same way, they can teach each other (and us) how to go about making a way.

One striking way in which Heidegger shows us how to be on our way involves the question, What is called thinking? asked in its second form: How is it that what is called thinking has become so called? It seems that this is nothing other than the historical way of asking, What is called thinking.[27] If so, the scholarly task would be to spell out the way Western philosophy began and developed. Heidegger's treatment of this supposition is very instructive. He does not attempt to disprove it, "not because we are indifferent to that impression, but because it cannot be dispelled by talking about it instead of setting out on the way of our question" (167). Specifically, Heidegger does not attempt to set out the correct answer; rather he attempts to get us to hear and respond to the call. That is, instead of staying within the way of thinking where the historical supposition reigns, he trys to help us leap to another way. He leaps from the sphere of representational thought to originary thinking.

But, then, to answer the question in its second, or any, form, he would need to start over. This is precisely what he does in the middle of Part II (167). He begins anew by jumping over to Parmenides and his way of thinking—held in fragment six, which experiences and responds to the call in a thoughtful way: "One should both say and think that Being is."

When he approaches Parmenides' saying, Heidegger continues to contrast the two major ways in which we might try to think that saying and then develops the route, *via* multiple meaning, to the one inevitable way. It might appear that thinking requires that we "take a position somewhere along the road, and there make conversation about whether, and how, earlier and later stretches of the way may be different, and in their difference might even be incompatible"; actually, we respond to the way only when we remain underway; we need "to be underway on the way in order to clear the way" (169).

The first way belongs to those who never set out on the genuine way, "but merely take up a position outside it, there forever to formulate ideas and make talk about the way" (169). A little later Heidegger adds that this is the realm of conversation, which "consists in slithering along the edges of the subject matter" (178). It seems clear that Heidegger would identify this way as that of the common view of thinking. Here, for example, we might suppose that from some "objective," that is, historical or philosophical stance outside the way, we could know what Parmenides' saying means. Yet even if we are careful not to follow this path, we still may not be on the proper path; we may be between ways in our search for the necessary and only way. Again, this way is not made by the thinker. This was true for Parmenides and Nietzsche, too. Nietzsche's tale of the wasteland "itself traces and clears the way"; Parmenides' saying is addressed to him, calls to him, "and even speaks to him of ways" (175). Obviously, this path is that of originary thinking, where we try to "take up a thinker's quest and to pursue it to the core of this thought's problematic" (185), and it is the rare and difficult way of thinking.

As noted, Parmenides' saying shows him some ways. Just when we are between the two ways of thinking treated above, we also encounter a crossroad with more ways. So we not only have to think Parmenides' ways, but must try to do so in the originary and not in the supposedly "objective" or usual way.

Parmenides is shown three ways: "one which thinking must go before all other ways; one to which thinking must also pay heed as it proceeds; and one which remains impassible to thinking. The calling calls thinking to the crossroads of way, no way, and wrong way" (175).[28] Initially it seems that Parmenides' three ways overlap with the two ways of thinking treated above. The way that we should take before all others would be the originary way. The wrong way, which we need to heed but not follow, would be the way of representational thought. And then there is the possibility that there is no way of thinking. Indeed, in fragment seven, Parmenides does intend to keep us out of the dead-end way of thinking and also warns us "against the other way which is also open, besides the genuine way, the one that mortals usually follow" (199)—the way of mere chatter, as opposed to reflection.

Of course, Parmenides is speaking not only of ways of thinking, but, finally, of Being. The three ways are the ways which we might try to think—and that means think Being, as fragment two makes clear. The impassable way to thinking is "that IT IS NOT, and that IT is bound NOT TO BE."[29] Here there is no way for thinking to go. In addition, IT IS NOT cannot be THAT which calls for thinking (and also presumably calls to Parmenides in his saying), because, as Parmenides' saying tells us, this is "a path from which no tidings ever come."[30] The way which we should heed, but not follow, is the one mortals usually do follow, even though it does not lead to what is to-be-thought. Heidegger holds that the warning against the usual human way of confusing TO BE and NOT TO BE is not a simple rejection; rather, it calls on us to be careful. (Similarly, Heidegger's own warning about traditional, representational thinking does not aim to disapprove of that thinking; but to think it in regard to what is called thinking.) This common route is the wrong way for thinking to go. The one way which thinking must go is "that IT IS and it is not possible for IT NOT TO BE." This is the way of what calls for thinking.

In the end, Heidegger's two ways and Parmenides' three ways together point to the same, necessary way:[31] after considering but avoiding the impassable way, after heeding the (too?) accessible but wrong way, Heidegger and Parmenides teach that the path of originary thinking is the path IT IS, which calls for thinking. We respond to this genuine way by attempting to get underway thinking the duality originarily. Here we learn to do so from the way Heidegger thinks the four forms of the question, What is called thinking?

If Heidegger is teaching us to think, and if we are to learn to think by seeing how he makes this way and by getting explicit pointers in the matter, then there is the question of just where he is and where he is going. This also is the question of where we are and of where we are trying to learn to go. Heidegger teaches us that we need to discover and explore what we are *already within*. In fact, Heidegger's whole effort is to lead us to see, or at least catch a glimpse of the whole sphere within which we are learning to think. He is teaching us to learn to think by learning how to think what we already are within. That is the point of the *figura*. He teaches us to trace its delineation for ourselves; that is, he teaches us to discover where and how to make our way.

We could say that we are learning to think about and within what lies before us. Of course, the natural world lies before us. In some obvious way, nature, which we are within, provides the basis for this metaphor of learning to think what we are "within." But, it really is not a metaphor because we are with what is already laid down before us. And it is not just nature that literally is laid down, and then thinking and saying which are somehow metaphorically laid. As Heidegger teaches us, what is said and saying itself are laid down and lie before us. So we are taught how to make our way within what is said.

This means that Heidegger teaches us to make our way within the multiple meanings of the sayings of poets and thinkers, before all else. He shows that we need to do this first by taking up the sayings of Nietzsche, Hölderlin, and Parmenides and secondly, by learning to understand their sayings. But before we can learn to understand them, we have to become aware that we live within them, that they speak to us. The sayings of the early Greeks, for example, give testimony to what calls for thinking and they themselves respond to that call. We need to learn to listen to what is said.

Yet Heidegger teaches us that this does not mean that we learn to hear merely what men have said. Indeed, if we merely inquire into the subjective expressions of poets and thinkers, by means of biography, philology, or psychology, we will miss what is said. That is because what the thinkers and poets say is itself within a sphere; that is, they and we make our way within a realm that is not merely human. As Heidegger shows us, we already and always move within the duality and language, too. What humans say makes its way within language; language is a way within the duality. Heidegger teaches, then, that we can learn multiple meanings within the duality because the presence of what is present prevails and calls for saying and thinking; the duality "speaks throughout language, and maintains for it the possibility to tell, to state" (322). But more immediately, or at a simpler level, we learn to hear and understand what words say as we make our way within language. That is, (as discussed in section 1 of this chapter), language is not a human plaything or tool; rather, language plays with our speech. Accordingly, we must learn to listen beyond speakers' narrowly intended meaning to what words tell by transplanting our listening to, for example, the domain of Greek language. In short, we must learn to let language and words lie before us.

Heidegger teaches us that originary thinking aims to show, recall, and hold the unaccustomed; it aims to recover originary meaning by way of exploring the multiple meanings and the single unitary meaning behind them. This is what Heidegger does over and over in the lectures with such words as "think," "thank," "memory," "call," "language," and "dispose." He teaches us to hear what the words tell us in their richer language. And clearly he goes about his task of thinking and saying not as he would for himself, but in a way that will enable us to learn and follow:

> It would be most in keeping with the way on which we have set out with our question, if we were not to leave off all asides and warnings, and tried to trace in thought what the saying tells us. But today, when we know too much and form opinions much too quickly, when we compute and pigeonhole everything in a flash—today there is no room at all left for the hope that the presentation of a matter might in itself be powerful enough to set in motion any fellow-thinking, which, prompted by the showing of the matter, would join us on our way. We therefore need these bothersome detours and crutches that otherwise run counter to the style of thinking ways. This is the necessity to which we now bow when we now attempt, by circumscribing the matter in ever narrowing circles, to render possible the leap into what the saying tells us. (171)

Before we learn what a saying says, we must learn that and how we always move within it: the saying is prior to thinking.

We see, then, that when Heidegger teaches us to see and understand multiple meaning he also is teaching us both what it is within which we make our way and also how to make our way. We learn to think within the complex whole, that is, the duality. Within the duality we learn to move in the common, representational modes of thinking and in an originary, recalling manner. More importantly, we learn to make our way *from* one *to* the other and how it is that the former is a reduced, partial thinking and saying within the latter. This movement we learn, then, is nothing merely historical (of which more will be said shortly), but a movement within what is.

When learning to inhabit this sphere of multiple meaning, one learns that all the meaning, and especially the single unity behind it, is not—indeed, cannot be—said or thought. It is neither said nor thought at any one time, nor in all times taken together. That is to say that we learn that we finally are called on to think the presuppositions of what is said and thought; we are called to think the unspoken. Of course, "presupposition" does not indicate anything merely arbitrary, but that within which a particular saying lies, that within which lies what is-let-lie-before-us. "Presupposition" means something like "the situation in which a thing is lying" or "the situation of the foundation" (200–201). Learning to hear the presuppositions, which are so *close* to us, includes learning that "they are so stubborn because they have their own truth" (152). Originary thinking thinks how they are not arbitrary or idiosyncratic but, in their way, necessary.

To learn to hear a thinker requires hearing beyond what he says (though not in skipping over it) to the origin from which his thought comes and toward which it moves; that is, "listening for what remains unspoken in it" (55), which Heidegger tries to teach us with Nietzsche and Parmenides.

There are stages of presupposition, then. The most obvious and superficial sort—and, perhaps, therefore the most difficult to overcome, if Heidegger's concern and effort in these lectures is correct—would be our own assumptions, assumptions about objective meaning, and so on. Next, there would be the presuppositions within which a particular thinker's or poet's saying and thinking lie. Then there are the presuppositions of whole groups of thinkers who belong together: "we must try to listen to an early saying which gives us evidence how much early thought generally responds to a call, yet without naming it, or giving it thought, as such" (168). Finally, there is the primal unspoken (even language belongs within something unspoken), the presupposition behind all others and behind all that is thought and said; this is the situation within which lies everything which lies at all.

> The thematic sphere of Western metaphysics is indicated by *methexis*, the particular being's participation in Being. . . . This sphere of metaphysics is grounded in what *metoche*, what the unique participle *eon* distinguishes with a single word: the duality of individual beings and Being. But in order that metaphysical thinking may first of all discern its own sphere, and attempt its first steps in that sphere, "It is useful to let-lie-before-us and so the taking-to-heart also: beings in being." (223)
>
> However, *no* further inquiry and thought is given to the duality *itself*, of beings and Being, neither to the nature of the duality nor to that nature's origin. The duality emerges only up to the point where the *emmenai* of *eon*, the Being of beings, can be taken to heart. (224)

Learning to think multiple meanings, then, means learning to make our way to the unity behind what individual thinkers and poets and groups of thinkers and poets think and say, until we at least arrive in the neighborhood of the final unity behind all particular multiple meanings and their locally unifying meanings. But, we can arrive at that duality only through its call which speaks in language and in what the thinkers and poets say and think. Because of this, learning to make our way is learning the art of dialogue. We try to learn to move from thoughtlessness to thoughtful address and listening: all genuine thinking speaks to the thinking which preceeds and follows it. We try to learn the art of dialogue with men, and, ultimately, in a very strange way, with the duality.[32] "Every dialogue becomes halting and fruitless if it confines itself obdurately to nothing but what is directly said—rather than that the speakers in the dialogue involve each other in *that* realm and abode about which they are speaking, and lead each other to it. Such involvement is the soul of the dialogue. It leads the speakers into the unspoken" (178). This is what Heidegger is trying to do with us.

Since Heidegger is attempting to teach us to hear and understand by showing us how to move from the place we commonly are to a strange—even foreign—place, he naturally explains what we are doing in terms of a radical movement. We don't learn to think by effortlessly meandering, but by an artful leap: "In contrast to a steady progress, where we move unawares from one thing to the next and everything remains alike, the leap takes us abruptly to where everything is different, so different that it strikes us as strange" (12); "there is no bridge here—only the leap" (8). The leap we are learning is a leap in meaning and relation, where we move from representational or originary thinking across to a think-er's thought to what words tell and to the duality.

This leap is "the leap of a single vision"; but "leap and vision require long, slow preparation" (232–233). We suppose that Heidegger has prepared and that we are only beginning to learn how to. There is a great difference, then, between what the teacher does and what we do. His leap is heuristic; following it is part of our preparation for our own leaps. Normally, he moves more agilely and surely than we do. He leaps ahead of us. (Because he is aware of how hard it is to learn to leap, Heidegger makes a proper teacherly concession to our situation and graciously provides us with some helpful bridges to use in the meantime, as we are to learn to leap. This is what over a fourth of the book consists of: bridges for us learners—*die Stundenübergänge*, literally "passages," "cross-ings," "foot bridges," "viaducts," or "transitions" between les-sons.)

But it is not only Heidegger who thinks; if we follow him, we do too. Insofar as we try to think along we try to make some leaps of our own. And Heidegger intends us to. That is why he not only thinks out loud in front of us in his book, but also carefully shows us how to think (or, at least, how to learn to think); he sometimes implicitly and other times explicitly tells us what to do. This is how *What Is Called Thinking?* means on the third level. As he puts it, "We shall never learn what 'is called' swimming, for example, or what it 'calls for,' by reading a treatise on swimming. Only the leap into the river tells us what is called swimming" (21). We are asked to leap along with him. He shows us how, telling us, "We therefore shall take a few practice leaps right at the start, though we won't notice it at once, nor need to" (12, cf. 171). In the largest sense, we took those practice leaps when we tried to follow what he said and the way he said it. That is, the first two levels of the book's meaning actually were lessons in how to think, even though we may not have noticed it when we followed them. But, now, we can explicitly see what Heidegger has tried to get us to do.

Learning to leap is a gathering. We learn to come together with Heidegger, and he attempts to gather us (of help us gather ourselves) together with other thinkers, language, and the duality. (Keep in mind, of course, that this gathering-thinking is not simply a conceptual activity nor merely a human process.) Thus, the way which we are trying to learn is a way across meanings, a way between persons, sayings, relationships, and situations, within the duality. (Recall the *figura*.) Thinking and saying are movements between. That is why the way of thoughtful saying and hearing—dialogue—is the way of *trans*-lation and *inter*-pretation of what we already belong within and together with.

Every thinking along with another thinker involves translation, though this is more obvious in some cases than in others. For example, if we try to learn a way of thinking from what Parmenides, Nietzsche, or even Heidegger say, we must translate what they say to us in order to understand it. The translation of saying from one language to another is an obvious example. But it is merely an example because we also have to translate the earlier sayings of thinkers in our own language into our language as it currently is used. In fact, when we assume that we already understand the meaning of a saying merely because the same term is used, we are most likely to misunderstand it. That is, it is obvious that we must be careful to hear what *legein* means; but "logic" seems to speak clearly to us, though, in fact, we may not really understand it at all.

If we are to learn to think, we must similarly hear and understand what our teachers say; that means we must also translate their sayings. To be able to hear, we have to become aware that everything must be translated, perhaps especially what seems obvious; to be able to understand we must learn to hear what is laid before us without disturbing its essential nature. Becoming aware of this is facing, though not in itself overcoming, the first barrier to learning thinking: assuming that we are already hearing and thinking. He also shows other barriers that we need to become aware of and pass beyond.

When translating, we must be careful in at least two respects, he tells us: "The first concerns the content of the saying. The second concerns the manner" (178). We have already seen that we must move from what the content appears to be, that is, from the obvious, to what is astonishing, that is, to the unaccustomed and even unspoken. Second, this means we must understand how the saying is said, its careful and specific order and relations. Indeed, the way it is said is the same as what is said. But, granted that we must learn to hear both content and manner together, in their unity, if what is said is not simply to slip by us, isn't all this obvious? Perhaps, but by treating it Heidegger teaches us all that translation involves not only the saying that is to be translated, but also our own presuppositions.

For example, do we assume that *logos* and *logic* mean the same thing? Do we assume that Hegel's, Kant's, Aristotle's, and Parmenides' use of terms which designate logic and being are the same, or that their assumptions are the same? How are they all related? Here Heidegger teaches us that all thinking and all learning of thinking—including translation—is interpretation. We may assume that we merely need to learn the art of translating, "but every translation is already an interpretation" (174). Note that he says "already." We do not translate and then interpret what we have translated; rather, every translation is *already* an interpretation. And, of course, what is said in our own language also needs to be interpreted.

This shows us some of the difficulties which every interpretation has to deal with. For example, our assumptions about the relation of subject and object, derived from our relation to the history of representational thinking, especially since Descartes and Kant, not only enter into our interpretation, but form our understanding and expectation of interpretation itself. Thus, Heidegger calls attention to one "illusion" of representational interpretation:

It is that we imagine we are approaching Parmenides' saying in an objective manner and without presuppositions when we take cognizance of it without any intimations. . . . But this "cognizance-taking" without intimations and questions, and seemingly not burdened with any prejudice, is in fact an interpretation as charged with presuppositions and prejudices as is possible in this case. (176)

Of course, the opposite is a presupposition too; that we can approach a saying only in a subjective manner with our own idiosyncratic presuppositions is the historicist/relativistic side of the absolutist/objectivistic view. But Heidegger clearly is trying to teach us to move beyond either alternative, as we saw in section 1.

How is this possible? That we lose track of meanings and that meanings change seem obvious. It would appear that language and past sayings are a matter of history. The solution, then, apparently would be found in the historical sciences, such as philology. We would aim, for example, to recover the correct meanings of words. This, in turn, presents another apparent dilemma. How can we base philosophy (supposedly a supra-historical knowledge) on merely historical insights, on the history of language, for example?

Heidegger's response is based on the difference between originary thinking and the common view of language, history, philosophy, and science in general. As he argues when passing from representative to originary thinking, what is needed is not more or better knowledge. The historical treatment of language and thought, however correct, remains within the sphere where the past is treated as something finished, which, once gone by may either be examined objectively or seen as part of an everchanging flow of events (depending on which view one takes).

Only as we pass beyond the sciences to originary thinking can we understand language, the thinking of thinkers, and even history itself. In this passage, we move beyond the concept of history to think the essential nature and origin of the spheres which must be thought, and which include that of history itself. Specifically, we would try to hear what words tell, without relegating them to "what was." "With these words ('thinking' and 'thought') something has entered language—not just of late, but long ago. But though it entered language, it did not get through. It has gone back into the unspoken, so that we cannot reach it without some further effort" (133). While we must, then, go back into history of language, we do not have to go back by the way of historical sciences.

Similarly, "what a thinker has thought can be mastered only if we refer to everything in his thought that is still unthought back to its originary truth" (54). Again, what is past is not relegated to the category of what is disposed of; the originary remains fruitful. Parmenides and Heraclitus, Plato and Aristotle, Hölderlin and Nietzsche give "voice and language to what now is—but in a language in which the two-thousand-year-old tradition of Western metaphysics speaks—though in a form transposed more than once, timeworn, shallowed, threadbare, and rootless" (75).

Even while he argues that the originary still provides food for thought, Heidegger is not proposing that recovering origin involves the attempt to live in the past. For example, we need to think originarily what *thank* means. It may appear that we merely have excavated a discarded heirloom of language. "But," Heidegger tells us, "can we in this way call the word back into the spoken language. No! Then why do we try at all to draw attention to what the word states, since we have to concede that the treasures of language cannot be given artificial currency in a usage somehow refurbished?" (153). The answer, of course, depends on our seeing that thinkers and words are not mere artifacts for an anthropological and archaeological view of thinking. Recollective thought holds the opposite: "Let us be honest with ourselves: the essential nature of thinking, the essential origin of thinking, the essential possibilities of thinking that are comprehended in that origin—they are all strange to us, and by that very fact they are what gives us food for thought before all else and always" (45). Consequently, interpreting a text is an originary task and never merely a historical problem. The best historical science (which may seek certainty about constantly changing views) is not yet originary thinking.

This has at least two implications: interpretation is not merely the comparison of interpretations, and the assumptions of representational thought block interpretation. First, we do not genuinely interpret by objectively comparing different interpretations in order to scientifically demonstrate their common objective features, nor do we merely compare them to show their changes and to chart the prevailing interpretive assumptions at any given historical period.

The project of a correct account of interpretations is the proper aim of science; but, it is not itself interpretation, that is, thinking. At the least, interpreting a thinker means learning to think his presuppositions, even back to the unspoken, as we have seen. Second, Heidegger argues that traditional representational thought prevents hearing what, for example, the early Greeks said and thought because it assumes the Greeks used concepts the way representational thinkers did and that earlier concepts were interchangable with later ones. For example, Heidegger argues than when *legein* and *noein* become ratio which becomes reason (as in the *Critique of Pure Reason*), the Greek essence of what is thought is lost and obscured, at least in part because later, derivative concepts are used to explain the originary. Thus, modern representational thinking, in stubbornly holding on to its concepts, blocks its own access to the origins and essential character of thinking.

Accordingly, we do not learn to think if we try to translate what our teachers say into our own terms. This translation interprets their thinking *via* the way we think and transposes it into what we think. We need to learn to move in the other direction. We need to learn to interpret what we think and say and what our teachers think and say in *their* terms. That is, we need to translate our understanding into, and interpret it in light of, their originary thinking and saying. This would apply to us as individuals and as members of a culture. As to the latter, Heidegger's description and critique of traditional interpretation does not claim that philosophy since the early Greeks is false or mistaken, but that it does not question, nor genuinely achieve what is called thinking. (Indeed, we need to reflect on how Greek thinking prepared for the development of representational-conceptual thought.) What is needed for interpretation, then, is the art of originary thinking. In other words, learning to interpret is learning the *way* of originary thinking, as Heidegger demonstrates in translating and interpreting Parmenides' saying.[33] Of course, this does not tell us how to interpret the Greeks only; we must learn to interpret by way of recalling originary thinking even when the thinking we are translating is very close to us. (Indeed, then it may be more important and difficult than ever.)

Since translation and interpretation require that we enter into a dialogue with the thinkers and even that we enter into their unspoken, we need their cooperation. Indeed, we need their help. For their part, they help us by giving us hints. For example, Heidegger says, "Fortunately, Parmenides himself, by his manner of stating, gives us a hint which helps us to bring out the manner in which 'being' and 'to be,' belong together" (219). They participate in meanings which refer to each other because what they state always has to do with the duality. Thus, while Parmenides does not answer the question, What is to be understood by thinking? if we hear him properly, he helps us question it.

The same is true for Heidegger. The whole book might be understood as a hint to help us learn to interpret thinkers and to think ourselves—hence, Heidegger's concern with *clues*, which are strewn through the lectures. To note only two more examples, we may get clues from representational thinking, when he says philology might "give us a clue on occasion," (138) and clues from the originary meaning of words (150). So we must find clues, but even more importantly, we must be able to find what they hint at. That is, we must learn to let clues be clues: "To receive a clue is difficult, and rare—rarer than we know, and more difficult the more we merely want to know. But clues also have forerunners, to whose directives we respond sooner and more easily, because we ourselves can help prepare them part of the way" (138). (What Heidegger says here seems to be a forerunner which hints at, and depends for its intelligibility on, the *figura*, which in turn seems to be a clue derived from and concerning what must be thought.) Heidegger, then, teaches us to perceive clues by helping prepare their forerunners in his own thinking. These lectures aim to help us respond to hints which we might otherwise miss, and thereby to what is hinted at—the origin of the hints.

Hints and clues help us to question. That is, they are essential to interpretation, which aims to raise as questionable what is to be thought. As we have seen, this means not that we merely notice what is to be thought or add it to the stock of knowledge, but what we find a way to let its problematic speak to us. Here what often seems to be irrelevant or pointless may function to focus the

question, for example, as is the case according to his own understanding and claim, with Heidegger's circuitous translation of
Parmenides' saying. Because we can hear the question and think
what needs thought only when we are on our way within what calls
for thinking, Heidegger's teaching of translating and interpretation
is directed toward moving us into this sphere. Thus, nothing is
gained if by translation we mean merely replacing one concept with
another without thinking both through. As Heidegger stresses,
"The translation is still no translation if we merely replace the
words *eon* and *emmenai* with our own terms 'being' and 'to be' or the
Latin *ens* and *esse*. . . . What is missing?. . . What is still needed?
That we ourselves, instead of merely transposing the Greek terms
into terms of our language, pass over into the Greek sphere" (226,
cf. 233).

Learning to think is learning to make our way within the
sphere to which we belong. Interpretation is learned and takes
place in this sphere; also it helps hold us there. Recall that every
translation is already an interpretation: "Every interpretation must
first of all have entered into what is said, into the subject matter it
expresses. Such entering is in our case presumably not as easy as
entering an orchard and there to speak of a tree. To enter into what
is said in the phrase 'being is' remains uncommonly difficult and
troublesome for the reason that we are already within it" (174).
That is, as a way, thinking is translation and interpretation of what
we are already within; as a leap, originary thinking moves within
what it already belongs to. Immediately, or initially, we may
belong with a saying that already is laid down; translation then
"makes the entire saying audible in what it says" (209). But
finally, we belong within the gathering of the duality. The thinking
Heidegger is teaching a way within this whole, a way of recovering the
belonging to take it to heart.

To recover this belonging, we must learn to let it lie before us;
this involves learning to let lie before us the saying and thinking of
the poets and thinkers and learning to interpret their work in a way
that allows what is said to lie before us as it is in its nature. For
example, it means letting Greek, Roman, or medieval words themselves directly tell us what *they* designate. Of course, such interpre-

tation requires a great deal of ingenuity. As Heidegger shows us in this book, letting a saying of Nietzsche or Parmenides lie before us is very difficult. Heidegger's translations and interpretations are full of strategies to help us remove obstacles, face assumptions, pass beyond conceptual thinking, listen for what is unspoken, and so on.

This kind of interpretation often looks odd; it is always difficult, slow, and indirect. But Heidegger is teaching us that it is necessary for the interpretation that originary thinking seeks. Though it seems peculiar and strained, even incorrect to one-track thinking, originary interpretation is not arbitrary. It may be, however, that moving us from the obvious to the strange, as we have seen, inevitably will appear arbitrary; yet, in fact, it is careful and heuristic. Actually, in order to let a saying lie before us, the interpreter must eschew all willful maneuvers and devote himself to the saying itself and to what it gives in its own way. It may appear that Heidegger is playing with words in his translations; but he shows us this is not so. Consider, for example, how convincingly he shows us the originary meaning of "call" in its Biblical setting so that we clearly can see how arbitrary *our usual* assumption is (117). And recall how he teaches that it is not the willful human use of terms as tools that is the source of meaning; rather, he shows how the sayings of great thinkers and poets (in response and service to something greater than themselves) and how language itself should be our proper concern. Moreover, he shows how both thinking and teaching require the teaching of originary interpretation:

> We cannot deal here with the preparations needed to make that leap of vision which transposes us into That which speaks from his word. Here we can state directly only what such a leap sees. Whatever has been seen can be demonstrated only by being seen and seen again. What has been seen can never be proved by adducing reasons and counter-reasons. Such a procedure overlooks what is decisive—the looking. If what is seen is put in words, its mention by name can never compel the seeing look. At best, it can offer a token of what a seeing look, renewed again and again, would presumably show more clearly.
>
> Therefore, when we speak of our transposition into *eon*, and call it that which is seen, such a statement always remains a questioning

statement. It looks immediately like a mere assertion, made purely on a whim. That appearance cannot be dispelled directly. (233)

Now Heidegger is not saying that we simply should accept without reason what he says. The whole of his book shows that that would be a thoughtless view, for the aim of all he says and does is to help us become thoughtful about what he says. Heidegger is actually making a simple point: either we hold that he sees more than we do and that he can teach us, or we do not. Of course, we might not be sure right now; but, if we decide he is not trustworthy, no clever, airtight arguments on his part will convert us into learners or him into a teacher. In any case, our trust would not involve believing that he has seen or said, or could say, all that is needed to think what is called—or calls for—thinking. What goes on here is more modest.

His presupposition, then, in the entire book, in all that he says—and in the translation and interpretations—is that there is the teaching and learning of thinking *here*. Parmenides and Nietzsche teach Heidegger to think; as he learns to think, he and they teach us to think. In brief, the assumption of the book—barely spoken—is that That which calls for thinking calls on us to learn thinking (this means it calls for the teaching of thinking, too). This is the proper expectation which opens the book to us: with it we can begin to encounter Heidegger and what is called thinking; without it we can only go counter to and confront them.

More importantly, he asserts, "But all of the great thinking of the Greek thinkers, including Aristotle, thinks non-conceptually. Does it therefore think inaccurately, hazily? No, the very opposite: it thinks appropriately, as befits the matter. Which is to say also: thinking keeps to its way of thinking. It is the way toward what is worthy of questioning, problematical" (212). Heidegger has prepared us for this from the start. Perhaps, without being aware of it, we were moved to be open to learning by the initial lecture, which both set the homely, heuristic tone and, implicitly, set out the central thought. On the first pages, Heidegger noted that man perhaps "wants too much when he wants to think, and so can do too little" (3), and that our world's "course of events seems to demand rather that man should act, without delay. . . . What is lacking, then, is action, not thought" (4). So it seems. This thought is echoed when we are almost finished trying to translate and interpret, that is, to think "this undeniable peculiarity of the Greek word *legein*, that it means at one time 'to lay' and at another 'to tell.' It is idle. It is even useless" (205).

But now that we have been taught to prick up our ears at what *seems* so and to think about what "use" and "thought" mean, perhaps we also appreciate what "action" means and why Heidegger says, "And yet—it could be that prevailing man has for centuries now acted too much and thought too little" (4). Now that we have tried to think the difference between representational, metaphysical thought and recollective, originary thinking, we see that, in the tradition, thinking and doing are understood in the same way (in terms of grasping, forming, willing, and so on). That is, the efficient production, application, and profit of the processes of thinking and acting are congruent with, and devolve from, Being understood as Willing.

In striking contrast, especially in tone, originary thinking is presented by way of homey and reverent terms ("thank," "call," "devotion," and "take to heart," for example); this thinking also calls for action, but action which is notably non-willful and non-aggressive: we need to let-lie-before-us, take-to-heart, seek the fitting response, and so on. This is not the will to power, but the heart's desire to belong reverently. This originary action has been, in fact, going on throughout the book. Heidegger has not forsaken action for thought; rather, he teaches us to pass over from the action of the traditional way to an originary kind. That action, the appropriate response that results from thinking, not from thoughtlessness, which results from the slow way, not the quick, has been described to us by Heidegger, who also has been telling us something of what to do and how. Insofar as we have learned to begin to think, he also has evoked thinking from us. We have learned perhaps, how to go along with him. The book acts, then, to move us toward the habit of this deeper action; Heidegger acts by teaching us the craft of thinking, as well as by thinking himself.

He told us about this in the first lecture when he spoke of

learning thinking and the cabinetmaker's apprentice. Recalling what was said about thinking (especially how the activity of forming concepts to grasp reality is distinct from remembering and appropriately responding to what is given to us), now we may hear what Heidegger initially said of teacher and learner:

> His learning is not mere practice, to gain facility in the use of tools. Nor does he merely gather knowledge about the customary forms of the things he is to build. If he is to become a true cabinetmaker, he makes himself answer and respond above all to the different kinds of wood and to the shapes slumbering within wood—to wood as it enters into man's dwelling with all the hidden riches of its nature. In fact, this relatedness to wood is what maintains the whole craft. Without that relatedness, the craft will never be anything but empty busywood, any occupation with it will be determined exclusively by business concerns. Every handicraft, all human dealings are constantly in that danger. The writing of poetry is no more exempt from it than is thinking.
>
> Whether or not a cabinetmaker's apprentice, while he is learning, will come to respond to wood and wooden thing, depends obviously on the presence of some teacher who can make the apprentice comprehend. . . . (14–15)
>
> We are trying to learn thinking. Perhaps thinking, too, is just something like building a cabinet. At any rate, it is a craft, a "handicraft". . . . All the work of the hand is rooted in thinking. Therefore, thinking itself is man's simplest, and for that reason hardest, handiwork, if it would be accomplished at its proper time.[34] (16–17)

From the very beginning of the lectures, Heidegger has been prompting us to raise questions and thereby to begin to think. He has tried to teach us the originary habits of head, heart, and hand so that we might learn more properly the art of habitation within the gathering duality.

Consider this image of the *thinking* teacher. We find a thinker making his way to and fro because thinking turns out to be movement between man and Being, within the duality. But the thinker is not a hermit who keeps to himself. Just the opposite, the thinker thinks aloud so that we may learn thinking. The thoughtful movement is the teacher's way of teaching, and we learn to think by seeing the way the thinking teacher goes. What does the "way" of the thinking teacher include here? First of all, "way" means his course of movement, with its own sites and sequence of passage. We learn how his thinking goes; we follow the way it goes. We learn the way to get where thinking and teaching go. Secondly, "way" indicates his style. We look at the way he goes about his teaching and thinking. Third, "way" speaks of the way to go about a task; that is, it has to do with the knack of thinking. Heidegger teaches us how to go about thinking and learning.

Now, these ways of the thinking teacher are not accidentally related to the substance and style of *What Is Called Thinking?*, nor are they gratuitously included in the book. Indeed, the subject matter—Being, beings, human being, thinking, saying, and so on—is presented to us by the teacher; it appears and is gathered together for us only insofar as the teacher thinks before us to show us the way to learn thinking.

If the way of the thinking teacher lays out the substance of the book, that way also organizes it. But earlier it appeared that the principle of organization or *figura* was "the gathering—giving all at once and the belonging together of the presence of what is present, the human, and thinking and saying, where thinking and saying are within the duality and moving to and fro between the duality and the human," which, sketched in a teacherly manner, looked like the following:

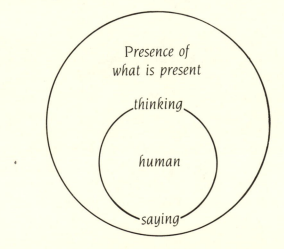

How to reconcile these two insights?

It is precisely in the course of the teacher's thinking that the substance of the book is gathered together and laid before us; at the same time, in the course of this movement, the *figura is delineated*. As the teacher is underway thinking and teaching, his thoughtful teaching reveals the otherwise unspoken or concealed figura. Indeed, this is the only way the figura is embodied in this book! But, this means that the action of the thinking teacher, as he gathers together Being, beings, man, thinking, and saying, traces out the *figura*, and the *figura* is a kind of map of his movement. That is to say, *the figure of the thinking teacher and the figura coincide. The abstract figura is the same as the human figure of the thinking teacher in action. Further, both show the same: the figura indicates the pattern of what is called thinking; the figure personifies the process of thinking, or traveling the way of what is called thinking.*

The *figura* is the active personal figure in *stasis*; the personal figure in action is the *figura* in movement.[35] In short, the persona of the thinking teacher (or his action in level three of the book) thinks and lays out before us the central organizational principle of the book (the *figura* of level two). (Of course, this also indicates a further unity in the book because it shows how the second and third levels come and belong together; recall, too, that the first and second levels themselves coincide.)

Accordingly, there is a sense in which the thinking teacher is as central to Heidegger's *What Is Called Thinking?* as Zarathustra is to Nietzsche's *Also Sprach Zarathustra*. Heidegger notes how Nietzsche thinks the bridging central to all he says: "The superman goes beyond, overpasses man as he is, the last man. Man, unless he stops with the type of man as he is, is a passage, a transition; he is a bridge; he is a 'rope strung between the animal and the superman.' The superman, strictly understood, is the figure and form of man to which he who passes over is passing over" (60). Deliverance from revenge is the bridge crossed by him who goes across. (106)

It is Zarathustra who paradigmatically passes to and fro on this tightrope when he teaches the eternal recurrence of the same, the superman, and the deliverance from revenge (106). As a result, he personifies the passage itself: he is an image of the doctrines he means to convey. Similarly in *What is Called Thinking?*, the thinking teacher teaches us that thinking and saying are movement within the duality, that is, they are ways of gathering and dwelling in the midst of the presence of what is present. But since he teaches precisely by gathering and moving back and forth within the duality so that we can watch him and thereby learn how to move this way ourselves, *the thinking teacher—the same as the figura—embodies the truth which the book says, shows, and aims to achieve.* Finally, teaching and thinking are the same; that is, they belong together because they both strive to learn our relation to the duality and to take it to heart.

Heidegger seldom speaks of love (perhaps because "love" is the commonest and most worn of words, even more thoughtlessly used that "being"). He does, though, speak of it once in the second lecture, in a way fitted to the thought of teacher and student. Heidegger quotes from Hölderlin's poem "Socrates and Alcibiades":

> Who the deepest has thought, loves what is most alive,
> Who has looked at the world, understands youth at its height,
> And wise men in the end
> Often incline to beauty. (20)

Then he adds:

> We are concerned here with the line "Who has most deeply thought, loves what is most alive." It is all too easy in this line to overlook the truly telling and thus sustaining words, the verbs. To notice the verb, we now stress the line in a different way that will sound unfamiliar to the common hearer: "Who the deepest has *thought*, loves what is most alive." Standing in the closest vicinity, the two verbs "thought" and "loves" form the center of the line. Inclination reposes in thinking. . . . What the line tells we can fathom only when we are capable of thinking.[36] (20–21)

4. AN OBSCURED VISION

We have learned that to interpret the multiple meanings of what is said and thought is to make our way within the duality which already gathers us and to which we already belong. Because we already belong within it, the gathering duality is what lies-there-before-us so that we may take-it-to-heart. The third level of the lectures, then, arrives back at the same place as the first two. Further, what Heidegger says about what is called thinking (level one), how he shows us what he says (level two), and the way he teaches us to think (level three), all arrive at (and expose as their assumption) a unified source. That is, the first three levels of meaning both move toward and derive from a fourth level of meaning. Specifically, all that Heidegger says and does in this book already moves within and presupposes a prior gathering. This means not only that the three levels of meaning in the lectures together articulate an ultimate vision, but also that the first three levels originate from That which the vision intends. As noted, Heidegger can say, think, and teach insofar as he has begun his own "leap of vision which transposes us into That which speaks from": that is, *eon* or into That which calls for thinking (233). Heidegger acknowledges the relation of vision and saying-doing in a letter to William Richardson where he says, "He alone can fulfill who has a vision of fullness."[37]

The fourth level of the book, the vision which these lectures present, or better, what is envisioned in them, is not given by any set of lines or captured as a message here or there. Rather, it and its unity are behind and prior to what is said and thought. It is what the aspects all point to or hint at. "Our attempt to indicate what the words 'thinking,' 'thought,' and 'memory' say might serve to point at least vaguely toward the realm of speech from those unspoken sphere those words initially speak. Those words bring to light situations whose essential unity of nature our eyes cannot yet pierce" (14). In thinking, we try to follow the directive of what shows itself to us in this vision: "Our discussion will be freer, not by being more unbounded, but because our vision achieves an open vista into the essential situations we have mentioned, and gains from them the possibility of an appropriate bond" (142).

But is what ultimately calls for thinking finally envisioned in this book? It may seem so because Heidegger names not only That which calls for thinking, but also more fully the constellation of the duality, originary and representational thinking and saying, and the human. Yet, is this what is required for the vision? It does appear, given what we have heard thus far, that Heidegger succeeds in leaving representational thinking behind; but, we need to measure how far he manages to go. A careful questioning indicates that Heidegger's leap does not fully succeed in transporting us out of the metaphysical to a vision of what lies across the abyss, over on the other side from representational thinking.

Broadly, the "ultimate" which speaks here is the unity of the duality, thinking, saying, and the human. This is just what we have tried to hold in mind with the *figura*. Positively, this is unity—a unity of all that is said in *What Is Called Thinking?* And, as we have seen, this also is only a unity of what has been said so far concerning the Being of being; that is, no deeper or further meaning appears.

The limitation of what Heidegger says concerning the duality— which appears to be That which calls for thinking—may be experienced, if we do not exaggerate the point, in the restriction that the *figura* conveys. Thinking, saying, and the human are gathered and kept in the duality. Can we understand what this really says? The originary letting-lie-before-us and also taking-to-heart are enclosed by the Being of beings. That is, the former, which do succeed in breaking through the old ways of thinking and speaking with a freshness and energy, are still confined to movement within the duality. Even where that means the Being of beings, not just being or Being, the language is hobbled by the metaphysical; the vision is limited.

The failure of *What Is Called Thinking?* becomes clearer if we think of this book in light of "A Dialogue on Language" which was presented only a few years later. Recall that, as we have seen, in addition to the historical report made in "A Dialogue on Language," that work moves back and forth between metaphysical and originary thinking and saying, as does *What Is Called Thinking?* But in contrast, "A Dialogue on Language" broke through to *a vigorous vision* of Saying. While this was folded back into the rest, so that there was a unity, the vision freshened the whole and provided a glimpse at least, as Heidegger says there, of the unbounded region.

Such a luminous breakthrough does not occur in *What Is Called*

Thinking? It is as if *What Is Called Thinking?* functions at the second level found in "A Dialogue on Language." After the success of the freeing translation of "thinking" and "saying" (as "taking-to-heart" and "letting-lie-before-us"), the stoppage in the "being" of beings is frustrating. This also occurs in the ending of *What Is Called Thinking?*: the final pages focus on the duality; yet rather than maintaining a pregnant meaning, they more plainly stop.

The style of *What Is Called Thinking?* makes sense in light of the lesson learned from "A Dialogue on Language" and its final return to thinking. There we saw that even successful vision did not dismiss our own responsibility to think and say as best we can. Unlike mystics who might lapse into silence after vision, the partners in the dialogue resume their proper saying as thinkers. *What Is Called Thinking?*, even without vision, must do this, too. Rather than lapsing into silence, it honestly assumes the responsibility of doing the best it can to say, think, and teach—though it finally is unable to say That which is needed.

How is it that the cluster of duality, thinking, and saying is not ultimate? What does this entail? At the least, Heidegger fails to pass altogether beyond metaphysics. He does move from thinking Being and being metaphysically to the duality, which he thinks (aiming at the originary) as the "presence of what is present." Here he manages to go back to the early Greek *eon* and *emmenai*, back through the long history of metaphysics. He translates the duality, to be sure; but, by his own standards, he still holds on to Being and being. Consistently, he attempts to say and think back and forth from Being and being to What gives both—the truly originary. Though he does think many words originarily, (for example, "needful," "think," and "say," the hardest to think), "the duality" does not really get translated originarily. Heidegger moves to the Greek presence of what is present, and thus finally stays in the metaphysical, now dragging Being back into an earlier epoche. Still thinking *via* Being, Heidegger neither succeeds in stepping back beyond the Being of beings nor forward to what is coming originarily. Because he does not manage to go on to say the still-coming and still-calling-for-thinking in non-metaphysical terms, the attempt to arrive originarily at That which calls for thinking falls short. It does not arrive at the point of seeing That which calls for thinking—the origin of the cluster of duality, thinking, saying, and the human.

Heidegger himself recognizes this failure both explicitly and implicitly. Toward the end of the lecture, after all he has said of the duality, he adds forthrightly: "It remains undecided whether in the 'presence of what is present' there will appear That which constitutes the presence of what is present. It would be a mistake, then, for us to take the view that Being meant merely, for all time, the presence of what is present" (235). The word "merely" should be enough to help us hear that the lectures have not yet fully clarified, in words, the final vision. "That" speaks of it, too. This inquires after the element in which everything seen so far belongs together.

Consequently, in *What Is Called Thinking?* either no ultimate vision comes, or it comes so veiled that only the barest hints can be found. Those struggling, incomplete hints do come, just before the final responsible continuing and concluding thinking of the duality in the last pages. This structure, which parallels that of "A Dialogue on Language," further underscores the failure here and the success achieved in the later dialogue.

With these hints in the penultimate sections of the book, Heidegger tries to show what is finally useful, that is, what admits into essential nature and keeps what has been admitted safely there. Finally, Heidegger hints that the primal That which calls is a dynamic gathering together of what already belongs together.

Though only briefly, Heidegger gives glimpses of how man dwells with That to which he belongs and within That which gathers. For example, we live where storms "show on the face of the sky" (188). If we try to hear what that says originally (obviously far from any representational meaning) we might attend to passages from Hölderlin's poetry. The hymn "The Ister River" speaks of the dwelling of mortals on earth, the last stanza of which Heidegger glosses thus:

> There is no welcome where no meal, no food and drink can be offered. There is no stay here for mortals, in the sense of dwelling at home. If mortals are to be made welcome and to stay, there must be water from the rock, wheat from the field. . . .

Shafts are no more necessary to the rock than furrows to the earth. It belongs to the essence of welcome and being at home that it include the welling of water and the fruits of the field. . . . (190)

Things have an essential community here and are not thought as independent existents. . . .

This essential community is in turn determined by the nature of welcome and stay. The welcoming, and the staying, are what marks the dwelling of mortals on this earth. But dwelling, in its turn, is not grounded within itself . . . . (193)

Heidegger goes on to speak of what happens "*within* that realm of being which opens up when the earth becomes a habitation. The home and dwelling of mortals has its own natural site. But its situation is not determined first by the pathless places on earth. It is marked out and opened by something of another order. From there, the dwelling of mortals receives its measure" (191).

Heidegger meditates on another of Hölderlin's hymns, "The Titans," which develops the situation, placing mortals dwelling on earth under the face of the sky:

"Under the firm measure" means for Hölderlin "under the sky." According to the late poem that begins, "There blooms in lovely blueness," the face of the sky is the place where the unknown God conceals himself. "Under the firmament," under the sky so conceived, there is the site where mortals inhabit the earth. (194)

To say and think what is useful is to try to let lie what grants us habitation as mortals on earth, under the sky and God. This, which is kept safely for us, requires that we respond by taking it to heart and safeguarding it. This is what is called for, for the gathering of what properly and essentially belongs together.

The lectures, then, attempt to envision a fourfold gathering, and thereby hint, but only hint, at our originary home and way of dwelling. If it could be let lie before us and taken to heart, the vision itself would ultimately point to that gathering and our belonging within it.

Thus, there is yet a deeper failure in Heidegger's attempted originary saying, because words which are necessary to think That which calls for thinking in its deepest meaning are successfully brought to our attention, but without being thought through. Words break off. That is, they are spoken, which helps; but, they are not really said, which hinders. Specifically, "gathering" and "belonging together" clearly are crucial to Heidegger's project. These words promise an originary manner of moving beyond representational concepts in order to vibrate with their early Greek counterparts such as *Logos* (the unifying of many into one) and also to speak originarily for the future. But Heidegger does not manage to have them say.

He employs them in the place where metaphysical or traditional Greek terms would appear and goes on to use them to work at saying the whole. This is crucial because what is most at stake, and what *What Is Called Thinking?* can most contribute, is the saying of the nature of thinking, saying, and the duality (or beyond), which means how these gather and belong together. It is just here, at the point of saying the inmost, that Heidegger strangely remains at the surface of the words. This is even more striking than in the case of "the duality." There Heidegger does remain within metaphysics—even if with a new thought. But with "gathering" and "belonging together" he has spoken originary words, quite unlike the "presence of what is presence," and yet he cannot, or does not, think them through originarily and use them to think the real issue. If he had done so, he would have made the leap of vision. I say "or does not" and "strangely" because Heidegger says more about "gathering" and "belonging together" in *Early Greek Thinking*, composed between 1943 and 1952. Why does he not say more in *What Is Called Thinking?*, composed between 1951 and 1952? He easily could have.

In sum, the book is a failed leap. For all his success in attempting to jump and in going some way into the previously obscured or forgotten, (1) the limitations indicated by a binding *figura*, that is, the confining of some originary saying within the boundary of what remains metaphysical, (2) the staying with the Being of beings, and (3) the lack of originarily working out and using "gathering" and "belonging together" all prevent a full originary going back to the not-yet-metaphysical or forward to the no-longer-metaphysical. Heidegger keeps one foot in the meta-physical, and so cannot leap fully. Or, it is as if once he leaps from the bank of representational thinking, he lands well enough, but only on the penultimate duality, short of the opposite shore—short of an ultimate vision of That which finally gives and says what calls for thinking. Rather than achieving a fourth level of meaning, a vision of the unspoken realm from which the first three levels of meaning come or are given, Heidegger's leap appears limited to the first three. Not that this is any small feat. Yet without blaming Heidegger for the failure, we must acknowledge it.

Heidegger also recognized, even within *What Is Called Think-ing?*, the limitation of what is said about That which calls for thinking in hints he gave and in the struggle he made to move through the fog. Again and again he asserts that we still are not thinking. It is a mistake to hear these observations as mere echoes of a Platonic irony and modesty, as useful only for bringing to mind and explaining the dual metaphysical and originary thinking, or as nothing other than a heuristic technique to move us to learn thinking.

They do have meaning at these levels, but finally at the fourth level, Heidegger's disclaimers simply are honest descriptions. He knows he only sees so far and says so; he is quite aware that vision is called for but does not come in *What Is Called Thinking?* As noted, he does not believe that such a failure, which is a failure to think, is a matter for self-reproval; instead, it is a situation or experience which describes how we stand in regard to That which calls for thinking. We must do our part, to be sure. But this matter also depends on what really must be thought, which, Heidegger holds, "keeps itself turned away from man since the beginning" (7). It withdraws from us; therefore, no one is to blame. Still, we are responsible—called on—to learn to think what we nonetheless are related to, that is, to be open to what withdraws and yet remains near (14, 17, 25–26). Looking for what withdraws is looking into the "veiled" (17). He admits that his attempt does not see into the final unity (141). He says that "a fog [*der Nebel*] . . . arises from the region of what is most thought-provoking" (14). In a fog there is partial disclosure, but it only is partial; vision is obscured.

Even if we focus on the limitations of Heidegger's own seeing, the failed vision is not merely a matter of the shortcoming inherent in his particular text and project, and accordingly, acknowledged here; rather, it is a problem which plays across all he wrote, which can be seen from a comprehensive comparison of his works. Though it is beyond the scope of this book, a study of the Heideggerian *corpus* shows that there are several major sets of work which vary in substance and style.[38] Here we can note that there are works which, while central to his thought and development, still remain metaphysical (this would be the case with the early traditional and scholarly study *Kant and the Problem of Metaphysics* and even the revolutionary *Being and Time*). Another sort develop an originary manner of saying and thinking while also exploring—or going back through—the history of metaphysics. Examples of this bifocal vision are "A Dialogue on Language" and *What Is Called Thinking?* and also works such as *Der Satz vom Grund*. In others, such as "Language," "Language in the Poem," and "The Nature of Language," Heidegger explores and learns from poetry, that is, from a poetic-originary way of saying. In still others, he speaks originarily, on his own, without also doing so metaphysically, as in "Building Dwelling Thinking." That is, if we look at everything Heidegger wrote and the way he wrote each work, we find that in some works he did succeed in breaking through to and maintaining the originary; in others, because of both inability and the choices of approach and subject, he remains within metaphysics.

In this overall situation, *What Is Called Thinking?* is very important because it is a watershed from which it is possible to go back into metaphysics and traditional scholarship or over into originary thinking and a new manner of saying and reading. For this reason alone *What Is Called Thinking?* is worth careful study and perhaps indicates why, as Heidegger himself acknowledged, it is one of the most neglected of his works: it attempts to lay out both representational *and* originary thinking and thus says a substantial amount that is foreign or of little interest to each kind of scholar. In a lecture, presented ten years after *What Is Called Thinking* was published and entitled "On Time and Being" (a kind of reversal of the early *Being and Time*), Heidegger acknowledges and explains the failure of works such as *What Is Called Thinking?*:

> The task of our thinking has been to trace Being to its own from Appropriation [*Ereignis*] by way of looking through true time without regard to the relation of Being to beings.
>
> To think Being without beings means: to think Being without regard to metaphysics. Yet a regard for metaphysics still prevails in the intention to overcome metaphysics. Therefore, our task is to cease all overcoming, and leave metaphysics to itself.[39]

The final failure at the fourth level of meaning, or failure of final meaning exhibited in *What Is Called Thinking?*, is nothing "self-contained," like a flower which simply fails to appear; rather, it is a case of the whole having a modified meaning, as happens when a rose has so many petals missing that its appearing as what it should be is compromised. Since the vision is not found as a discrete "part," but only as a deeper meaning in and through the first three meanings, it is obscured by their failures. At the same time, since visionary meaning informs the first three levels, concealment of vision means concealment in what is said, in how it is said, and in what is taught. Still too concerned with the metaphysical, *What Is Called Thinking?* achieves only an obscured vision.

CHAPTER FOUR

Still Learning to Read, Think, and Say

This book was intended chiefly to be a patient listening, not a critique of Heidegger, because we cannot learn if we do not first listen and also because it is presumptuous to suppose we know so much that we can criticize him from our own vantage point before listening to him. But after trying our best to listen to him and to accommodate ourselves to his language as he teaches us to do, we still need to question the meaning of *What Is Called Thinking?* What problems of language and thinking does the obscured vision call to our attention? Whatever is pointed out will, as we have seen, run throughout what he says at all four levels, especially at the basic level—his saying concerning representational and recollective thinking.

It is not so important here to go back to see what specific problems arise from each instance of failure concerning Heidegger's use of "gathering," "belonging together," and "the duality," for example, though that could be done. Finally, those specific shortcomings together simply fail to think and say; they fail to help us hear and learn what needs to be thought.

Since I am not Heidegger, it would be presumptuous to pretend I could say what he failed at, to as it were, pick up where he left off and reveal to the reader what "gathering," "belonging together," and so on really mean. For that we have what Heidegger himself says, in other works. Therefore, it's better to look to see *how* and why Heidegger's thinking and language both remain involved in the realm of traditional metaphysics and what those points of belonging have to do with both his *success* and *failure* at the originary, which also means with what his task is at the end of *What Is Called Thinking?*

195

Proceeding this way also will show us how we could go back to work through the specifics of what Heidegger says in order to question, for example, Being, Willing, the presence of what is present, gathering, and so on. Further, it would explain in a coherent way why different sorts of readers have specific, but varied criticisms of *What Is Called Thinking?* and would indicate what they might want to pursue.

Heidegger is in need of a new language and way of thinking. This does not mean that he is capable of inventing new words, for as we have seen, language, understood originally is no mere human expression or creation. Rather, an originary saying would be found through a recollection, that is, by thinking back through what language says in order to retrieve a way of saying what is needed.

At times Heidegger succeeds, as happens with "need," "call," "think," and "say." At other times he only partially succeeds, as when he finds "gathering" and "belonging together," yet merely leaves them partially retrieved without working out what they say. In all these cases, in fact in his whole attempt at originary thinking and teaching, two needs remain paramount. First, Heidegger needs a dynamic language. Though we will only later see why this is so, it is an obvious feature of *What Is Called Thinking?* Simply put, if we are to stop thinking of beings, and especially of Being as the ultimate being, we need to find a way to think and talk which does not begin by forcing us to reify. The most obvious need is to shift from a noun-bound way of saying to a verbal mode. The usual use of nouns reinforces our thoughtless habit of always thinking of beings; shifting to verbs and verbal forms can help teach us another way. The traditional use of noun-being seems to be the result of the historical development of traditional thinking; breaking it is a step in retrieving originary saying, which appears to have been more verbal and active. For example, according to Heidegger, this occurs in the transformation of *Logos* through logic and dialectic to the logistical (153 ff. and 238 ff.) and, most of all, in what participles say—those powerful forms which have both a substantive sense (as a noun) and a verbal sense (220 ff.). Not surprisingly, he meditates on the story of the participle of participles: being.

This need for a dynamic language already involves the second need, the need to pass from a representational manner of saying, which is willful, to an originary manner, which is non-willful. But this does not just mean avoiding the modern approach by way of the distinction of subject and object. No longer understanding what is called thinking by way of will means avoiding a way of thinking by way of will, which itself is willful, and also means overcoming the understanding of Being as Will and of thinking as part of the willful. Here we strike a root problem in *What Is Called Thinking?* In his attempt to find dynamic language, Heidegger says that thinking "calls for" and "needs," "demands" and "gives," "commands" and "wants." These verbs appear to be part of the language of will, that is a voluntaristic or personalistic language of the traditional metaphysics from which he is attempting to leap free.

The basic question concerning the failure of language in *What Is Called Thinking?*, then, has to do with the relation of its "originary" language to its resources in the language of our tradition. Three specific possibilities need to be explored: (1) does Heidegger's language personify or anthropomorphize his subject matter, (2) does it avoid anthropomorphism only to continue a metaphysical-representational tradition of affirming Being in voluntaristic terms, now as willful Being which returns to covertly consume its own origins and seduce us into submission, or (3) is it, is some other way, still related to our traditional language but nonetheless genuinely on the way to the originary?

In attempting a dynamic language, Heidegger encounters a problem inherent in the structure of European languages. As noted, shifting away from reifying representational thought involves de-emphasizing nouns and emphasizing active verbal saying. But the use of verbs involves or at least implies subjects. The most obvious subject is the human being since the obvious association, speaking of thinking or saying, for example, is with the human. It is important to notice how Heidegger includes the human without reducing everything to a merely humanized realm. This especially is significant because earlier misunderstandings and barriers, created up by those who interpreted Heidegger as an existentialist or subjectivist and *Being and Time* as a work in philosophical anthropology still may prevent us from hearing him.[1] According to such interpretations, Heidegger began with the human and, moving from *Dasein* to

Being, began both a career and a cultural movement that anthropomorphized Being. In fact, it was to overcome the still inadequate language of *Being and Time* that Heidegger shifted his manner of saying in *What Is Called Thinking?*, a work which shows how one-sided such a "subjectivist" interpretation is. In fact, it should now be clear how Heidegger specifically denies that we can ever begin with the human and then proceed toward Being. In terms of the *figura*, such a partial assumption (part of a humanized view) would be thought as human being moving toward Being.

But this is precisely what Heidegger argues is one-track thinking. Of course, just as he refutes the one-sided movement from the human to Being, he also refuses to substitute the opposite movement which would begin with Being and later proceed to the human. Nor can we simply add the two together to arrive at the correct sum of both (79–80, and as we have seen, in earlier sections). (This would also mean that it is a simplistic mistake to see Heidegger's career as having two neatly distinct stages, where he supposedly moved from the human to Being in the first half and then back from Being to the human in the second. Such a view fails to see that what may appear to be one directional, is, in fact, nothing other than the partial, and early, elaboration of what could be seen and said, at any one time, of a more complex and complete understanding.)

Actually, Heidegger's work aims to deanthropomorphize thinking, our approach to ourselves and Being, and our understanding of all that gathers together. One passage which very nicely illustrates this deanthropomorphization, which aims to think and thereby free us from the assumptions of our two-thousand-year-old tradition, occurs where Heidegger argues that with the originary word "memory," it still appears that heart and disposition are something naturally and specifically human. But even if this is so, he goes on, memory is "not exclusively, nor even primarily," human (150). He then elaborates how the definition of memory as the gathering of thinking that recalls requires us to think together the recalling, what remains to be thought, and their gathering (cf. above, chapter 3, sections 1 and 2). Here, in the space of a page, we see the elaboration of a sphere beyond any anthropological view; indeed,

Heidegger absorbs such partial views and makes sense of their development by way of his at least partially successful seeing and saying.

That means that *What Is Called Thinking?* explores the ways in which our emphasis on the human is derived from a prior saying of the duality. That is, words such as "logic," "need," "use," "history," and so on, once spoke originally; then gradually in Western metaphysical history, they were translated and reduced to their current anthropomorphically understood meaning.

But this understanding could indicate something more disturbing. If Heidegger speaks of the duality as the originary subject of his verbs and employs verbs which appear to be voluntaristic or personalistic, is he not saying that it is Being's will which now reigns? If so, he would, after all, be a follower of Nietzsche, and like Nietzsche, circle back to read Being-as-Willing into the history of Greek philosophy.

This is not the case. Because of the language he attempts to use, that is, because of the source and its manner of saying which he adapts, his language appears to look voluntaristic just as it looks mystical and poetic. As we shall see, it is the connections with the religious, the mystical, and the poetic, not finally with the metaphysical-willing, that creates this appearance.

Consider how *What Is Called Thinking?* does not simply remain with a voluntaristic, metaphysical language. On the one hand, as the first sections of chapter 3 already have shown, Heidegger does move beyond metaphysical talk of will in the originary use of key words such as "need," "call," and "use." That is, if we continue to hear voluntaristic language when we read such key words, it is not because Heidegger has not tried to say otherwise; need is what is fitting to the nature of, what allows to come to its own nature and relationships; call is the coming forth as laying out of what is called—a name lays out a thing as it is, That which calls brings forth. As noted, Heidegger fails to translate all representational verbs in this way, so that "gathering," "belonging together," and others are not said safely over on the originary shore. But insofar as it is achieved, the originary does overcome voluntaristic connotations.

Secondly, although parts of *What Is Called Thinking?* remain concerned with metaphysics and thus say things in that language, other parts are successful in going beyond the philosophy of Being as Willing. That is, because Heidegger does focus on Being as Willing to a considerable extent, it could seem that all that he says is thought in terms of Will, that not only Being is voluntaristically said but so too is the duality. Granted, "the present of what is present" still does echo Being and being and the historical-metaphysical meaning of words. But to interpret in the end Heidegger's saying as voluntaristic is to disregard all that has been demonstrated above, that Heidegger does indeed begin to move (which means *does* move in parts of *What Is Called Thinking?* and especially in "A Dialogue on Language") beyond the metaphysical tradition, even if he does not fully leap free from it. In other words, persisting in following what appears to be voluntaristic language insists on dragging a red herring across the trail of our thinking. It does so because it misleads us into going back into the history of metaphysics just when, following Heidegger, we are trying to get beyond it. That is, it leads us to the "wrong" place in the sense of returning only to the single-track of the metaphysical which holds us back from the originary trail.

Of course, insofar as *What Is Called Thinking?* continues to think Being, it is necessary to stay with the history of metaphysics. That is necessary in any reading because of the failure of *What Is Called Thinking?* It also is necessary, on quite different grounds, in any learning of originary thinking, which must start from where we are, from within the still dominant metaphysical realm. This necessary scholarship, which would trace out in detail and depth the relationship of Heidegger's thought to the history of Being, obviously cannot be done here. Even so, it is one thing to continue to study the metaphysical and another to hold that Heidegger remains caught in a voluntaristic view. He may not have gone much beyond Being in *What Is Called Thinking?*, but he has gone beyond a voluntaristic saying. Further, the obscured vision is not all he has brought to language. The "four-fold," even though only hinted at in *What Is Called Thinking?*, in *Discourse on Thinking*, and in "A Dialogue on Language" all show his movement.

Though I am convinced of this, it must be said that Heidegger does compound the misunderstanding himself in what he says and does and in what he does not say. Heidegger attempts to do so many different things simultaneously in *What Is Called Thinking?* that he has difficulty holding them all together. He strains to keep from going off on otherwise legitimate and necessary trails which, while important in themselves, do not lead where this lecture series is trying to go. For example, when he thinks the history of metaphysics where Being is thought as Willing. Here at the end of the first part he shows where he (or we) could go, and where he (or we) should go to *keep* on the path to what is called thinking. Similarly, in the penultimate lecture of the first part, he notes that we could attempt to understand historically what Leibniz, Kant, Ficte, Hegel, Schellig, Schopenhauer, and Nietzsche said about the Being of beings—about Willing (91), or that we could try to understand these thinkers originarily. Now, we know he does not intend to undertake a scholarly, historical understanding. But in *What Is Called Thinking?*, neither does he pursue Being as Willing originarily (though he does so elsewhere, for example, in *Der Satz vom Grund*, two years later), and for the purposes of learning thinking, he breaks off this tact.

That is, while this is a necessary task, here it misleads. Earlier, in the fourth lecture when thinking Being as Willing in Nietzsche's work, Heidegger advises his students to postpone reading Nietzsche and instead study Aristotle for ten to fifteen years (73). This takes place along with his admonition to find, then lose Nietzsche. The time for the learner to find Nietzsche (and Being as Willing) is not yet; the time to lose Nietzsche is at hand for Heidegger, for otherwise he misleads the learner. Thus, after keeping with Nietzsche in the final lecture of the first part, he does break off. The second part starts off anew, without Nietzsche and continues that way. Heidegger sees that he is spending too much time on Being as Willing and is providing an unhelpful example. Here Heidegger remains too much concerned with metaphysics, which he is not yet beyond; he even suggests that he is not yet to originary thinking, saying, "you must concede that the teacher's attempt may go wrong" (25–26). He is at a crossroad before us; he chooses one way, and we may or may not follow his path. That is, it is not wrong to follow the other way, but it is misleading because from there we should not be able to make a leap to the originary and that which calls for thinking. We need to learn from this clear lesson. We could pursue the task of criticizing Heidegger's *What Is Called Thinking?* by way of Being as Willing, but to do so, even as a necessary, legitimate task, would lead us over to another project. It would keep us stuck in the metaphysical. If we would not be misled by this treatment in the project of learning originary (not scholarly) thinking with this book, we should follow the new lead. We need to see both sides, the metaphysical-traditional and the originary; but the real project is to attempt to pass from the first to the second, which means temporarily giving the first up.

Another misleading section is that in which Heidegger goes off on a tangent concerning Nietzsche and the European political situation (65–69). Or, as an example of misleading by omission, Heidegger fails to spell out and say what "gathering" and "belonging together" originarily mean when he could, and instead allows the impression of voluntaristic overtones to linger. And, more as a failure, by keeping the "presence of what is present" in terms of the Being of beings, what has been said of Being and being *via* willing naturally continues to echo.

Beyond Heidegger's mistakes and our stubborn refusal to relinquish reading voluntaristically, however, there is a deeper reason for the impression of a false scent; the real danger is the actual "source" of much of *What Is Called Thinking?* Heidegger's dynamic language appears to be voluntaristic not because he continues to think Being as Willing, but because, without any acknowledgment, *What Is Called Thinking?* is built on the Western tradition which uses a dynamic, personal language. That is, the Judeo-Christian tradition, with its personal God who wills and acts, is the real source of much of what Heidegger thinks and says. Derived from this unacknowledged source, his verbs appear to speak of Being in terms of willing (which itself is a representational derivative and reduction, drawing in part from the same source). In other words, *What Is Called Thinking?* utilizes a manner of saying which appears personalistic because it adapts for its own purposes much of the manner and language of the Judeo-Christian tradition.

This means that our critical question of the problem of Heidegger's language and thinking and its relation to metaphysical thinking takes on a new dimension. Granted that the issue of the relation of *What Is Called Thinking?* to the tradition of Will in Nietzsche, Schelling, et al. needs to be thought through, that still would take us in another direction than learning to read Heidegger and fathom the sense his originary thinking makes. Our special task involves a larger and deeper issue concerning Heidegger's language and thinking: *how does he learn to hear, think, and say? What is the origin of what he originarily says and the manner of his saying and teaching too? What has he beheld, even as his originary vision remains veiled?*

Furthermore, if we listen to the lectures thoughtfully, we find they not only speak to us with their own voice, but bear with them an echo (which they barely hide). When we pay close attention to the way Heidegger thinks and speaks, we find more than the manner or mode of his thought; we also find that "from which and to which what is said is attuned" (37).[2] Consider three theses concerning this attunement. The evidence for the first thesis generates the other two although the latter can be no more than recommended here. First, then, both the procedure and the structure of *What Is Called Thinking?* correspond to the fourfold hermeneutics practiced by the Church Fathers and in the Middle Ages. Heidegger interprets what is called thinking by adopting the fourfold method of scriptural exegesis. This correspondence itself points to another one: Heidegger's lectures, thinking and saying, and That which calls for thinking are secular analogies to scriptural exegesis, the Bible, and God, respectively. Finally, because his method is a secularized version of biblical hermeneutics and because four levels of meaning are attributed to his subject (the duality, thinking, and saying), four levels of meaning are incorporated into his text with the result that, by a kind of slippage, *What Is Called Thinking?* is a sort of secular scripture. Indeed, in "A Dialogue on Language" Heidegger acknowledges the debt his thinking owes to biblical studies; elsewhere he indicates that thinking is not identical to faith, yet belongs to it.[3] Consider, then, how the structure and style of Heidegger's interpretation of thinking exfoliate polysemous meaning in a way which corresponds to medieval hermeneutics, how this may be but one off-shoot of a plant which itself is entwined with religion, and how Heidegger's text may be a secular scripture.

To begin, the four questions, or the four forms of the one question, What is called thinking? correspond to the four meanings of Scripture: the literal, the allegorical (or figural), the tropological, and the anagogical.[4]

The literal sense of Scripture, *sensus litteralis*, had to do with the conventional meanings of signs, that is, with the things and events which they signify. This would include the discursive, cultural, and rhetorical aspects of signification. Accordingly, the literal meaning of Scripture is nothing "reduced," nothing merely "literal," as we might use the word today.[5] Rather, it was all that an author could intend, including metaphysical and parabolic meanings. At this initial and foundational level, the Bible tells us about what has been done and said. *Sensus litteralis* teaches history. This account of what has happened enables us to follow the unfolding of the sacred in the course of human history and therefore to understand the meaning of these events.

A secular version of this literal sense would concern itself with words and what they mean.[6] Again, without any reduction in meaning, this level would have to do with the structurally crafted and poetic, as well as the referential and discursive aspects of a text's meaning. Of course, the full intention of any writer of special skill and ability, that is, the literal meaning of the text, will be complex and rich. As an example, in a philosophical treatise, what the author tells us concerning the things, events, and relationships which words signify would be this plain or literal sense. And clearly the first question which Heidegger asks operates at precisely this level. He first asks and then answers, What is it which is called by the word "thinking"? or, What is it which is named thinking? What is thinking really? As we saw earlier, the initial concern of *What Is Called Thinking?* is to tell us about thinking. It intends to explain to us what "thinking" usually means and also what it really, or originarily, means. When we read *What Is Called Thinking?*, we initially look for and discover what Heidegger says about all this, and what Heidegger has said concerning the word "thinking" and, the nature of thinking is the literal sense of his book.

But the Church Fathers accepted not only the historical meaning of Scripture, but its spiritual sense (*sententia*). Following Philo, they developed techniques for reading, that is interpreting, the fuller meaning of what was taught. They explained how it was that in addition to the meaning which any human author could indicate concerning things, people, and events, there was a deeper meaning which was not a matter of convention. They believed that while man could make words mean things, God—and only God— could make those things themselves mean other things. God, then, provided a spiritual sense for them to understand. As this *sententia* developed into three spiritual senses, the medieval scholars developed an appropriate threefold method of exegesis.[7] Hence, the complex hermeneutic of the Middle Ages responded and corresponded to the literal and triple spiritual senses of Scripture.

The first sort of spiritual interpretation to grow out of the literal level was called allegorical or figural.[8] (This is unavoidably confusing because "allegorical" does not mean what we mean by "allegory"—the latter is part of the literal sense. Further, the differences between what the medievals meant by "allegorical" and "figural" were vague for a long time after Augustine. Finally, the figural sense contains the allegorical, not *vice versa*.) The figural sense is so called because it involves the prefiguration of events in Christ's life. For example, the crossing of the Red Sea was taken to prefigure Christ's baptism; Abraham's sacrifice of the ram prefigured the human nature and sacrifice of Christ. There are two basic aspects of this figural or allegorical meaning. First, there is the unfolding story of Christ, who fulfills all that happened before and all that was foretold. That is, the meaning of Scripture lies in the drama of the Incarnation. But, of course, Christology is not merely biographical. Secondly, there is the doctrine which the history of the Incarnation teaches. A secular adaptation of this figural sense would have to concern the explanation behind what was said at the first level. It would inquire into how and why the plain sense is as it is, and thereby would provide a fuller interpretation of what the author says.

The second question of the book asks both How is it that a psychological process is that which usually is called thinking? and How is it that what "thinking" really names is an originary recalling or gathering? These inquiries go beyond what Heidegger has to say, for obviously Heidegger himself did not arbitrarily name either the human processes or the originary gathering "thinking." He has told us that it is so; he has given an account of what is a fact. But then, by way of asking, "What is called thinking?" in the second form of the question, he goes on to ask how it is that that which is called thinking is so called. In answering that question, Heidegger tells us how this has come about. That is, he explains the way thinking is understood in the tradition and why it is understood in just this way. Interpreted in the second way, then, the question, What is called thinking? asks about the doctrine of thinking; it inquires about the paradigm(s) for thinking which our tradition rests on. Here Heidegger interprets the history of what is called thinking so as to reveal both the two major incarnations of thinking and the doctrine of thinking.

The next sense of Scripture is the tropological. If we contemplate the image of Christ and the doctrine of the Church, we realize that understanding them entails action. The doctrine is not only to be taken up in belief, but also to be enacted in our lives. Thus, this meaning teaches morality. *Sensus tropologicus sive moralis* answers our question, What should I do? or How can I live this doctrine? Secularized, this sort of meaning would have to do with proper human conduct. How should we act? How can we act? What is human nature so that such action is possible or necessary? In the largest sense, this inquires after the moral universal which would emerge from the paradigms and doctrine which we imaginatively contemplate. The secular meaning is the human vision which emerges from the work. Heidegger also asks, What is called thinking? in this version of tropological sense. He interprets the question in its third variation to ask, What does thinking call for? when he explores what thinking requires from us. Heidegger simply is asking what thinking, understood first according to the traditional doctrine of thinking and then according to the possibility of originary thinking, means for our lives. How are we to think this way or that? Here we want to learn how to think; we want to know what we should do.

The final spiritual sense of Scripture is the anagogical. It follows from the earlier levels: (1) history teaches (2) doctrine, which (3) we attempt to live; if we believe and live the doctrine, (4) we move toward our final end with God. The anagogical meaning then is eschatological. It indicates the final relation or state of the saints with God in heaven. In a secular version, (1) what is said about thinking has a fundamental philosophical meaning and history which also (2) instructs us about the unfolding of thinking and of the doctrine of thinking, which (3) we attempt to live by learning how to think ourselves; if we take thinking to heart and attempt to think originarily, (4) we will move toward our final (philosophical or thoughtful) end. That is, if we understand and also take up originary thinking, we would participate in the event of thinking. The secular cosmic vision corresponds to the anagogical. Here we would see all that we might hope for. With the fourth version of the question, Heidegger asks about the ultimate and its relation to the human. He asks for what is beyond the merely human and for what enables the human to come into its nature. What is That which calls for thinking? is the final meaning of the question, What is called thinking? When he answers this fourth question, Heidegger interprets the origin and end of thinking as finally meaning the duality in relation to man. Heidegger's elaboration of That which calls for thinking and sets it underway and which is understood as the duality gathering man to itself, obviously then is a secular *sensus anagogicus*.

In sum, Heidegger asks what is called thinking in four ways which interpret thinking in a manner adapted from biblical exegesis. In its first form, What is called thinking? inquires after the literal sense; in its second form, after the figural or allegorical; in its third form, after the tropological; in its fourth, after the anagogical sense. But the work even more deeply and fully instantiates the fourfold hermeneutic. All four questions, or all four ways of asking one question, are plainly given and answered by Heidegger. That is, for all their intricacy, the four levels of meaning just reviewed are what Heidegger himself says concerning thinking. All he says about representational and originary thinking finally is the literal sense of the lectures.[9] Because of this, we get a *hint* that the whole book, not just the four questions, devolves from the hermeneutical procedure. In chapter 3 above it was argued that *What Is Called Thinking?* has four levels or phases. If the entire first level of the four—what Heidegger says concerning thinking, according to the four questions— actually corresponds to the literal level, we might expect that *What Is Called Thinking?*, as a unified text, itself has four kinds of meaning.

Even as we found that Heidegger has a great deal to *tell us* concerning thinking, we also saw that the lecture series does not merely tell us what is called thinking; it also *shows* that thinking to us. Heidegger presents us with the movement or style of his thinking, and in chapter 3 above, we tried to see how (beyond any abstraction of what Heidegger says, or its first or literal phase) the whole lecture series is structured to embody what he has to say. But this is a second, figural sense. Here the style of the thinking is presented to us so that we can see how it unfolds. But that means it is exemplary. The teacher is an *exemplar*. If this level shows that the teacher *does* what he *says*, and if we are to understand the book in this phase by watching how he goes about thinking in order to understand how his thinking and his talk coincide, then the book presents a doctrine concerning thinking: a thinking is the gathering together of what already belongs together. Further, the figural sense is not only doctrine, but includes the way the doctrine is ordered. That is, in biblical exegesis the figural sense is both Christology and Christ as the Incarnation or embodiment of the doctrine. Put another way, Christ is the figure who focuses and embodies the sense of what is said and done in *Scripture*.

The same occurs in Heidegger's book. The sense of what is said and done concerning thinking is focused and ordered by the *figura* which lies behind what Heidegger says and what he does. It is a *figura*, then, in a profound sense: it is the central organizational principle of the text and of the doctrine of thinking. Because of this, it (or the equivalent figure of the teaching thinker described above in chapter 3) is to *What Is Called Thinking?* as Christ is to the Bible!

We saw that the lecture series has a third phase which results from the first two. Because in phase two the book achieves the thinking which it tells us about in phase one, a fusion occurs; in turn, this unity rhetorically acts upon us. That is, Heidegger does say what thinking is and he does think himself; insofar as we genuinely follow what he says and does, we are not spectators observing something foreign to us but are drawn in to participate. The contemplation of the first two senses can result in learning how to go about thinking. Because Heidegger displays what he says in the way he does, he clearly intends to teach us how to think.

The lectures have this further sense, then: the teaching and learning of thinking occur right here. We are invited to learn the skills which Heidegger not only displays (phase two), but which he actively, explicitly and implicitly, teaches (phase three). Insofar as Heidegger teaches thinking and we learn to think, the text addresses our concern about what we should do. This is the tropological sense: it treats the way to live the doctrine of thinking—the way to think originarily. In addition, the book presents a vision of the whole of thinking. In fact, it insists that the traditional way to think (an attempt to perfect and clarify representational concepts, or to extend their grasp) is only partially valid and must be unlearned. The more responsive thinking (thinking which responds to What calls for thinking) is originary. This vision of originary thinking and its partial "derivative" (representational thinking) yields an understanding of the human and of human limitations. Thus, the vision of thinking is a human, tropological vision; but, it is not merely that. It also opens beyond itself: the way to think involves passing beyond any merely human interest or use. Accordingly, from the first three phases a fourth is generated.

Finally, the book attempts to present the comprehensive vision of the duality, man, thinking, and saying—or, perhaps, of the fourfold gathering—even though it ultimately fails (see chapter 3, section 4). It also indicates how those who learn to think originarily (and, in their way, those who think representationally) belong to the gathering of what already belongs together. Specifically, in the fourth phase, *What Is Called Thinking?* works to describe what the *figura* and the way of originary thinking point to: That which calls and still is calling for thinking. That which gathers, or the duality gathering itself, or something even beyond these, is the final, eschatological meaning of the work. Although only glimpsed obscurely, that which calls for thinking is the origin and end of what is called thinking; it also is the anagogical sense of *What Is Called Thinking?*

The medieval biblical hermeneutic, then, clearly provides the procedure which Heidegger uses in his own secular, thinking way, to interpret thinking. Again, all that Heidegger says concerning what thinking is, interpreted according to the four modes of the question, What is called thinking?, is the text's plain or literal sense; the way the text, in its second phase, does what it says, fusing style with substance, especially as focused by the master *figura*, discloses a figural or allegorical sense; the third phase, in which teaching and learning to think are actions happening here, is tropological; and, the fourth phase, which would envision the ultimate gathering of what belongs together, is anagogical.

This correspondence obviously involves the following sort of relation: Heidegger's interpretation of *What Is Called Thinking?* is to its subject (thinking) as medieval exegesis is to its subject (the Bible). But just as obviously, the Bible is a sort of middle term. That is, it is a book, spoken and written, to be heard and read, by men in order to achieve union with God. And correspondingly, Heidegger, says that thinking and saying are middle terms. Thinking and saying are the ways in which man and That which calls for thinking (Being, the duality, the fourfold-gathering) belong together. Thus, the whole situation, according to Heidegger, appears analogous to the religious paradigm. We could sketch this:

What Is Called Thinking?	*biblical exegesis*	
thinking and saying	::	Bible
That which calls for thinking		God

Note further that Heidegger's lectures themselves embody the four sorts of meaning, but *not* in a way which is discursively or logically straightforward. That is, they do not present the four meanings of thinking in anything resembling the order of a commentary, gloss, or traditional explication. Just the opposite. The four senses are so interwoven, so fused, that the book stands on its own as a saying and has such a complex, substantial meaning that it must be thought through carefully (not quickly "disposed" of). That is, because it has four sorts of meaning fused together, *What Is Called Thinking?* seems to require a reading according to a secular fourfold hermeneutic. But that would mean that *What Is Called Thinking?* is a secular scripture—clearly the object, not of faith, but of originary thinking and reading.

The central role that the second level[10] (the figural) plays in the book supports these theses, especially the major one. The figural sense incarnates and focuses the literal sense; the tropological and anagogical arise out of contemplation of the figural (specifically, they arise as a result of contemplation on the image or figure which embodies the literal sense and organizes the doctrine). In *What Is Called Thinking?* the figural plays an unusually major role—this in addition to the pervasive power of the master *figura* (which is an aspect of the figural sense). This figural sense is appropriately central to Heidegger's project. In the Middle Ages, the second sense of *Scripture* was sometimes understood to be figural, sometimes to be allegorical.[11] Though the complex and troubled history of the distinction is beyond our scope here, the essence of the difference bears directly on Heidegger's thought. Throughout the development of biblical exegesis, there has been a tension between two religious events: creation and Incarnation. To simplify, the creation implies the principle of hierarchy; the Incarnation, the collapse of that principle. The hermeneutical practitioners and theoreticians who emphasized hierarchy favored the allegorical sense; those who emphasized the incarnational or horizontal principle favored the figural. These differences had major implications for the theory of signs and for the relation of the literal sense to the spiritual senses.

Heidegger favors the incarnational model and the figural sense, as evidenced by his extensive use of the *figura* or *Gebild* to incarnate the sense of thinking (detailed in chapter 3), by his insistence on the historicity of both sign and what is signified (as seen in his discussion of the words "thinking" or "being" and the continuing historical event of That which calls for thinking), and by the horizontal or containing fulfillment of meaning, when, for example, thinking and saying are gathering *within*, (described in chapters 2 and 3).[12] But Heidegger does more than sound the figural sense and the incarnational model. When he operates in accord with this hermeneutical principle, which holds (a)that literal truth is needed and retained by the spiritual senses, (b) that the relationship between *figura* and its fulfillment is horizontal, and (c) that the *figura* is an empty form which is filled (its fuller meaning is *within*), Heidegger is deemphasizing the alternative. That is, he is choosing against the hierarchial principle, the principle that has laid at the heart of traditional transcendental metaphysics ever since Plato! By insisting on maintaining the historical sense, Heidegger refuses the traditional philosophical claim that knowledge be atemporal; by insisting on the horizontal figural relationship, he refuses the idea of transcendental Being and the unreality of this world; by filling in the *figura* and by seeing thinking and saying as part of a gathering within, he quietly collapses the vertical scheme of metaphysics. Thus, Heidegger's thought is stylistically and substantially figural rather than allegorical; it is thoroughly figural.

If Heidegger is a genuinely figural thinker, we can expect to find more instances of this secular adaptation, which holds out against any onto-theological hierarchy, indeed three more manifestations of the figural are found in his book.

As briefly noted, the figural sense developed in biblical hermeneutics to include typology. A type is a historical person, thing, or event, which (1) both retains its own independent meaning and also (2) prefigures Christ. To elaborate the prefiguring relationship, the type signifies Christ, and Christ fulfills the type. The type, then, is both something in itself and also points to Christ or to something which is part of Christology; Christ or a Christological event or thing involves or fulfills the meaning of the type. Further, a genuine type must have both a formal resemblance to what it signifies and also be historically connected to it. These conditions, for example, hold between Moses and Christ, the ram which Abraham sacrificed and Christ, Noah's arc and the Church, and the passage through the Red Sea and baptism.

What Is Called Thinking? contains its own typology. What Heidegger says about originary thinking in the book's first or literal phase (his second set of answers to the question, What is named thinking?) prefigures what he does in the book's second phase. *What he tells us* about originary thinking *is a type of what he does*, of the way he goes about thinking. As a type, originary thinking—understood by Heidegger to be recollection, memorial gathering, and a taking and keeping at heart—does have its own independent meaning. We are told what thinking is and has been. That is the plain or historical sense of the type, what is said concerning originary thinking. But, because it is a type, originary thinking also signifies that which is not yet fulfilled. What is prefigured (what we are told about) must also occur in a more complete way; it must be incarnated. This occurs in the lecture series. Originary thinking, announced in the lectures' first phase, is fulfilled in the second phase when Heidegger does what he earlier said. Thus, in the second phase we find the prototype embodied in Heidegger's style of thinking.

A second manifestation of this figural dimension can be seen when one considers the second question of the book's literal phase (How is it that what is called thinking has come to be so called?) a type of the entire book. That is, the originary account of the history of thinking prefigures everything Heidegger does and says, fulfilling the originary story of thinking. Heidegger insists that the originary story or history of the relation of the duality and man, which includes thinking and saying, is the proper meaning of past, present, and future events. Accordingly, his originary account has its proper independent sense. But the story clearly tells of the forgetting and the withdrawal of what calls for thinking, of the reduction of thinking in our metaphysical tradition, and of the attempt to recover originary thinking in our metaphysical tradition, and of the attempt to recover originary meaning by means of a thinking which recalls and gathers. In short, the story is not finished. It points ahead to the event of thinking, which would achieve this recalling and gathering. Thus, the account of the history of thinking (from its beginnings, down through the tradition, and finally moving toward the stage when we learn to think, though we are not yet thinking) prefigures originary thinking; the event of originary thinking would fulfill the meaning that the historical unfolding foreshadowed.

Specifically, then, the first two phases of the book are intimately bound together by typology. The second phase of the book is the way it is because the thinking which Heidegger *does* is part of the drama whose story (or perhaps, plot) was told earlier in the first phase. Heidegger's actual originary thinking—what he does in the book's second phase—plays out the story which already is underway long before he joins in and which includes what he does as a part of the entire story (that is, as part of the drama of the unfolding duality and the gathering of human thinking and saying into the duality). Put directly, the originary account of thinking (the whole originary story) is itself part of the story of thinking; accordingly, originary thinking necessarily includes its own activity and essence in its account of thinking. It indicates why and how thinking, now attempting to become originary, will go; Heidegger's originary thinking begins to fulfill that project.

Generally, since the other phases of the book (the teaching of thinking in the third phase and the vision in the fourth) also are facets of originary thinking, they too fulfill the type. That is, the story of thinking is a type, presented in the book's first phase of meaning and fulfilled in the second phase (when Heidegger does what he says), in the third phase (where Heidegger teaches originary thinking), and also in the fourth phase (where the unity of duality and man is envisioned). Accordingly, the book's first level presents the type—originary thinking—of the rest of the book. *What Is Called Thinking?* fulfills that type because it gathers together what already belongs together (phase two), teaches us, gathers us together with that gathering (phase three), and obscurely envisions the gathering of what already belongs together (phase four).

A third way typology works is in the typological relationship between ordinary, traditional thinking, and originary thinking. In fact, we saw, over and over in chapter 3, how Heidegger begins with the partial or "reduced" originary understanding of a word, concept, thing, or event and then goes on to develop the full originary sense. Here, each of these belongs to a kind of "old testament" (their meaning according to traditional metaphysical, representational thought) and also to a "new testament" (their meaning when thought originarily). Further, each is an "old testament" type which is fulfilled in the "new testament."[13] For example, the "logic" of representational thought is fulfilled in the *logos* and *legein* of originary thinking. Notice, too, that the requirement that the type have formal resemblance to and historical connection with what it is a type of is fulfilled here—indeed, these relationships are stressed by Heidegger. Recall just a few of these types: "thinking," "memory," "language," "history," "use," "bridge," and "dispose." In each case, the historical, traditional meaning remains; it is not undone. But also in each case that traditional meaning points beyond itself; it is a prototype of some originary meaning. Again and again, Heidegger argues that though something does mean this or that, it does not mean *merely* this or that, but also something more complex and profound. For example, thinking is a human activity; but, it is not merely a psychological process or human activity. Finally, it is a *gathering* together of man and duality. This procedure or typological style both anchors us in what the tradition does say and think and also opens us up to the originary meaning which satisfies or completes the type. For another example, the anthropological movement of traditional thinking from man to Being is a type of the originary duality (the relation of Being and human being, both given at once by way of thinking and saying). The complete *figura* fulfills the partial "movement from man to Being by way of human thinking and saying" and renders it intelligible, both as to its historical reality and development and to its incompleteness.[14]

The figural procedures of the book, then, involve the literal or historical sense of what is said; indeed, the procedures require and sustain that meaning. The clear and crucial importance which the *story* of thinking has for Heidegger, coupled with the connection between saga or saying and thinking, prepare us for a parallel which Heidegger seems to develop between the story of thinking and the Bible.[15]

It is not necessary to sketch the main events and characters of the Old and New Testaments. Think, for instance, only of the three main events of the Bible, creation, Incarnation, and the last judgment. God created the heavens, earth, and all that belongs to the earth, including man whom He made to be free, free even to sin and thus turn away from his origin and Who nonetheless continued to love and sustain him. Christ was made man and freely died that man might come back into the proper relation with his creator, and thereby gain heaven. In the end there will be the final coming, wherein people will be put into their proper place, and, especially, the good will be reunited with their God. The medievals often spoke of these three stages of human history as innocence (from the creation to the fall), wayfaring (from the fall to the end of the world, with the Incarnation and Redemption as central turning points), and glory (man united with God after final judgment).

Heidegger's story of thinking proceeds with a strikingly similar "plot." In the beginning was the duality, and the duality was with man. But man, who was needed by the duality and was able to think the duality, was also free to forget it and to turn away. And he did. The duality became more and more forgotten as man developed his own tradition of thinking, by which he could ever more powerfully grasp anything and everything as an object, and as That which calls for thinking withdrew into concealment. But, even after What calls for thinking withdrew, some relation to man remained, and man continued to point toward the withdrawal. Somehow, it came about that What had been forgotten came back to mind; What was unspoken and unthought for so long, finally grew closer to man. There was the event—or the possibility of the event—of originary thinking. In originary thinking what long ago was rent asunder is again gathered together: man and the duality are gathered together. In originary thinking—the gathering together of what already belongs together even while apart—there is a reconciliation. This prospect must reverentially be let be, and our lives will change accordingly. Someday, a day which we have not even begun to achieve, man and That which calls for thinking will be fully together. But for now, long before that final union, we can take only a few preliminary steps. As a community of dedicated thinkers we can try to stay on the right path of thinking, so that some of us might achieve the thinking which gathers and belongs. For now, we are not yet thinking; we are not yet fully gathered to what gathers us.

Of course, put this way, Heidegger's story of the history of the duality, man, thinking, and saying seems silly or trite. It also seems incredibly presumptuous; after all, a conscious secularization of things religious is one thing, but this is too much. But in fact, it may be only my presentation, not Heidegger's work, which makes it seem so. If we are humble enough to admit that we have not experienced what Heidegger has, we need to admit we are not capable of judging him. Here I mean to point out what apparently is going on in *What Is Called Thinking?* and elsewhere in order to point to what we must understand, *not* reduce what it means to what we see at first glance. What needs to be understood is that Heidegger apparently tells his story in a way which parallels the religious story central to Western culture. Somehow the story of That which calls for thinking and sacred history are the same; at the least, they are in the same neighborhood or are intertwined with each other.

Here, it is worth noting that the Incarnation as interpreted by Kierkegaard, for example, seems to play a part in *What Is Called Thinking?* Because God loved man so much, according to Kierkegaard, He acted so that man could freely love in return.[16] If he appeared in all His majesty and power as "King," he might be feared or even respected, but He would not be embraced or loved, for who could think themselves worthy to love such a One. Accordingly, He lowered himself so that He would not intimidate His beloved, so that His beloved could love Him in return. That is why Christ came so humbly: The Incarnation is He who calls for, and makes possible, loving. In Heidegger's apparently parallel account, man is somehow also essential to That which calls for thinking.[17] Though thinking is nothing merely human, it is human because it is a way of belonging together which holds between man and the duality. It is useful—both necessary and "wanted"—to the duality that man both let-lie-before him and take-to-heart-too the presence of the present. Thus, what is unthought and unspoken moves so that it may someday be thought and spoken.

The similarities between Heidegger's story and interpretation, on the one hand, and the Bible and biblical interpretation, on the other, extend even further. For example, we can gather together a variety of features which alone may not be proof of this parallelism, but which support the major evidence cited so far and thus further recommend the thesis.

In *What Is Called Thinking?* we saw that Heidegger controls the tone of what is said. For example, he presents an excited state of will and power when treating Nietzsche, but replaces this with a restrained, restful tone when he speaks of Aristotle, and, later, of Parmenides. The measure changes throughout. At first there is the quickening pace of surging, barely constrained energy; later, the movement is much slower and calmer. Finally, however, Heidegger speaks in a voice which is not modernly dynamic, not classical, not "oracular." That is, a fourth tone pervades the work: Heidegger's own voice (or, perhaps, that of originary thinking) is noticeably *homey*. When Heidegger speaks originarily we hear a dialect of thinking, as it were, a dialect of long-standing, rural life. Here the lectures are full of talk of craft, hand, heart, thanks, food for thought, paths, leaping and swimming, gifts, foothills and moun-tains, wood and trees, home and play, the useful, rocks and earth, furrows and chasms, waters and rivers, calling and being called, keeping and guarding, and so on. Compared with the polished, sophisticated speech of Nietzsche, with the supple, authoritative language of Aristotle, or with the venerable, "paratactic" saying of Parmenides, Heidegger's homey language is strikingly like that of the Gospels. It strikes our ear, after we have heard traditional, metaphysical language for so long, as being like the language of the New Testament. To mention only a few of the obvious similarities: Heidegger speaks of epiphany (10), our ears being opened (48), reverence (72), delivery from sin (105), being called to hope (123), giving thanks (139), devotion (140 ff. and 163), the heart (141), tidings that overtake all our doings (145), offering (146), the source of call and radiance (168), testimony (168), what hails from (187), the gates of knowledge and the great hall where all that can be known is kept (207), the gleaning of grapes (208), and leap and vision (171, 232 ff.).

To elaborate only one aspect of all this, Heidegger develops *thinking* in language long associated with the Gospels and the religious tradition which followed from them. Thinking is thought as memory which, in turn, is spoken of in terms of "devotion" and "thanks" (138 ff., 163). Devotion (a constant concentrated abiding with something) (140), and thanks (the heart's core, "the gathering of all that concerns us, all that we care for, all that touches us insofar as we are, as human beings,") (144), are they not religious in tone? Consider further the following examples:

> In its original telling sense, memory means as much as devotion. This word possesses the special tone of the pious and piety, and designates the devotion of prayer, only because it denotes the all-comprehensive relation of concentration upon the holy and gracious. (145)

This helps us to interpret a gesture which occurred at the beginning of the book.

> The hand reaches and extends, receives or welcomes—and not just things: the hand extends itself, and receives its own welcome in the hands of others. . . . Two hands fold into one, a gesture meant to carry man into that great oneness. (16)

These hands joined together are those of people settling matters with a handshake and thanks (146); they are the hands of a couple joined together in the wedding ceremony, who become who they are as they take their vows. But before all else, these are hands joined together in prayer. Heidegger's talk of gift and giving, which "delivers us to thinking," clearly calls to mind the Lord's Prayer. It is perfectly natural, too, for Heidegger to explain what "call" originarily means with a gloss from the New Testament, after writing that "to call means to get underway": "In the older Greek version of the New Testament, Matthew 8:18, we find: . . . Seeing a large crowd around him, he called to them to go to the other side" (117). Further, Heidegger explains, to be called to thinking is a calling—a vocation. The call to be the servants of the "being" of being (235) echoes the call which came individually to Mary and Jesus, for example, and which they answered with "Thy will be done."

Obviously, too, Heidegger expects that when we read of thinking as memory, and of memory as taking to heart and keeping the memory safe there, we will think of the religious prototype of such language: Luke 2:51. The passage relates what happened immediately after Jesus "taught" in the temple in Jerusalem: "He then went down with them and came to Nazareth and lived under their authority. His mother stored up all these things in her heart." This itself echoes the Old Testament. Genesis 2:15 says: "The Lord God took the man and placed him in the garden of Eden to till it and to keep it."[18] And is heard again in the *Sayings of the Fathers*, in which Anthony the Great tells us, "So whatever you find your soul wills in following God's will, do it, and keep your heart."[19] In the Christian tradition, these ways of thinking develop using the same images that Heidegger turns to, including the connection between thinking *via* laying before or letting lie, taking to heart, keep, and memory and That which gives us food for thought. In an Advent sermon, St. Bernard reflects on this line from the *Psalms*, "I have laid up your words in my heart: that I may not sin against you," and says:

> But how are they to be kept in our heart? Is it enough simply to preserve them in our memory? To those who only do this the apostle says: *Knowledge puffs up*. And, further, forgetfulness easily obliterates a memory. You must keep the word of God in the same way as it is best to keep your bodily food. For this is living bread and the food of the spirit. While earthly bread is in the cupboard it can be stolen by a thief, gnawed by a mouse, or simply go bad from being kept too long. But if you eat it, what have you to fear? Keep the word of God in this way: for blessed are those who keep it. So let it be taken into the stomach of your mind and pass into the things you care for and the things you do. Eat what is good and your soul will enjoy prosperity. Don't forget to eat your bread, lest your heart should dry up. If you keep the word of God like this, there is no doubt that it will keep you.[20]

Here we also might note Heidegger's positive references to Eckhart[21] and Pascal, his critique of a logically conceived Absolute God (157), and the comparison of the problematic character of thinking with the unconditional character of faith (177). While thinking and faith are not identical, Heidegger shows us that they are related. His secular, originary use of religious language and ideas gives expression to the fact that they belong together.

Finally, we might note one last correspondence: the hands clasped together in "a gesture meant to carry man into the great oneness" (16) remind us that originary thinking, because it is recollective, is a form of meditation, akin to prayer (especially when prayer is seen to be, not any asking for things, but an event of grace and union). Think, for example, of the correspondence between originary thinking (which attempts to open us to belonging with That which calls on us to think) and Ignatian meditation (which attempts to open us to God's love and will)—a method Heidegger would have known intimately from his seminary days with the Jesuits. (After attending the Gymnasium at Lake Constance, he went to Bertholds Gymnasium in Freiburg-im-Breisgau and next studied as a Jesuit novice in Freiburg.) Here I cite only one of the most famous features of Loyola's method, meditation beginning with place. Of course, this itself already is within an old tradition. For example, the love for place is found in Anthony the Great's reaction to the Interior Mountain and is carried on in the recollective prayer of St. John of the Cross as well as in Ignatius.[22] In *The Spiritual Exercises*, the "image of place" is a consistent prelude to meditation. Here Ignatius instructs us how to *"recall to mind"* the physical place (for instance, a temple, mountain, road, hell, or the soul in the *body*) which provides the scene for spiritual action.[23] The parallels between this technique and Heidegger's way of thinking are suggestive. Note that the biblical passage which Heidegger cites to originarily think "call" (Matthew 8:18) is a passage which holds Jesus' lament for a place where He belongs and in which we learn about the hardships of apostolic calling: "Foxes have holes and the birds of the air have nests, but the Son of Man has nowhere to lay his head" (Matthew 8:20). Heidegger is well known for his topology of Being, which Pöggeler explains as "a saying of the place, and thus a thinking of the trust, of Being."[24] We only need to recall Heidegger's concern with sphere, realm, abode, and place of mortals in *What Is Called Thinking?* (178, 190 ff., and chapter 3 above). Heidegger, as a good Jesuit, begins by imagining place, and proceeds toward the highest vision the soul longs for—the sphere of the unspoken.

The *figura* also attempts to sketch the *place* of the duality. It, too, is an image which is the focus of meditation in Heidegger's lectures. By going over and over the *figura*, we try to explore the scene of man's relation to the duality, that is, of the drama of the unfolding of the withdrawal and gathering together of the duality and man. Specifically, we can begin with a meditation on, or by way of, the *figura* which renders the place in a concrete way, and can be varied so that we can think of the whole story or any part of it. For example, we might think of the partial movement from the human to Being (the anthropological movement of much of traditional thought), or of man as the site of the event of Being, and so on. Here, the *figura* hold and fixes thinking within the scene of what the *figura* delineates: the scene of the duality, or better, of the event of gathering. Even if the scene turns out to be the event (the gathering underway), it still is a "placement." The static, then, becomes dynamic as we move through the scene in thought; in this thoughtful action we may experience the meaning of the drama. In short, the whole of *What Is Called Thinking?* is a kind of meditation, and if we understand that it is meditation that the *figura* focuses on, then it appears that the lectures move from place to deeper meaning, just as Ignatian meditation does.

Again, the religious analogues in *What Is Called Thinking?* should not be taken to explain Heidegger's thought and language, much less to categorize and thereby dispose of them. Rather, the correlations support the thesis that Heidegger's originary thinking in *What Is Called Thinking?* corresponds to medieval hermeneutical ways of thinking and interpreting. In addition, all of these relations might indicate that it would be worthwhile to explore Heidegger's work in terms of the religious sources he seems to draw from and/or as a kind of secular scripture. As noted, it is not simply the case that Heidegger explicates the fourfold meaning of what is called thinking, though he does do that, in such a way that produces a certain fusion of meaning in a new work. That is, his own text does not remain a discursive commentary, but assimilates the four sorts of meaning into its own original texture. Heidegger's work is composed in such a unified, organic way that, like the food we eat which becomes our body, the four sorts of meaning become the very substance and style of the book itself: the work, as a whole, transforms the multiple meanings of thinking into its own tissue, which itself has multiple meaning. By a process of incorporation, then, *What Is Called Thinking?* itself becomes a polysemous text, which, in turn, if it is to be understood properly, must be read hermeneutically. Thus, *What Is Called Thinking?* shifts into place not only with the texts of Parmenides and Nietzsche, but also with the Bible, too. Because of its connection with the Bible and its tradition, *What Is Called Thinking?* becomes a sort of secular scripture.

If *What Is Called Thinking?* is a secular scripture, we must question the relationship between Heidegger and this religious tradition, including Heidegger's use of it for originary thinking.

There have been two phases in the scholarly interpretation of Heidegger's relation to religion. The difference between them is important because the second state of this scholarship can open to a genuine questioning of what the recollective use of religion might be. The first phase of scholarship largely belongs to traditional representational thinking; the second also may, *or*, it may learn to become originary. The critical interpretive possibilities, then, replicate Heidegger's distinction between metaphysical and originary thinking.

The relationship between Heidegger's work and religion and theology has long been evident. The first phase of scholarship, which is still being practiced, is particularly interested in that relation since the 1920s, and especially since the publication of *Being and Time* in 1927. Given, for example, Heidegger's youthful religious training, his early academic teaching of and research into Christianity, his fruitful interaction with theological colleagues in Marburg, and the enormous impact of *Being and Time* upon theologians, the mutual influence of Heidegger's work and Christian thought naturally were investigated early on.[25] However, perhaps the classic statement of the issue has been put by Rudolf Bultmann, himself deeply influenced by Heidegger, in his "New Testament and Theology":

> Above all, Heidegger's existentialist analysis of the ontological structure of being would seem to be no more than a secularized, philosophical version of the New Testament view of human life. For him the chief characteristic of man's Being in history is anxiety.

Man exists in a permanent tension between the past and the future. At every moment he is confronted with an alternative. Either he must immerse himself in the concrete world of nature, and thus inevitably lose his individuality, or he must abandon all security and commit himself unreservedly to the future, and thus alone achieve his authentic Being. Is not that exactly the New Testament understanding of human life? Some critics have objected that I am borrowing Heidegger's categories and forcing them upon the New Testament. I am afraid this only shows that they are blinding their eyes to the real problem. I mean, one should rather be startled that philosophy is saying the same thing as the New Testament and saying it quite independently.[26]

This issue was traced out by Macquarrie in *An Existentialist Theology*, to note another influential work, and the theme is taken up again by Michael Zimmerman in *Eclipse of the Self*. The common feature of such works is their assumption that Heidegger is an existentialist and *Being and Time* is a work in philosophical anthropology which elaborates the structure of human experience, interpretations based on the perspective of *Dasein*. To be sure, more is glimpsed; Macquarrie, for example, notes the importance of being for Heidegger, and Bultmann notes religion's and philosophy's common concern. But what is noticed is just as soon dropped; persistently, issues of Being are thought out as part of the doctrine of the human.

Thus, Heidegger is seen as detheologizing. His relation to religion is understood as a secularization where secularization means, in the modern anthropological stance of the Western tradition where God is dead, to take over religious language without God in order to speak of the structure of human existence or *Dasein*. In this view, Heidegger is also thought to use religious language in a reduced form: religious terms, ideas, categories, concepts, and so forth are utilized, or made lively, as part of an existentialism. In turn, the now vivid existential insights are reused by theologians for their own purposes; theologians are given a basic way of seeing experience which can be elaborated religiously. Hence, Heidegger and theology are seen in interaction as both attempt to talk about authentic human life.

There is, in fact, little doubt of the borrowing in Heidegger's early work. For example, St. Paul informs Heidegger's view on time and existence; *kairos* appears in *Being and Time* as *Augenblick*, and so on. The problem here is that while historical sources often are traced correctly, the truth of what Heidegger is saying just as often is missed. Thus, a second phase of scholarship developed, precisely insofar as the assumption concerning Heidegger's meaning changed. As it became clearer that there was more to Heidegger than *Being and Time*, or, better, that Heidegger really meant something different because he was no mere existentialist or philosopher of human existence, a deeper interpretation was required. No longer seen as a metaphysician (not even a metaphysician concerned with Being as opposed to a philosophical anthropologist concerned with human being), Heidegger is reinterpreted as an originary, meditative thinker.

Here the questions of his relationship to religion and theology and of mutual influence are asked differently and more adequately. The result of these recent works shows that the influence of Christianity is very complex and runs throughout Heidegger's career. From the large and growing literature, we might note that Thomas Sheehan maintains that Heidegger's early thought, about temporality, for example, is derived from the New Testament experience; that Michael Zimmerman discusses how Heidegger's understanding of self developed and was overcome in the end after a lifetime of struggling with the Judeo-Christian tradition; that Reiner Schürmann and John D. Caputo trace out the mystical elements in Heidegger's thought; and that in a much under appreciated work, George Steiner points out Heidegger's consistently religious vocabulary and pietism as the seventeenth-century source of the phrase "thinking as thanking." Some of these scholars follow the issue back to the early Heidegger and *Being and Time* or before; but now they do so with a sense of the whole Heidegger, that is, of Heidegger as one who moved from an early position oriented toward the human and metaphysical to a later position which, while still belonging to a unified or single thinking, clearly passed over to a different set of concerns, or really, to concerns which only gradually emerged for him and his readers.

This involves a change in assumptions. What earlier had been ignored, or noted but forgotten, is precisely what counts. The task becomes one of seeing how Heidegger became an originary thinker over his entire development by critically tracing out his influences and adaptations. His sources and the way they are found in his work are understood in the light of his lifelong engagement with religion and theology. In this mature scholarship the issue concerns the parallels between the two. Heidegger's use of religious themes, language, and so on is seen as informing his understanding of Being and its relation to man. Secularization is seen as a movement attempting a whole vision, or mythology, where Being (or ultimately, That which gives) and the human are parallel to God and his human creatures.

Our raising and questioning the parallels between Heidegger and medieval biblical hermeneutics moves within—or begins with —this second phase of inquiry. This body of recent scholarhip points out that what I have argued just now is not an isolated event. That is, it is supported or corroborated by other scholars in that its results are at least congruent with studies undertaken with otherwise quite other concerns, approaches, and results. This hermeneutical dimension of *What Is Called Thinking?* may be peculiar to that book, or at least it may not so far have been found in other works, but that is unlikely; it is not so peculiar. In addition, that Judeo-Christian thinking and saying remained a lifelong interest and source for Heidegger underscores the importance of fully exploring and understanding the matter. Recall that Heidegger does not suppose that traditional historical scholarhip should cease; rather, he wants to show that, however necessary it is, it is not the only way of thinking—it is not yet recollective or remembering. Thus, what we began to consider in tracing out parallels becomes a deeper questioning.

Such questioning can be deeper because, beyond the scholarly study of the influence and interaction of Heidegger and religion, we still need to learn to ask about Heidegger's originary thinking. And, as he teaches so exhaustively in *What Is Called Thinking?*, originary thinking never is a matter of mere historical influence to be traced by historical or philological science, because the latter, no matter how precise, remain representational. How, then, do these parallels question and aid in passing to an originary manner of thinking? They bring before us the question of the relation between Heidegger and religion, its experience, scripture ("Saying"), and understanding-interpretation. The task becomes asking how religious thought and language enter or pass over into originary thinking for Heidegger. In doing so, how do they remain apart? Are they the same—how do they belong together? The question of secularization, then, takes on another meaning: does such an originary saying retrieve and say the same as religious language? How or how not?

While not all scholars who work in the second phase of investigating Heidegger's relation to religion move over from traditional scholarship to an at least attempted originary questioning, some, like Professor Caputo, do. For example, he considers the relationship of Eckhart's mysticism and Heidegger's memorializing thinking in order to see what retrieving use Heidegger makes of mysticism and to look more fully at both Heidegger and religion. Without attempting to recapitulate his work here, we can note that he answers the question of relation by showing that Heidegger uses mysticism as a model for originary thinking. Specifically he argues that when Heidegger sought a more adequate way to think and say what was needed concerning Being and thinking, he found he could proceed by working out an analogy: what Eckhart said concerning God and the soul was analogous to an originary thinking of Being and thinking:

$$\frac{God}{soul} :: \frac{Being}{thinking.^{27}}$$

This, in turn, raises or involves other major questions. Is Heidegger, in another way than we considered earlier, humanizing or personifying Being? What tone or chill comes when a religious vocabulary is used without the "guarantee" and consolation of a loving-divine source? The point here is that the important questions concerning the parallels between *What Is Called Thinking?* and medieval biblical hermeneutics move us to the same place as do

Caputo's questions arising from the parallels of mysticism and Heidegger's thinking. However, rather than take up the question of how religion in general comes into play for originary thinking, for which we have no preparation here, we need to ask, Why and how do the medieval hermeneutic and scripture come into play for originary thinking in *What Is Called Thinking?*

I would like to show that the reason Heidegger develops a secular scripture and persists with an easily misunderstood relation— a belonging-together with religion—is that it enables him to retrieve, or attempt to retrieve, a way of saying whereby the necessary vision of That which calls for thinking would come. That is what *secular* means here: to originarily retrieve a way of thinking and saying. In short, we find a realistic practical manner of going about his task. He needs a source which is rich enough and appropriately able to say what needs to be brought to language. Specifically, why does Heidegger, after listening for twenty-four years to comments and criticism from scholars comparing his work to Christianity, often in narrow and mistaken ways, and after commenting on this misunderstanding no end himself (for example, throughout "A Dialogue on Language"), nonetheless persist in thinking through Christian ways of interpreting and saying and why does he cast *What Is Called Thinking?* in a way which echoes this source?

There are four major reasons why, given the nature of the subject matter of thinking and saying, he would find it very useful to adapt a version of hermeneutical interpretation. First of all, it provides a way of reading and interpreting multiple meaning in a full way, more adequate to its subject matter than the contemporary alternatives. Specifically, hermeneutics includes, even insists on, the historical level first, which is critical to Heidegger's understanding of What comes and gives in time; in addition, it holds that historical sense within an ultimate context and spells out the implications for what should be taken to heart and how we should act. That is, the historical drama, the taken to heart, and how we act, all "flow" from the eschatological—from That which gives and comes. This same method has long been applied to Greek texts, too. Thus, the hermeneutical approach allows a fuller, more complex disclosure of the saying of both traditions which Heidegger originarily enters.

Second, hermeneutics is an instance and model for the integration of the many into the one. It is itself, like the *Logos*, an exemplar for the *gathering* which proves to be a key originary thought in Heidegger. It gathers, in a dynamic way, what belongs together: meanings and subject matter, interpreter, et cetera. Further, it does so in a way which is incarnational rather than hierarchical, and thus is congruent with the project of an originary immanence rather than metaphysical transcendence. And this incarnational model includes both the historical (the past which is still coming) and the eschatological (the future, ever coming).

Third, hermeneutics is a wonderful gift for the teacher. Hermeneutics explicitly works on behalf of the pupil in lessons, for congregations in sermons, and for the prayerful in meditation. That is, it is designed and meant for learning and meditation—the uses the teacher needs. Here he finds a language for and a way of interpreting and presenting which is simple and yet profound, rich and also aimed at being taken to heart. In short, it is heuristic, a proven way for learning.

Fourth, the assumption of hermeneutics about language is just what Heidegger finds compelling: reading and interpreting finally do not focus merely on a subject's text, because language is nothing merely human. As we have seen, the medieval assumption is that while men can make words mean, hermeneutics allows interpretation of more than text; it opens to subject matter, and through the text which things are, to That which sends meaning, that is, to That which says and calls for thinking. (Of course, this does not diminish the problem that Heidegger's saying is no divine work or word; but, it does show why hermeneutics would be a model for thinking and saying.)

Note that throughout the development of his thought, Heidegger persists in keeping the historical. Despite misunderstandings and the dangers of historicism, as we have seen in the detailed treatment of "A Dialogue on Language" and *What is Called Thinking?*, he originarily thinks though history; further, time remains a major concern in his work from *Being and Time* through "Time and

Being." This is because originary thinking thinks the epochal unfolding of That which calls for thinking, for example, as the history of metaphysics and as the still coming Origin. As Professor Caputo notes (though making a different point):

> Secular means having to do with the *saeculum*, the ages, the times. But the 'times' are to be understood, for Heidegger, in terms of the mission (*Geschick*) of Being, and the mission of Being in terms of the event of Appropriation (*Ereignis*). The secular character of Heidegger's thought consists in his unwavering concern with the history of the West, with its "epochal transformations," with the "future" of the West which is, for him, bound up with and hidden in its first beginnings in the Greeks.[28]

To oversimplify, this concern with the historical destiny of the West is quite unGreek (which also means quite unlike Christian theology as determined by the Greek), but, it is very Judeo-Christian. This does seem to be the case if we focus on the two experiences of time. As Mircea Eliade, the distinguished historian of religion and interpreter of the sacred, shows, traditional sacred time is reversible; here, primal mythical time again becomes present. Hence, it appears to be circular in that rites and rituals can bring it back or recover it now, and hence, we can have a regeneration, achieved through a return to the time of origins. This also is the realm of mystical experience of the eternal. Eliade points out that in contrast, Judaism leaves cyclical time behind. The Old Testament tells the experience of God not in terms of cosmic time, but in terms of historical time. That is, the Hebrews experienced the meaning of history as an epiphany of God. In Christianity, time becomes linear: it is understood as having meaning as a line from Creation and Fall, through the Redemption, to a final redemption.[29] Actually, the matter is more complex. It needs to be noted that while the Judeo-Christian experience involved a different experience of history than the Greek, Christianity continued to struggle with both experiences of time—the experience of the "eternal" or cyclical and that of the historical. As Eliade points out, linear and cyclical views of time and history both remain in conflict well into the seventeenth century (the era of Descartes). For example, in Joachim of Floris we find the history of the world divided into three great epochs and an "immanentization" of the cyclical theory.[30]

Now, Heidegger, too, has aspects of each theory. On the one hand, as noted, he sees an unfolding of the destiny of the West— the history of the Giving—concealed in time. Yet, he also attempts to think originarily the still coming origin and attempts to return to the originary. The abiding origin is neither reduced to nor beyond time. This would further explain, in part, why Heidegger utilizes the hermeneutical tradition and a Christian scripture. He needs and wants to keep historical time as the epiphany of That which gives. Unlike the Platonically or neo-Platonically understood eternal, That which calls and comes is immanent. It is analogous to the Incarnation. In addition, Heidegger needs and wants to think what the origin of time is. That is, far from any reductive historicism, Heidegger does not want to stop with history and time, but to think the origin—That which itself gives—and this also means "gives time". In "On Time and Being," written late in his life, Heidegger holds that it is not time which gives, but the event of appropriation itself (*Ereignis*): the ultimate source of history, which is not thereby eternal or ahistorical, but prior and most originarily within history, and still coming.[31] That is, Origin, coming in the future, is thought eschatologically. So, as historically immanent (incarnate) and as source of history and coming in the future (eschatological) That which calls for thinking needs to be thought, at least partially, hermeneutically.

If we pursue the issue of how Heidegger learns originary saying it may be that he is not so much interested in any secular scripture, that is, in any secularization for its own sake, as in finding the needed way of thinking and saying. Simply, it may be that the way he proceeds and the models he uses, are unavoidable for what needs saying. Clearly he seeks, and needs, a *dynamic* language. He finds it in Christianity. But that is not the only place he finds it, nor are scripture and hermeneutics his only models. A brief look at this will shed more light on why his originary language appears voluntaristic.

The God of Christianity is, of course, understood to be a personal, active God. Thus, in speaking of His action in history, the Bible uses a very active, personal language. But what is important for Heidegger's use may not primarily be the subject of Christianity (God-Christ), but the dynamic language which says the unfolding of religious events. The obvious analogy of Being and God may mislead us. That is, if we begin by thinking of Heidegger's secular scripture as a way of substituting Being for God, we assume the orthodox interpretation of Heidegger as at the end of a line of metaphysicians, where metaphysics is playing out and down. But the later Heidegger seems interested in Christianity just where it does not appear to be metaphysical, in its primal writings and in Eckhart, for example. That is, in order to think originarily and to avoid casting all in terms of beings and Being, Heidegger seeks in Christianity the model for nonrepresentational saying. Now, Christianity did not avoid representational thinking for two thousand years and Eckhart, too, often spoke the language of traditional metaphysics; but, is all Christian saying metaphysical? Certainly, Eckhart does step out of metaphysics on occasion as Professor Caputo argues.[32] In its nonrepresentational language, Christianity speaks of the dynamic of history in a way which emphasizes the drama of God and the person or soul, to be sure, but not by way of self as subject or object. This dramatic dynamic between God and soul is like the dynamic between That which calls for thinking and mortals. Heidegger, however, attempts to think that dynamic itself in his adaptation of language. For example, he takes over Eckhart's *Gelassenheit* to speak of the releasement necessary for thinking. But this releasement is precisely the giving up of self and voluntarism (a problem which Heidegger is explicitly concerned with and critical of); this requires giving up any representationally understood subject.[33] As Caputo notes, it is pre-personalistic. For another example, Heidegger speaks of graciousness originarily and is careful to show in "A Dialogue on Language," how that should not be taken in terms of willful action (in either an aesthetic or religious version of the metaphysical). And, he uses *Ereignis* to say What gives being and Being, the dynamic giving or endowment itself.

This also may be adapted from Christianity's saying of the advent of Grace; even so, as professor Zimmerman contends, such saying (a) aims at overcoming any terms tinged with a personalistic conception of God in favor of an ontological-historical language, (b) bespeaks the advent itself, and (c) avoids describing *Ereignis* as an agent.[34] Note, too, that Eckhart's idea of the Godhead (*Gottheit*, which is closer to *Ereignis* than to "God") is, as Zimmerman observes, "the abyss which lies beyond the personal God of creation" and is without personal characteristics (this divine abyss is "nameless and will-less").[35]

This is difficult and dangerous. If Heidegger is looking for a dynamic language which can say an ultimate vision, he naturally would look to Christianity, but, he also is open to the same difficulties that Eckhart, for example, encounters in speaking of God's need (*brauchen*: to need or use). The verb, even if originarily understood, does not speak of a happening without raising a whole tradition of misunderstanding.[36] As we have seen in analyzing *What Is Called Thinking?* "need" means "let into" and "preserve in essence" (187), which is not at all voluntaristic, though it is a helping. Furthermore, that it is the dynamic language of Christianity, especially its verbs of the unfolding of the sacred in history, which Heidegger attempts to retrive, is supported by a comparison with another of his originary sources—early Greek thinking.

At first, it might seem that this would emphasize, if not a secular bent in Heidegger then a pagan one.[37] But finally, it is not Zeus who interests Heidegger, but the *Logos*, which is more ultimate than the gods themselves. Although it then might appear that, just as Heidegger might translate God into Being, he simply takes *Logos* in the same way, as the noun of all nouns, this can be dispelled with a look at what Heidegger makes of the Greeks, that is, of his originary use of what is said there. That his interest is in a vocabulary of action (but not of personification, neither by abstracting from the gods nor by personifying concepts) is clear. Many of the originary verbs which appear in *What Is Called Thinking?* are heard here; in "*Moira*," for example, he uses "involves," "grants," "take heed of," "call for," "use," "govern," "resigns," "liberates," "required by," "respond to," "bestows," "alloting," "dispensing," "needs," "maintains," "supports," "let belong," and "unfolding."[38]

When Heidegger takes up what Parmenides says about *Moira*, he is taking up something which underlies *What Is Called Thinking?* The lecture was meant to be part of *What Is Called Thinking?*, but was not delivered. Perhaps it was not delivered because *What Is Called Thinking?* had not yet gotten to its subject matter. This could be so because *What Is Called Thinking?* does not get beyond the presence of what is present, which still thinks by way of the Being of beings, though it hints at something more ultimate. *Moira* asks after precisely that. Heidegger explains that what is said concerning *Moira*—and this is critical—"reveals to the thinker the breadth of vision fatefully reserved for the path he treads" (*EGT*, 98). And what is the vision which failed when *What Is Called Thinking?* could not see beyond Being and being—the vision Heidegger alluded to at its end? *Moira*, apportionment. Heidegger tells us that *Moira* says the destining of disclosing of the duality, it has dispensed the destiny of Being; and it appears more primal than the twofold, for apportionment "allots by bestowing and so unfolds the twofold" (*EGT*, 97). Note, the deep thought here is not of another being. *Moira* is not something else besides beings and Being: rather, *Moira* names the way and coming: the bestowing apportionment or the dispensing destining.

Heraclitus speaks this same way. He speaks in a way which appears to name being or Being, but Heidegger shows how what appears as noun speaks as verb. *Logos*, according to Heidegger, is the laying; it is *aletheia*, the unconcealing (*EGT*, 66 and 71). Thus, *Logos* is lightning, not a physical phenomena or process, but a flashing disclosure. Laying and lightning belong together because *Logos* is the collecting laying down of itself and other things (*EGT*, 93). That is, *Logos* as gathering, belongs with fire (*pur*), sun (*Helios*), lightning (*keraunos*), and the eternal living fire (*kosmos*).[39] Here too we hear of *Logos* as the truly fateful governance, of lighting governance and the "purely apportioning event" (*das reine Ereignis*) (*EGT*, 72 and 123). Later, in a seminar on Heraclitus, Heidegger considers how fire is apportioned, and how jurisdiction belongs to *dike*.[40] This raises two issues. If Heidegger uses the model of Judeo-Christian scripture and hermeneutics because of its dynamic language which says the historical and eschatological unfolding of a sacred drama, he seems to use early Greek thinking as part of the same play: in Parmenides and Heraclitus he finds a dynamic, highly verbal language which also brings to the fore apportionment and governance (*Moira*, lightning, *Ereignis*).

It is of the greatest importance to see that Heidegger himself understands the Greek sayings which he closely attends here as the way to an originary saying. As he says repeatedly in the Heraclitus seminar, primal Greek saying is "not yet metaphysical" and speaks, or would be retrieved in a "no longer metaphysical" thinking. The dynamic language would be a way to such thinking. Then, too, the use of—or need for—thinking back behind Being and being to the more ultimate dispensing destiny is explicitly said to be nonrepresentational and nonvoluntaristic (as was the case with *Gelassenheit*). For example, his explication of Heraclitus' thought of "steering," is understood originarily not as a process (compare this with what Heidegger says of thinking), but as a noncoercive steering by the gods.[41]

Other questions follow from seeing that Heidegger may have been seeking the same in, or back behind the saying of both Christianity and early Greece. In looking to these two sources in order to find what is needed to originarily think what is held in ultimate vision, Heidegger seems to pass beyond a representational speaking concerning voluntarism to an originary saying of the fateful, of destiny. But is this not ultimately metaphysical? Does it not repeat Augustine's path, out of the Greek and Christian traditions? Has Heidegger found a language in his two models which helps at all or does it leave him stuck in the language of will and subject, that is, in metaphysical language?

The question of the fateful in Heidegger's thought, even if it does finally overcome the metaphysical tradition, which it does not do in his early works, deepens in regard to his later works when they are seen as an originary recovering-thinking of what is found in primal Christianity and early Greek thinking. That is, the question of the fateful raises the question of a link between the

Greek and Judeo-Christian and their belonging with Heidegger's way. The fateful keeps Being, being, and human being, without taking any of them as its starting point: the fateful (*das Geschick*) "lies behind the happening (*Geschehen*) which makes history (*Geschichte*)"; that is, the fateful has the originary sense of setting in readiness and order, of disposing in light of belonging.[42] That is why the fateful is thought with *Logos*, the laying out and letting lie before us, that is, "the assembly of that which sends everything into its own" (*EGT*, 72).

Though it is a question which first begins to open here, it should be noted that Heidegger himself held that such fatefulness, thought spoken of by way of "seemingly willful language," was no fatalistic concept nor was it, originarily thought, voluntaristic (*EGT*, 72). Of course, that remains to be seen, especially since in *What Is Called Thinking?* Heidegger was not yet free of metaphysics. In any case, the fateful—a matter of sending and that which is sent—belongs close by the subject matter of *What is Called Thinking?*: that which is called and calls for thinking.

We need to be cautious, however. Though it is necessary to explore Heidegger's originary secular language, here we can do no more than raise issues as possibilities or hypotheses, in the sense of something thrust forward as a possible support. One way to try to think about Heidegger's use of the Greek and Christian and their relationship could proceed by persisting in our focus on his deliberate keeping of the fateful, historical, and religious, despite the enormous difficulties and misunderstandings that result. Why does he persist when it would be so much easier to discard what his critics find troubling, to say the least? This returns us to the issue of the sense in which his writing is secular.

Suppose that his work is secular, where that indicates "different from the religious." That would mean that he can not speak out of a religious experience, that is, point to God as That which says and calls for thinking. A student once asked him, in a letter, whence his thinking about Being received its directive.[43] We too, after listening to the tone of his voice and the substance of what he says, and after reflecting on the parallels between his language and thought and the Bible's, might ask on what authority he speaks as he does. Of course, we would not expect the answer would be "on God's authority"; rather we expect it might be "on that of That which calls for thinking." For Heidegger at least appears to speak with authority, an authority that disappeared from the Greek tradition with Heraclitus and Parmenides. When Heidegger does answer the student and us, however, he tells us that this question is not the right one. No one, he points out, asks on what authority Plato spoke as he did; so, too, the question is not appropriate of any thinker. No person provides anything like his own credentials or justification, nor can he or she claim to have any; yet, this does not make thinking arbitrary. Rather, it is a matter of genuine and proper response to That which calls for thinking; it is a matter of learning the craft of thinking. That is, the question we need to ask of one who sounds like a secular prophet is, What is called thinking?

Thus, even while Heidegger's language and thinking tred a path parallel to religion's, the differences between originary thinking and saying and religious activity do not disappear—indeed, they are vivified. And as a result, we are led back to Heidegger's question, What is called thinking? That is, as a result of these correspondences, his thought should be more problematic for us than ever. How strange that he should think and speak this way. How can we learn to let these features of this thought and language lie before us so that we can take them to heart? Can we follow their hint in order to come close to what they point to?

Here he would need to go back through religious saying to that which governs the gods themselves to discover That which calls for originary thinking. His need to recover the most primal would then account for his need for the early Greek. But because he thinks that the coming of the originary necessarily involves an unfolding of and in history, the Greek is not enough. This accounts for his need for and appropriating use of the Judeo-Christian and the hermeneutical interpretations which keep the literal-historical meaning and also the cosmic vision. And in the thought of the Greek fateful-dispensing destiny and Christian eschatology, he finds a common joint, which for all the vast differences, points to . . . to what?

The answer may lie in another distinction which we can think by using the work of Mircea Eliade. We often suppose that to call Heidegger's thought secular is to separate it from the sacred. But as noted, the secular is differentiated from the religious; the sacred is differentiated from the profane. The profane is just what Heidegger seeks to overcome. The profane, as Eliade shows us in his phenomenology of religion, largely is understandable negatively, as the absence of sacred power, as the desacralized cosmos. It is where existence is understood, for example, metaphysically in terms of subject and will; it is where we have the homogeneous, neutral and relative, or indefinite, merely natural space and time, and non-multiple, non-exemplary meaning and one-track thinking.[44]

What then, of Heidegger's attempt to say the sacred? The sacred is the ever-coming, exemplary source that powerfully informs the world with multiple, homologous meaning. The sacred is the originary: it is that which sends and comes in time. As experienced by Judeo-Christianity, its epiphany happens in history; here we have the event of the immanent—the manifestation of the mystery of immanence.[45] To say such a source, Heidegger would need a way to achieve regeneration to the time of origins, where for historical, no longer cosmic time, this means "to what still comes now, in the future." Thus, the history of Being would be the covering up of the epiphany of the sacred which needs to be overcome by a thinking that can retrieve the multiple meanings, the homology of thinking and saying, and both with That which exemplarily calls for thinking and saying.

So, whereas the *secular saying* of the *profane* is nothing other than the metaphysical saying of Being, for example, as Will, and where the realm of the *religious saying* of the *sacred* belongs to prophet and priest, the *secular saying* of the *sacred* belongs to poet and thinker. Hence, for all his use of philosophy and religion, Heidegger finally remains closest to the poet, who also works the same fields. In short, to find a way of saying, Heidegger seeks a secular version of the originarily religious; that secular saying, however, seeks to say the genuine originary gathering realm—the sacred. So, what calls for thinking and the manner of saying belong together; the sacred and the secular might name what Heidegger tries to learn to gather in both language and thinking: the secular saying of the sacred. Of course, this may only appear to be so. That means it needs to be questioned.

In terms of the historical unfolding of Being, it might be that the medieval, Christian metaphysical theology reduced God to Being and in doing so kept (at least an aspect of) the sacred as subject-matter, but lost religious saying and thinking. The modern epoch further reduced Being from any sacred reals to the merely profane. (Is it possible that the sacred may not be able to be kept without religious saying, save in an echo, by poets?) Thus, the recovery of the sacred would require a retrieval of the primal Judeo-Christian and early Greek. Heidegger's honest attempt, starting where we are, could not pretend to a religious language, but could seek to be an originary secular saying. Whether such a truly secular language would be possible is what Heidegger seeks to learn and teach. *How could any language say such an ultimate Source?* What would such a language be like?

Again and again, then, we are brought back to the need for and character of dynamic language (as found, for example, in the Greek saying of *Moira* and lightning that attempts to move and stay in a dynamic language, "prior" to any reifying transfer to noun and being.) Though such language is dynamic, it need not be understood as personalistic or voluntaristic. Heraclitus, for example, speaks of *Logos*, but means nothing personal thereby. He also speaks of time in seemingly anthropomorphic terms: "Time (*aion*) is a child playing a game of draughts. The Kingship is in the hands of a child."[46] But, far from projecting anthropomorphic language onto time, this precisely forces us to try to think of time and the fateful in their originary, not yet representational, and thereby non-subjectivistic, character.[47] The play is that which is without reason, representationally understood; it is the mysterious play of language itself, toward which we are called to originarily release ourselves (118–119 and compare the mirror play of the fourfold).[48]

That Heidegger is sensitive to the misreading of such dynamic language is seen in his concern with the Christian understanding and use of the early Greek. That is, because of the Christian tendency to interpret, for example, Heraclitus, by way of God and

creation, Heidegger calls into question specific Christian translations. Challenging Clement of Alexandria's interpretation of lightning in terms of an omniscient supra-sensible God and questioning
the impact of fragment 64 ("Lightning steers the universe")
handed down by the Church Father Hippolytus, he moves beyond
issues of historical-philological determinations of correctness in
order to non-representationally hear what is said.[49] What matters is
what speaks originarily in the Greek, which Heidegger as well as
the Church Fathers sought; or, better, it is what Heidegger (going
back through the Christian and Greek) and what the Christian and
Greek themselves, each in their own way, attempted to think and
say. Thus, in drawing upon the Greek, just as in adapting the
Christian, Heidegger is seeking a nonsubjective, nonwillful way of
exploring the primal unfolding.[50]

In addition, insofar as biblical hermeneutics falls within the
realm of theology, not religion, then it is part of the onto-theo-
logical way of thinking. If this is so, biblical hermeneutics too is
part of the story of thinking and is to be recalled and recovered in
an originary manner; it too belongs to and should be gathered into
originary thinking—which is a sphere separate from faith. Another
possibility is that biblical hermeneutics may be religious, not theological, and then might be "prior" to the onto-theo-logical, just as
early Greek thinking is; on this model, religion and religious
hermeneutics would need to be recovered just as is the case with
primal Greek thought—which was not conceptual-philosophical.
In fact, if this is how it is, early Greek thinking and primal
Christianity both are originary, and must be held in thought by the
thinking that recalls origin. That originary thinking would need to
recover the ways of both Greek thinking and Christian religion.

Whatever our final understanding and critique of Heidegger
amounts to, this much seems clear: according to Heidegger's own
thinking, the Greek, the primal Christian, and his own attempted
originary thinking all belong together because they attempt to say
the same. That is, in order to say the most primordial, the same
way needs to be taken by all these vastly different modes of saying.
Thus, for Heidegger to find a no-longer-metaphysical way to say
what is needed, he needs to make use of the not-yet-metaphysical

saying of Judeo-Christianity and the early Greek. Not surprisingly, poetry, the third major mode of nonrepresentational thinking for Heidegger, also struggled with these same sources, which remained coming as origin in Hölderlin, for example. That is, when Heidegger turned to Hölderlin in the 1930s to find a language which he did not have but needed, Heidegger heard what he needed in Hölderlin, words like "hint" (*der Wink*), "stillness and silence" (*das Schweigen*), *Ereignis*, near-far (*Nahe, Ferne*) and so on[51]—he therein also encountered the Greek and the religious. Since Heidegger was a thinker, not a poet, he could not simply adopt Hölderlin; instead, Hölderlin was a no longer metaphysical model insofar as he pointed to and said two other not-yet-metaphysical models: the Greek and simple religion.[52]

As a result of these insights, we can conclude that understanding Heidegger's attempt to use these sources originarily does not require assuming that he is using a degenerating language, or that he somehow must be sneaking a secular version of God and creation in under the covert name of Being or the presence of what is present. Some of *What Is Called Thinking?* is metaphysical; yet, some is not. (We have seen, for instance, that the originary is not.) Thus, we need to shift our focus; we need to remember how difficult it is for anyone to speak in a nonrepresentational way. To move beyond the language of Being and being is enormously difficult, so difficult that the overall failure of *What Is Called Thinking?* is not so important as the way Heidegger successfully moves. How could any language say the most originary which calls for thinking?

As noted in our detailed explication of *What Is Called Thinking?* in order to avoid thinking representationally (by way of subject), or in what stems from the subject (such as psychological processes), Heidegger deemphasizes nouns. Instead, he moves among verbal forms—for example, "say," "think," "lays," "takes to heart," "need," "use," and "call." Of course, normally, verbs imply a subject. The struggle then is to use verbs without letting them imply that the subject is being or Being, which would return us to metaphysics. That is, we need to learn to think of verbs without a subject. The need to insist on this accounts for Heidegger's odd habit of using the same word twice, which looks like a noun and a verb, and to insist that the subject is not a noun understood as a being or Being or in a personal sense: "Appropriation appropriates the mutually belonging" (*Ereignis ereignet*), "language says" (*Sagen sagt*), "World worlds" (*Welt Weltet*), "thing things" (*Ding dingt*).[53] Here we need to learn to let the dynamic stand. The dynamic is what is safeguarded and learned from the Greek and Christian: "*Logos* lays down . . ." ("*Logos legein*") and "In the beginning was the Word . . ."[54] The goal is to let language say actively, in a way which is both simple and profound, in order to touch the heart, that it might take up and safeguard what is said. Naturally, this is a difficult task and a demanding way to speak and write.

Another way Heidegger insists on the nonreification of what needs saying is at once more acceptably ordinary and more open to confusion. He uses an impersonal form of verbs. He attempts to say the dynamic impersonal as we would in "It is raining; it rains." Thus, he says, "It gives" (*Es gibt*, which as, Steiner observes, sounds close to American slang, "What gives with you"),[55] "That which calls for thinking," and "It is needful." This means that we cannot attempt to quickly ask what is the It, That, and so on, if we expect to find a final "gathering," or "belonging-together," "Saying," *Ereignis*, and so on.

The attempt to learn this is so hard that it not surprisingly fails; but, as we have seen in our detailed explication, it surprisingly succeeds when Heidegger fuses what he says and its manner in an originary way, for example, as happens with "Saying" in "A Dialogue on Language," with "needful" in *What Is Called Thinking?*, and with *Ereignis*. In sum, when Heidegger does succeed and where he holds his ground with an originary "It" and "That," it need not be the case that there is an any voluntaristic or personalistic subject smuggled in. Any secularization of primal religious saying and the not yet metaphysical is a use of a dynamic language precisely in order to talk at all. Heidegger finds that here he has what is needed to attempt (to learn) originary thinking. It may well be that such sources point out what would be the only nonmetaphysical way of language. That is, to retrieve an originary language to say an ultimate vision is to retrieve and keep dynamic language; but, dynamic language need not be metaphysical and representational.

The real questions are why is this so, how is it so, and what does it mean?

Granted that *What Is Called Thinking?* remains concerned with metaphysics, what we learn is that the *project* is to get back to the originary. Thus, our critique of Heidegger's work involves the honest assessment that he finally fails in *What Is Called Thinking?*, though he breaks through there in a way which he holds and improves in *Discourse on Thinking* and sustains best in "A Dialogue on Language." But this critique also involves seeing what and how he really is attempting. True, we can see that he searches for a nonvoluntaristic manner of saying. But that is not the main point. In seeking to find his own originary manner of thinking, he proceeds by attempting to retrieve through the Christian and Greek. This means he stays in the Western tradition. Note, this is quite another matter than staying with metaphysics; here, by keeping Western dynamic language and a concern with the historical, and perhaps, eschatological (the Christian does add a dynamic non-Greek understanding of time and history), Heidegger attempts, within our tradition, to release himself from metaphysics. To originarily think and say means to move back and retrieve from out of our tradition, to find the origin of the tradition which still comes in the future of our tradition. Originary thinking, too, is part of the unfolding of Western thinking.

In originary thinking the task is to hear the dynamic saying in a nonmetaphysical, nonwillful way. Back then, to our original project: to question what calls for thinking. We have to remain with Heidegger to think the history of Western representational thinking, the early Greek, the Judeo-Christian, the poetic, and, of course, Heidegger's own thinking and saying. That is, our patient reading of *What Is Called Thinking?*, which has tried to hear Heidegger, and our later criticism and questioning of his failure and obscured vision, both point to the tasks which still remain. Clearly, Heidegger still has a task, since he has not finally succeeded in *What Is Called Thinking?* And for us, as learners, specific homework remains if we would persist in trying to learn thinking.

The task for Heidegger is to pursue what comes forth partially in the originary thinking of *What Is Called Thinking?* That is, he must continue to originarily think the early Greek and the primal Judeo-Christian. By hearing what is said there, he could come to say his own. In addition, he has to listen to the genuine poets, poets such as Hölderlin, who drawing from the Greek and religious sources himself, finds a nonrepresentational way of Saying. This would not mean that Heidegger would become a poet, any more than it would mean he would become Greek or a Christian mystic; rather, it means he could learn by following the teaching of all three sorts of Saying. Heidegger himself sees this and points to his task in *What Is Called Thinking?* by taking up Parmenides, the religious language and manner of hermeneutics, and the poet Hölderlin. Heidegger is clear on where he must go in still learning thinking and saying.

As for our homework. Even after an entire book about Heidegger and about how to learn to read and think, we are still not through. All the talk about the difficulty of learning to think, the patience involved, and of our still not thinking was no mere ritual or set of platitudes. It stands. If we are still underway to learn to think, what Heidegger says and does in *What Is Called Thinking?* and our questioning criticism begin to bring before us four major questions, which we now are in a position to ask and to see as needing more sustained work to answer. That is the homework that follows *What Is Called Thinking?* In German, homework is *die Hausaufgabe*, "what is given for home." That is what *What Is Called Thinking?* gives in order to help us to learn to think.

The first major question which needs to be thought through fully is how originary thinking stands in regard to the Greeks, Judeo-Christianity, and the poets. This means more than scholarly tracing out of the relationships and influences among them, though that also needs to be done, for example, in regard to mysticism and pietism. More importantly, it requires an originary understanding of those three sources and Heidegger's thinking. What would "secular" mean in the end, if originarily thought? Is Heidegger's thought secular?[56] Can the originary be secular? (Reflection on what Eliade says about the sacred, secular, and *mythos* might help here.) What would the Greek and Christianity say, if originarily understood?

This raises a second, closely related, question. Does Heidegger succeed or fail to think originarily? Does a genuine Saying come from his work, or merely a bankrupt echo of a degenerating tradition which he swings into place while protesting that all is a misunderstanding? While I do not believe the latter is the case, given the freshness, power, and depth I find in his work, the question must be asked over and over by each of us if we are to do our part in questioning. (As we have seen, even if Martin Heidegger fails to sustain an originary thinking in the end, what he gives us is not merely the experience of another secular, philosophical-anthropological view; his originary moments do move, at least in places, beyond that.) Thinking through whether he was on the way of originary thought necessarily moves us beyond *What Is Called Thinking?*, "A Dialogue on Language," and *Discourse on Thinking* to his other works, to his whole corpus. A large project of exploration through that body of work is called for in order to measure the achievement of originary thinking.

Third, if Heidegger does succeed in an originary saying, even if somewhere other than in *What Is Called Thinking?*, "A Dialogue on Language," and *Discourse on Thinking*, what ultimate vision is let lie before us to be taken to heart? What is *That* which calls for thinking? Even in *What Is Called Thinking?*, Heidegger hints that beyond the duality we might hear It, the subject of the dynamic Saying we are trying to think—That which gives and calls for thinking. What would be said here? If what is named by "It" or "That which . . ." comes in history and remains in the future, how is it to be thought in a dynamic, but not metaphysical way? Can the secular, not-yet or no-longer eschatological "fateful" be thought originarily?

Fourth, can we ever learn to think originarily ourselves? That is, can we think Heidegger, the Greeks, and the others originarily ourselves? This is an enormously difficult task. First we need to listen and learn, that is, not rush. But, it is the final task, the real goal of our learning.[57]

Of course, the homework begins after we have finished reading this book and are, hopefully, still learning from Heidegger. Thus, while much remains for all of us, this book need not—cannot—do it all. Recall that the project was to show that Heidegger makes sense, that they way he makes sense is through the fusion of what he says and the manner in which he says it, and that Heidegger himself teaches us how to read his works.

That traditional scholarship is called for is not in question; [58] we also must learn to think originarily, to recover and take to heart what has been said and thought. The real lesson, however, is that before we engage in critical analytic scholarship or attempt originary thinking on our own, we still need to learn how to think. Thus, this book tries to stay true to what Heidegger teaches us: that we must first practice and learn to read in the way indicated, or some way close to it, in order to hear what thinkers say, and above all, to hear what Heidegger says, before we attempt to do other things with the text.

Simply put, we are not yet as able as Heidegger. In his example of teaching carpentry, he speaks of master and apprentice. Here, as learning readers, we are the apprentices; Heidegger is the master craftsman. This reading is the place to follow, not to assert ourselves. What is required of us in the end, an originary struggle with Heidegger himself, is not yet appropriate here. It would be unseemly, as Walter Biemel says, to pretend we are able, from the outside, to reproach Heidegger for his shortcomings or, supposedly from the inside, to speak for him as if we already know what he means: "This kind of speaking about Heidegger contains a precipitance that contradicts the style of his thought."[59] For now, we have a more modest task—to stand close by and see what is involved in learning thinking. We begin by trying to see whether Heidegger makes sense and, if so, how he does.

This is no false modesty: truly, "we still are not thinking." Recall, that "in no way" means we do not think at all. Having made it this far we all deserve a gold star or two. The deep meaning is that though we are still not thinking fully, we are learning thinking. That is what the gold stars really would be for.

Perhaps, if the way of reading and understanding presented here makes sense, or shows how Heidegger makes sense, we might have learned a genuine lesson concerning thinking: we may have found a patient calm which does not attempt to dispose of Heidegger and his texts too soon. The span of our lesson is none too long to let Heidegger lie before us. As Heidegger says of Nietzsche (and recall that Heidegger suggests ten to fifteen years on Aristotle, before we even take up Nietzsche): first find him, then lose him. We need to lose Heidegger in the end to think on our own; but first we must find him. An early epigram concerning Heraclitus applies to what we attempt of Heidegger: "Do not be in too great a hurry to get to the end of [his] book; the path is hard to travel. Gloom is there and darkness devoid of light. But if an initiate be your guide, the path shines brighter than sunlight."[60] If I have been right, Heidegger himself has become our guide in what he says and does concerning language and thinking. If we take to heart what he says and keep it before us instead of quickly disposing of it, we will have learned what is taught: to let the teacher teach and ourselves learn. Here, that is our task; it is our calling.

Notes to Preface

1. Martin Heidegger, *Nietzsche I* (Pfullingen: Verlag Günther Neske, 1961), p. 329. He also says, "All reflective thinking is poetic, and all poetry in turn is a kind of thinking." "The Way to Language" in *On the Way to Language*, trans. Peter D. Hertz (New York: Harper and Row, 1971), p. 136.
2. J.L. Mehta, *The Philosophy of Martin Heidegger* (New York: Harper and Row, 1971), pp. 66 and 79.
3. Hofstadter, translator, *Poetry, Language, Thought* (New York: Harper and Row, 1971), xvi.
4. George Steiner, *Martin Heidegger* (New York: The Viking Press, 1978), p. 9.
5. The two works referred to are David Halliburton, *Poetic Thinking: An Approach to Heidegger* (Chicago: The University of Chicago Press, 1981) and David A. White, *Heidegger and the Language of Poetry* (Lincoln, Neb.: University of Nebraska Press, 1978). Also, three essays have appeared since my writing this book, which take seriously Heidegger's style, the formal unity of his essays, and the exemplary role of his language: David Michael Levin, "The Embodiment of Thinking: Heidegger's Approach to Language" in Ronald Bruzina and Bruce Wilshire, eds., *Phenomenology: Dialogues and Bridges* (Albany, N.Y.: State University of New York Press, 1982), pp. 61–77; Graeme Nicholson, "The Coiling Pathway of Heidegger's *Essence of Truth*" in Hugh J. Silverman, John Sallis, and Thomas M. Seebohm, eds., *Continental Philosophy in America* (Pittsburgh, Pa.: Duquesne University Press, 1983), pp. 115–130; William Lovitt's welcome introduction to his translation of Martin Heidegger, *The Question Concerning Technology and Other Essays* (New York: Harper and Row, 1977), especially pp. xiv–xxiv.
6. Louis H. Mackey, "On Philosophical Form: A Tear for Adonis" *Thought*, 42 (1967): 259.

Notes to Chapter One

1. All page references to *Discourse on Thinking* in this chapter are given in parentheses in the text. All these quotations are from the translation by J.M. Anderson and E.H. Freund in the Torchbook edition (New York:

Harper and Row, 1966). Originally published as *Gelassenheit* (Pful-lingen: Verlag Günther Neske, 1959).

2. He also says "yes" by valuing the single idea in quite another way. See "The Thinker as Poet" in *Poetry, Language, Thinking*, pp. 3–4.

3. *Gelassenheit* means both a calmness and a releasement—a letting go and giving oneself up to. We might suspect then, that Heidegger is to tell us about releasement, instead of about thinking, perhaps. If so, the point holds: the topic would differ but not the assumption. Also compare p. 54 in the *Discourse* with p. 75 in *Gelassenheit*.

Notes to Chapter Two

1. All page references to "A Dialogue on Language" in this chapter are given in parentheses in the text. The quotations are from "A Dialogue on Language" in *On the Way to Language*, trans. by Peter Hertz (New York: Harper and Row, 1971). The German article appears under the title *"Aus Einem Gespräch von der Sprache"* in *Unterwegs zur Sprache*, (Pfullingen, 1959).

2. *Sein Und Zeit* (Tübingen: Max Niemeyer, 1972), p. 34ff.

3. Further, in a footnote Heidegger insists on his continued relationship with Husserl, explaining the dedication of *Being and Time* to Husserl and its later removal (see pp. 199–200).

4. For example, more needs to be known about Heidegger's relation to Japanese thought, and an identification of the Japanese inquirer in the dialogue might be made, since Heidegger notes that the present text originated from the visit of Prof. Tezuka of Imperial University in Tokyo in 1953–54 (note in English edition is on p. 199). Scholar-ship is also necessary to clarify the influence of Nietzsche on Heideg-ger and Heidegger's use of seemingly Nietzschian "ideas" as, for example, will, same, the careful weighing of words, play, gracious-ness. In this regard it is of interest to note the absence of reference to Nietzsche in the dialogue and the possible purpose for such an omission.

5. It should be noted, however, that the description of photography as objectifying is a complex matter, especially since photography me-morializes and may evoke thinking. As Heidegger notes in opening scene, which sets the tone: "I am happy to have photographs of Kuki's grave and of the grove in which it lies" (1).

6. A reader hoping to find Japanese art thought in its own terms is disappointed and frustrated in seeing European categories applied so that the Japanese experience vanishes. This happens, for example, in Makoto Ueda's *Literary and Art Theories in Japan*, (Cleveland: Case Western Reserve, 1967).

7. Cf. Heidegger on the transformation of things into standing-reserve (*Bestand*), for example, in *The Question Concerning Technology*, trans. by W. Lovitt (New York: Harper and Row, 1977), pp. 17ff.

8. For a report on "to gather" as the translation of *versammeln* see J. Glenn Gray, "Heidegger on Remembering and Remembering Heidegger," *Man and World* 10, no.1 (1977): 62–78.

9. The film itself appears to affirm the subject-object distinction and subjectivism of experience; but, actually, it helps us to understand that people experience and value things differently because these differences have their roots or bases in the ego or in the self image we have of ourselves. Thus, the film leads the viewer to the same conclusion that the dialogue arrives at later. Other interesting parallels between *Rashomon* and Heidegger's work that might be pursued are the role of the woodcutter and the opening scene of his walk on forest paths in the film and Heidegger's figure, *Holzwege*, or the multiple interpretation and versions of one event in the film and Heidegger's use of levels of dialogue and thought in the dialogue.

10. On "the same" and "the twofold" see *What Is Called Thinking?* which is the subject of the following chapter and *Identity and Difference* (New York: Harper and Row, 1974).

11. For example, language would be the flourishing-granting of the coming together of the twofold and man.

12. The three levels of the dialogue might be said to correspond to three meanings of the German word *von*. Or the levels might twine together the way they do in tandem with a play on that word, as it is taken to mean, in turn: (1) "about," (2) "concerning," and (3) "out of," or "from." Is Heidegger slyly implying, for example, that, at the third level, the dialogue is "by language" rather than "from the pen of M. Heidegger" by displacing the normal author's credit "*von* Martin Heidegger" with the "credit" which the title holds "*Aus Einem Gespräch*"—*von der Sprache*?

13. This is similar to Plato's dialogues, in which the most poetic and beautiful speech often occurs precisely when he attempts to "overcome" poetry.

14. For example, see Aristotle on the difference between "climax,

recognition, and resolution" in *Poetics* in *The Basic Works of Aristotle* (New York: Random House, 1941), p. 1452 ff.

15. Cf. "For if it is necessary to leave the defining something in full possession of its voice, this does in no way mean that our thinking should not pursue the nature of language. Only the manner in which the attempt is made is decisive." (22)

16. This to-and-fro pattern is similar to that of level two, but now expands to contain level three within it. Note that level three is much simpler in structure than the first two levels with their complex symmetrical arrangements of reporting and thinking. And, of course, finally level three is in the midst of level two and returns to it; level two itself is within level one. That is, the image shows the simple hidden deep within the complex, a safe place in which it flowers briefly.

17. This enables us to understand more fully the well-known saying: "I am telling you all this, but not in order to give the impression that I already knew then everything that I am still asking today. But perhaps there is confirmation here for you . . . of a phrase of (Hölderlin's), 'For as you began, so you will remain.'" (7) This does function biographically and historically when read as part of the second level, but finally the real point is not to merely report a return to early interests, much less to hint at any sort of historicism. Rather, understood at the second level, this says that the inquirer remains within and develops what thoughts he began with. Here we can recall (and interpret) the difficult lines I noted at the beginning of this essay: "Without this theological backgrond I should never have come upon the path of thinking. But origin always comes to meet us from the future. If the two call to each other, and reflection makes its home within that calling . . . and thus becomes true presence" (10). Further, thought by way of the (third level) experience which leads back to (second level) thinking, we can understand that what is thought is given to thought as a gift (think of language and the twofold), a gift given at the beginning perhaps, but which is only understood and fully appreciated in the end; this has to do with originary thinking: "In what sense do you understand 'originarily familiar'? You do not mean what we know first, do you? No—but what before all else has been entrusted to our nature, and becomes known only at the last" (33).

18. One might wonder whether the saying comes wholly from Heidegger or from beyond him, as Caputo suggests in concluding his *The Mystical*

Element in Heidegger's Thought (Athens, Oh.: Ohio Univ. Press, 1978), "Heidegger's writings must be for us not a body of texts to be subjected to a learned exegesis, but a voice which calls us to set our own reflection onto motion. And whose voice is it which calls to us from these texts? Is it only the voice of Martin Heidegger of Messkirch?"

19. Here I have translated *von* with "concerning" rather than "of" (which the English translation uses in place of its previous "on" and "from").

Notes to Chapter Three

1. In this chapter all page references to *What Is Called Thinking?* are given in parentheses in the text. All these quotations are from the translation by John Glenn Gray (New York: Harper and Row, 1968). Heidegger's lectures were originally published as *Was Heisst Denken?* (Tubingen: Max Niemeyer Verlag, 1954).

2. Throughout, I have transliterated the Greek; neither Heidegger's text nor Gray's translation do so.

3. There is, of course, more to it than this. It has been hidden from the beginning, and necessarily so.

4. In order to think about language as *legein* and saying we might reflect on how English holds the connection in "legend" and "lay." A "legend" is so called because it derives from Latin *legenda* ("what is read") and from *legere* ("to read"), which itself has an original meaning of gather or collect, derived from the Greek *legein*. "Legend" also means, for example, an inscription, and, in an obsolete verbal form, "to tell stories of." A "lay" is a short lyric or narrative poem intended to be sung, and "lay" once also meant the strain or tune itself. Suggestively, "lay" is connected in English to what Heidegger means by *noein* because as a part of the meaning of "lay" as to place or to put, it means "to lay ear to" and "to lay to heart."

   In this regard, it may not be accidental that Heidegger presents *legein* by way of a lecture series (*Vorlesungen*), rather than in a dialogue, for example. Both "lecture" and *vorlesen/Vorlesung* mean reading out (e.g. *lesen* means "gather, glean, pick," and *vor-lesen*, then, means "laying before us what is gathered"); both derive from *legere* and *legein*.

5. Compare this treatment of source and origin with the Japanese's experience of a "Wellspring of Reality" in translating German in "A Dialogue on Language," p. 24.

6. There is a disagreement about how to translate *eon emmenai*, or more precisely, Heidegger's translation of it: "*(das) Anwesen des Anwesenden*." Seidel uses "the presence of the presencing" and the "'to presence' of the presencing," (*Martin Heidegger and the Pre-Socratics* [Lincoln, Neb.: Univ. of Nebraska, 1961] e.g., pp. 84–85). In translating *"Moira"* (Parmenides VIII, 34–41), Frank A. Capuzzi uses "the presencing of what is present" (*"Moira"* in *Early Greek Thinking*, trans. D.F. Krell and F.A. Capuzzi [New York: Harper and Row, 1975] e.g., p. 92 ff.). Both of these seem happier translations than that of the English version of *What Is Called Thinking?* because the former two work to retain the participle form. Nonetheless, to retain the correlation with the English version, I generally have used J. Glenn Gray's "the presence of what is present."

7. See the argument of section two and three below.

8. *"Sprache und Heimat,"* in *Hebbel-Jahrbuch 11*, 1958–1960 (Heide, 1960), pp. 27–50.

9. Heidegger often is accused of whimsical, idiosyncratic, and false use of etymologies, for example. But, do the same scholars object to all such "playful" ways of thinking, for example, to Plato's? After all, in *Phaedrus* Plato thinks and speaks by way of fanciful etymologies about how we might "gain the ability both to think and to speak," (New York: Library of Liberal Arts, The Bobbs-Merrill Co., Inc., 1956, p. 55.).

10. Louis H. Mackey, *Kierkegaard: A Kind of Poet* (Philadelphia: University of Pennsylvania Press, 1971), pp. 259–261.

11. *"Sprache und Heimat,"* pp. 41–43.

12. Translated in "The Thinker as Poet" in *Poetry, Language, Thought*, p. 7. *"Erst gebild wahrt Gesicht./Doch Gebild ruht im Gedicht."*, *"Aus der Erfahrung des Denkens"* (Pfullingen: Neske, 1954).

13. Indeed, many Heidegger scholars implicitly assume this schema and dichotomy, for example, when they argue that he proceeds from man to Being in early "anthropological" works such as *Being and Time* and then that he, after the famous "reversal" decides to go the other way instead—speaking (presumably and presumptuously) from the vantage point of Being itself. See below and chapter 4, fn. 1.

14. I do not intend that the *figura* I present in these variations must be *the figura* of *What Is Called Thinking?*; however, I do contend that some

figura, which these delineations approximate, is the principle of organization of the saying and thinking in these lectures. As is obvious,
none of these variations is satisfactory in every case. Further, letting-
lie-before-us (abbreviated "saying") and taking-to-heart-too (abbreviated "thinking") may present the *figura* incompletely; they are not
meant to indicate all passage between man and the duality. If the
typesetter would allow, we would need to add, for example, the
corresponding "calls for thinking" and "lays out before us" or "gives
us food for thought" alongside what we have. Further, since Heidegger says elsewhere (see "A Dialogue on Language" in the previous
chapter) the duality (the sphere containing all others) is boundless,
we might leave off the outer circle. Again, the *figura* I delineate is the
best I now can do and is heuristic; nonetheless, we are—I am
arguing—being called on to discover the real *figura* in *What Is Called
Thinking?*

15. "Gathering" is not at all the same as "collect." See the article by J.
    Glenn Gray mentioned in chapter 2, fn. 8. There Gray also notes that
    "gather" has the same root as *gattern* (to join in marriage), which in
    turn comes from the Greek *to agathon* (the good).

16. The "orthodox" interpretation of *Versammlung* and *Ereignis* is that
    Ereignis ("the event of appropriation") is prior to and holds sway in
    versammeln, *Versammlung* ("the gathering"). See Walter Biemel, *Martin
    Heidegger*, trans. J.L. Mehta (New York: Harcourt, Brace, Jovano-
    vich, 1976), esp. chapter 9, and Otto Pöggeler, *"Sein als Ereignis,"*
    Zeitschrift fur Philosophische Forschung, XII/4 (1959): 599–632, trans.
    R.H. Grimm as "Being As Appropriation," *Philosophy Today*, 19,
    number 2/4 (summer 1975): 4.

17. On "pain" and the "rift" see "Language" in *Poetry, Language, Thought*,
    trans. Albert Hofstadter (New York: Harper and Row, 1971).

18. On "thing," "bridge," and "gathering" see "The Thing" in *Poetry,
    Language, Thought*, p. 174 ff.

19. Compare with what is said of "bridging" and "gathering" in "Build-
    ing, Dwelling, Thinking" in *Poetry, Language, Thought*, esp. pp. 152 ff.

20. Recall the poem mentioned in note 12 above, which says "Only image
    formed keeps the vision./Yet image formed rests in the poem."

21. See chapter 1, above.

22. This means that action attends or follows from thinking—or that
    thinking itself is action, as the following pages of this chapter argue.

23. Concerning the relation of habit and habitation (*WCT*, 36, 129), see
    section two above on dwelling.

24. This reduced sense of action needs to be thought by way of the difference between the ordinary and originary thinking, just as calling, et cetera, were above (see the first section of this chapter). Also, compare Hanna Arendt, *The Human Condition* (Chicago: University of Chicago Press, 1958).

25. On this leveling of one-track thinking see the first series of answers as compared to the second; especially compare the difference in the two sorts of thinking in regard to the "same": in the former it means merely the "identical" (see section one of this chapter above). This reduction also can be seen instructively in the interesting development of the meaning of "literal." See Anthony Nemetz, "Literalness and the Sensus Litteralis," *Speculum*, 34, 1959, 76–89.

26. On "dispose" and "settle," see the first section of this chapter.

27. On the distinction between history and origin, see below.

28. Heidegger says "no way" before "wrong way," but clearly he means that the second way is the "wrong way" and the third way is "no way" because the word translated as "no way" is *Unweg* (impassable or pathless), which clearly corresponds to the third way which remains impassable, (*ungangbar*) to thinking. In the German edition, page 108 corresponds to page 175 of Gray's English translation.

29. Except as noted below, the translation of Parmenides' fragment 2 used here is from Kathleen Freeman, *Ancilla to the Pre-Socratic Philosophers*, (Oxford: Blackwell, 1956), p. 42.

30. The translation of this phrase is A. P. D. Mourelatos' in *The Route of Parmenides* (New Haven: Yale University Press, 1970), p. 55.

31. Cf. Heidegger, *Einführung in die Metaphysik*, 2 ed., (Tubingen: Niemeyer, 1958), p. 84, trans. Robert Manheim as *An Introduction to Metaphysics* (New Haven: Yale University Press, 1959), chapter 4. Here Heidegger also treats Parmenides' sayings, but in a way which generated controversy and misunderstanding concerning nothingness (see chapter 2 above).

32. Cf. "A Dialogue on Language."

33. The connection between way, interpretation, and translation is very old. Hermes, as we learn from the first pages of the *Odyssey*, is the "wayfinder." Later, of course, it leads to hermeneutics. On Heidegger's originary recovery of 'hermeneutics' see for example, "A Dialogue on Language" pp. 29–30.

34. I once heard a farmer say about the changes in his craft, "Where there is less hand work, there is more head work."

35. Cf. Northrop Frye, *Anatomy of Criticism*, (New York: Atheneum, 1968), p. 82 ff.
36. Perhaps love, like thinking and saying, would be a gathering of man and duality. On learning to think, being capable, and inclining see *What Is Called Thinking*, pp. 3, 4, 141.
37. In a letter from Heidegger to William Richardson, "*Ergänzen kann nur, wer das Ganze erblickt.*" From William Richardson, *Heidegger—Through Phenomenology to Thought* (The Hague: Nijhoff, 1963), pp. xviii–xix.
38. This is the subject of my manuscript, *Heidegger and Homecoming*, prepared with the help of a Research Fellowship from The National Endowment for the Humanities.
39. Heidegger, *On Time and Being* (New York: Harper and Row, 1972), p. 24.

Notes to Chapter Four

1. See, for example, J.L. Mehta, *The Philosophy of Martin Heidegger* (New York: Harper and Row, 1971), esp. p. 110; Karl Löwith, *Heidegger-Denker in dürstiger Zeit* (Frankfurt: Klostermann, 1953); Walter Schulz, "*Uber den philosophiegeschichtlichen Ort Martin Heideggers,*" *Philosophische Rundschau*, I, 1953/54; Pöggeler, "*Sein als Ereignis*" and *Der Denkweg Martin Heidegger* (Pfullingen, 1963); William Richardson, *Heidegger—Through Phenomenology to Thought* (The Hague: Nijhoff, 1963).
2. Page references to *What Is Called Thinking?* are given in parentheses in the text in this chapter.
3. "A Dialogue on Language," pp. 9–11, *What Is Called Thinking?* p. 177, and "Phenomenology and Theology" in *The Piety of Thinking*, (Bloomington, In.: Indiana University Press, 1976).
4. The tradition is laid out masterfully by Henri de Lubac in *Exégèse médiévale: les quattre sense de l'Ecriture*, 4 vols. (Paris: Aubier, 1955–1964). For a synoptic presentation, see Louis H. Mackey, "Notes Toward a Definition of Philosophy," *Franciscan Studies*, vol. 33, annual XI, 1973, 262–272, especially section III. The latter essay is normative for the view of sacred and secular meaning presented here.
5. See Anthony Nemetz, "Literalness and the Sensus Litteralis," *Speculum*, vol. 34, 1959, 76–89.
6. See Louis H. Mackey, "Notes Toward a Definition of Philosophy,"

section III; Northrop Frye, *Anatomy of Criticism* (New York: Atheneum, 1968), and "Levels of Meaning in Literature," *Keynon Review*, spring 1950, 256–262; I. A. Richards, *Practical Criticism* (New York: Harcourt, Brace, and World, 1929); Kenneth Burke, *A Grammar of Motives* (Berkley: University of California Press, 1969); Richard Ellmann, *Ulysses on the Liffey* (New York: Oxford University Press, 1972).

7. In addition to works already mentioned, from the extensive literature see especially Beryl Smalley, *The Study of the Bible in the Middle Ages* (Notre Dame, In.: University of Notre Dame Press, 1964).

8. See Erich Auerbach, *"Figura,"* In *Scenes From the Drama of European Literature* (New York: Meridian Books, 1959), pp. 11–76.

9. It is interesting to note that there is a hermeneutical distinction which does not clearly correspond to Heidegger's double literal meaning (the traditional, representational account and the originary one). In fact, the literal sense is normally seen as having two aspects: the *littera* (the words, studied with grammar and rhetoric) and the *sensus* (the conventional meanings of those words). Northrop Frye develops these two aspects in a way which highlights their difference. He treats symbols as motifs (*littera*, the centripetal infracontextual relations) and as signs (*sensus*, the centrifugal referential sense). It is not clear, though, that the hermetic and representational emphases all correlate, respectively, with the originary and traditional answers in the literal phrase of *What Is Called Thinking?*

10. Despite my use of "level" to refer to the four aspects or phases of the text and to the four kinds of meaning, this does not imply that Heidegger embraces a hierarchical view. Just the opposite. I occasionally use "level" because it sometimes seems clearer to do so and because "level" and hierarchy are part of medieval hermeneutics. Clearly, as just noted, Heidegger himself is in the tradition of the Incarnational school; he speaks of "within," not of "above and below." Note, though, that the dynamic relation between levels of meaning (from the literal comes what you believe; from what you believe, comes how you act; by your action you get to heaven) also occurs in *What Is Called Thinking?* (from what is said about thinking comes the way Heidegger thinks; from the style of his thinking comes the learning of how think; from the teaching and learning of thinking emerges the vision of an originary gathering of what belongs together).

11. For example, see Auerbach and DeLubac, cited above.

12. Also recall Heidegger's remark cited in chapter 3, fn. 38: "He alone

can ful-full who has a vision of fullness." (*Ergänzen Kann nur, wer das Ganze erblickt.*) (Richardson, *Through Phenomenology to Thought*, pp. xviii-xix).

13. I argued above that what Heidegger says about representational, metaphysical thinking and originary, recollective thinking finally give rise to obscured vision. If we take representational thinking as an "old testament" and originary thinking as a "new testament," where the former prefigures the latter and together both yield the vision, we might underscore the parallel between Heidegger's thinking and meaning and that of the Bible by way of a remark of St. Thomas Aquinas, "Indeed, as Denis the Areopagite says: the condition of the Church is intermediate between the state of the Synagogue and the state of the Church Triumphant. Therefore the *Old Testament* was the figure of the New; the Old and the New together are the figure of celestial things. Therefore the spiritual sense, directed toward believing well, may be established on this figurative method according to which the *Old Testament* figures the *New*, and this is the allegorical or typical sense; in this sense the events related in the *Old Testament* are understood in terms of the Christ and the Church; or the spiritual sense may be established on this figurative method according to which the *Old* and *New Testament* together signify the Church triumphant, and this is the anagogical sense." *Quodlibet VII, a. 15*, cited in C. Spic, *Esquisse d'une histoire de l'exégèse latine au moyen age* (Paris, 1944), translated by William F. Lynch in *Christ and Appollo* (New York: New American Library, 1963), supplement four, p. 225.

14. The typological relationships between the major figures in the book, on the other hand, are not clear. Is Parmenides a type of Nietzsche or of originary thinking? Are Nietzsche (or the superman) types of the originary thinker (or, of the thinking teacher)? Or, is Parmenides the figure of what was and is no longer, Nietzsche the figure of what now is and long will be, the teaching thinker (Heidegger?) the figure of what is not yet?

15. On language or saying (which thinking takes to heart) as saga/story, see, for example, "A Dialogue on Language," pp. 47 ff. and above, chapter 2, sections two, and section three of chapter 3.

16. Kierkegaard, *Philosophical Fragments*, 2nd. ed. by Niels Thulstrup, translated by David Swenson, revised translation by H.V. Hong (Princeton N.J.: Princeton University Press, 1962), pp. 32 ff. Compare with Buber's idea that God "needs" man, for example, in *I and Thou*, Part Three (New York: Charles Scribner's Sons, 1958).

17. Cf. "A Dialogue on Language" where man is "needed and used by what calls on man to preserve the two-fold," pp. 32 ff.

18. Talk of the tree of the knowledge of good and evil follows immediately. It seems too farfetched, however, to connect this tree with those in *What Is Called Thinking?*

19. Owen Chadwick, *Western Asceticism* vol. no. II. (Philadelphia: Westminster Press, 1958), pp. 38–39.

20. In *Advent Sermons 5*; Minge, *Patrologia Latina*, 183, col. 51 B. C., translated and cited by Aelred Squire, *Asking the Fathers* (New York: Paulist Press, 1976), pp. 126–127.

21. See John D. Caputo, *The Mystical Element in Heidegger's Thought* (Athens, Ohio: Ohio University Press, 1978).

22. See Squire, *Asking the Fathers*, p. 8 and pp. 192 ff.

23. *The Spiritual Exercises of St. Ignatius*, translated by Anthony Matotla (New York: Doubleday & Co., 1974).

24. Otto Pöggeler, "Being as Appropriation," *Philosophy Today*, 19, no. 2/4, (summer 1975): 39. In the same article, Pöggeler helpfully considers Heidegger's thought in light of his orientation to the New Testament. For a listing of Heidegger's courses on religious figures and topics, see Richardson, *From Phenomenology to Thought*, pp. 63–671.

25. On Heidegger's early years see Michael Zimmerman, *Eclipse of the Self* (Athens, Oh.: Ohio University Press, 1981), pp. 3 ff., and Thomas Sheehan, *Heidegger: The Man and the Thinker* (Chicago: Precedent Publishing, 1981), pp. 3 ff.

26. Rudolf Bultmann, "New Testament and Theology," in *Kerygma and Myth* (New York: Harper and Row, 1961), pp. 24–25.

27. Caputo, *Mystical Element*, p. 143 ff.

28. Ibid., p. 227.

29. See Mircea Eliade, *The Sacred and the Profane* (New York: Harper and Row, 1961), especially pp. 68–111 and *Cosmos and History* (New York: Harper and Row, 1959), pp. 104–145.

30. Eliade, *Cosmos and History*, p. 228.

31. Caputo, *Mystical Element*, p. 228.

32. Ibid., pp. 199–201.

33. See Heidegger, *A Discourse on Thinking* and Zimmerman, *Eclipse*, p. 254.

34. Ibid., pp. xxv and 248 ff.

35. Ibid. and Caputo, *Mystical Element*, pp. 132 and 181.

36. Caputo, ibid., pp. 181–183.

37. On this topic see the stimulating work by Vincent Vycinas, *Earth and Gods* (The Hague: Nijhoff, 1961).
38. Heidegger, *Early Greek Thinking* (New York: Harper and Row, 1975), p. 91 ff. Hereafter references to this work will be given in the text in parentheses with the abbreviation *EGT*.
39. Heidegger and E. Fink, *Heraclitus Seminar*, 1966–67 (University, Ala.: University of Alabama Press, 1979), pp. 56–57.
40. Ibid., pp. 37 and 91.
41. Ibid., p. 8
42. George Seidel, *Martin Heidegger and the Pre-Socratics* (Lincoln, Nebraska: University of Nebraska Press, 1978), p. 23.
43. "A Letter to a Young Student," translated in *Poetry, Language, Thought* (New York: Harper and Row, 1971), pp. 183–186.
44. See Eliade, *The Sacred and the Profane*, especially the introduction.
45. George Steiner, *Martin Heidegger*, (New York: The Viking Press, 1979), p. 156.
46. Fragment 52, translated by Kathleen Freeman, *Ancilla to the Pre-Socratic Philosophers* (Oxford: Blackwell, 1956).
47. Caputo, *Mystical Element*, pp. 80 ff.
48. See Heidegger's "The Thing" in *Poetry, Language, Thought*, esp. pp. 179 ff.
49. *Early Greek Thinking*, pp. 104–105 and *Heraclitus Seminar*, pp. 5, 6, 23, and 127.
50. Zimmerman, *Eclipse*, p. 187.
51. See David A. White, *Heidegger and the Language of Poetry*, Lincoln, Neb.: University of Nebraska Press, 1978), 220 ff. and my manuscript *Heidegger and Homecoming*.
52. Seidel, *Pre-Socratics*, pp. 139 ff.; Steiner, *Martin Heidegger*, p. 141; my *Heidegger and Homecoming*.
53. See for example Heidegger's "The Thing," pp. 163–186. On Heidegger's use of neologism in *figura exymologica* see Erasmus Schöfer, "Heidegger's Language," in *On Heidegger and Language*, ed. J. Kockelmans (Evanston: Northwestern University Press, 1972), esp. pp. 287–293.
54. Seidel, *Pre-Socratics*, p. 93.
55. Steiner, *Martin Heidegger*, p. 58.
56. I take this as an open question, despite what Zimmerman and Sheehan argue, for two reasons. First, it seems open whether any really originary thinking—where the ultimate comes forth—could be secular in any ordinary sense. Second, that Heidegger remained

deeply religious despite all the scholarly evidence to the contrary is seen (a) in the inconstestably religious tenor of his work, which if anything, increase after *What Is Called Thinking?* (b) by his request for a priest to preside at his funeral (see Bernhard Weite, "Seeking and Finding: The Speech at Heidegger's Burial," in Sheehan, *Heidegger* pp. 73–75), and (c) by the tenable thesis that like many a "nonactive" Catholic, he remained at his place of beginnings (cf. "A Dialogue on Language") in a final, deep simplicity.

57. Not surprisingly, these four aspects of what is given for us to do flesh out the four levels of meaning: the first asks us to keep thinking through the meaning and history of what Heidegger and the tradition think and say; the second asks us to use the method of reading by way of substance and style on all Heidegger's works; the third asks for the whole vision which the corpus might let appear; the fourth asks that we stay learners, following the teacher's exhortation.

58. Also practically, the attempt to do all this now would require yet another entire book. For that, see the many already available, e.g., the works cited in note one of this chapter.

59. Walter Biemel, "Poetry and Language in Heidegger," in *On Heidegger and Language*, ed. J. Kockelmans (Evanston: Northwestern University Press, 1972), pp. 65–68.

60. Quoted in Steiner, *Martin Heidegger*, p. 11.

Selected Bibliography

I have included only a selected bibliography for two reasons. First, there are many standard, fuller bibliographies available. Second, the modest task of this book, an exegesis, makes direct and indirect reference to only a few of Heidegger's works necessary and implicates only a few more works on the methodology of reading.

I. Primary Sources

Discourse on Thinking. Translated by John M. Anderson and E.H. Freund. New York: Harper and Row, 1966. [*Gelassenheit.* Pfullingen: Verlag Günter Neske, 1959.]

Early Greek Thinking. Translated by David F. Krell and Frank A. Capuzzi. New York: Harper and Row, 1975. ["Der Spurch des Anaximander" from *Holzwege.* Frankfurt am Main: Klostermann, 1972, pp. 296–343. "Logos (Heraklit, Fragment B50)," "Moira (Parmenides VIII, 34–41)," and "Aletheia (Heraclit, Fragment B16)" from *Volträge und Aufsätze* 1. Pfullingen: Neske, 1954, pp. 207–282.]

With E. Fink. *Heraclitus Seminar 1966/67.* Translated by Charles H. Seibert. University, Ala.: University of Alabama Press, 1979.

Identity and Difference. Translated by Joan Stambaugh. New York: Harper and Row, 1969. [*Identität und Differenz.* Pfullingen: Neske, 1957.]

An Introduction to Metaphysics. Translated by Ralph Manheim. New Haven: Yale University Press, 1959. [*Einfuhrüng in die Metaphysik.* Tübingen: Niemeyer, 1953.]

"My Way to Phenomenology." Translated by Joan Stambaugh. *On Time and Being.* New York: Harper and Row, 1972. ["Mein Weg in die Phänomenologie." *Zur Sache des Denkens.* Tübingen: Niemeyer, 1969.]

On the Way to Language. Translated by Peter D. Hertz and Joan Stambaugh. New York: Harper and Row, 1971. [*Untergegs zur Sprache.* Pfullingen: Neske, 1959.] (The English edition changes the sequence of the essays and omits the first essay, which is translated in *Poetry, Language, Thought.*)

The Piety of Thinking: Essays by Martin Heidegger. Translated by James G. Hart and John C. Maraldo. Bloomington, In.: Indiana University Press, 1978. [*Phänomenologie und Theologie.* Frankfurt am Main: Klostermann, 1970.

Review of Philosophie der Symbolischen Formen, by Ernst Cassirer. *Deutsche Literature-zeitung für Kritik der Internationalen Wissenschaft*, Neue Folge, V. 1928. "Grundsatze des Denkens." "Jahrbuch für Psychologie und Psychotherapie, 1958, pp. 33–41. "A Conversation with Martin Heidegger," Anstosse: Berichte aus der Arbeit der Evangelischen Akademie Hofgeismar, vol. I, pp. 31–37.]

Poetry, Language, Thought. Translated by Albert Hofstadter. New York: Harper and Row, 1971. [*Aus der Erfahrung des Denkens*. Pfullingen: Neske, 1954. Der Ursprung des Kunstwerkes. Universal-Bibliothek Number 8446/47.

Stuttgart: Reclam, 1960. Also in *Holzwege*. Frankfurt am Main: Klostermann, 1950. "Wozu Dichter." In *Holzwege*. "Bauen Wohnen Denken," "Das Ding," and " . . . dichterisch wohnet der Mensch . . . ," in *Vorträge und Aufsätze*. Pfullingen: Neske, 1954.]

The Question Concerning Technology and Other Essays. Translated by William Lovitt. New York: Harper and Row, 1977. ["Die Frage nach der Technik" and "Die Kehre." in *Die Technik und die Kehre*. Pfullingen: Neske, 1962. "Nietzsches Wort 'Gott ist tot'" and "Die Zeit des Weltbildes." In *Holzwege*. Frankfurt am Main: Klostermann, 1950. "Wissenschaft und Besinnung." In *Vorträge und Aufsätze*. Pfullingen: Neske, 1954. *Vorträge und Aufsätze* also contains "Die Frage nach der Technik." "Sprache und Heimat," *Hebbel Jahrbruch*, 11, 1960, pp. 27–50.]

What Is Called Thinking? Translated by Fred D. Wieck and J. Glenn Gray. New York: Harper and Row, 1968. [*Was heisst Denken?* Tübingen: Max Niemeyer Verlag, 1954.]

II. Bibliographies of Heidegger's Works

Sass, Hans-Martin. *Heidegger-Bibliographie*. Meisenheim am Glan: Anton Hain Verlag, 1968.

Sass, Hans-Martin et al. *Materialen zur Heidegger-Bibliographie*, 1917–1972. Meisenheim am Glan: Anton Hain Verlag, 1975.

Sass, Hans-Martin, *Martin Heidegger: Bibliography and Glossary*. Bowling Green, Oh.: Philosophy Documentation Center, 1982.

Mehta, J.L. *The Philosophy of Martin Heidegger*. New York: Harper and Row, 1971.

III. Secondary Literature on Heidegger

Biemel, Walter. *Martin Heidegger*, Translated by J.L. Mehta. New York: Harcourt, Brace, Jovanovich, Inc., 1976.

Caputo, John D. *The Mystical Element in Heidegger's Thought*. Athens, Oh.: Ohio University Press, 1978.

Gray, J. Glenn. "Heidegger on Remembering and Remembering Heidegger." *Man and World*, 10, no. 1 (1977): 62–78.

Halliburton, David. *Poetic Thinking: An Approach to Heidegger*. Chicago: The University of Chicago Press, 1981.

Levin, David Michael, "The Embodiment of Thinking: Heidegger's Approach to Language." In Ronald Bruzina and Bruce Wilshire, ed. *Phenomenology: Dialogues and Bridges*. Albany, N.Y.: State University of New York Press, 1982.

Löwith, Karl. *Heidegger-Denker in dürstiger Zeit*. Frankfurt: Klostermann, 1953.

Mehta, J.L. *The Philosophy of Martin Heidegger*. New York: Harper and Row, 1971.

Nicholson, Graeme. "The Coiling Path of Heidegger's Essence of Truth. In Hugh J. Silveman, John Sallis, and Thomas M. Seebohm, ed. *Continental Philosophy In America*. Pittsburgh, Pa.: Duquesne University Press, 1983.

Pöggeler, Otto. *Der Denkweg Martin Heidegger*. Pfullingen: Neske, 1963.

Pöggeler, Otto. "Sein als Ereignis." *Zeitschrift für Philosophische Forschung*, 12:4 (1959) 599–632. Translated by R.H. Grimm. "Being as Appropriation." *Philosophy Today*, 19, no. 2/4 (summer 1975).

Richardson, William. *Heidegger—Through Phenomenology to Thought*. The Hague: Nijhoff, 1963.

Schulz, Walter. "Uber den philosophiegeschichtlichen Ort Martin Heideggers." *Philosophische Rundschau*, 1, 1953/54: 65–93, 211–232.

Seidel, George. *Martin Heidegger and the Pre-Socratics*. Lincoln, Nebraska: University of Nebraska Press, 1964.

Sheehan, Thomas, *Heidegger: The Man and the Thinker*. Chicago: Precedent Press, 1981.

Steiner, George. *Martin Heidegger*. New York: Viking Press, 1978.

Vycinas, Vincent. *Earth and Gods*. The Hague: Nijhoff, 1961.

White, David A. *Heidegger and the Language of Poetry*. Lincoln: University of Nebraska Press, 1978.

Zimmerman, Michael. *Eclipse of the Self*. Athens, Oh.: Ohio University Press, 1981.

IV. *Other Works*

Arendt, Hanna. *The Human Condition.* Chicago: University of Chicago
  Press, 1958.
Auerbach, Erich. "Figura." In *Scenes From The Drama of European Literature.*
  New York: Meridian Books, 1959.
Freeman, Kathleen. *Ancilla to the Pre-Socratic Philosophers.* Oxford: Black-
  well, 1956.
Frye, Northrop. *Anatomy of Criticism.* New York: Atheneum, 1968.
Lubac, Hendi de. *Exégèse médiévale: les quattre sens de l'Ecriture.* 4 vols. Paris:
  Aubier, 1957–1964.
Mackey, Louis H. *Kierkegaard: A Kind of Poet.* Philadelphia: University of
  Pennsylvania Press, 1971.
———. "Notes Toward a Definition of Philosophy." *Franciscan Studies*, 33,
  no. 9 (1973): 262-272.
Mourelatos, Alexander P. D. *The Route of Parmenides.* New Haven: Yale
  University Press, 1970.
Nemetz, Anthony. "Literalness and the Sensus Litteralis." *Speculum*, 34,
  1959, 76–89.
Plato. *Phaedrus.* New York: The Bobbs-Merrill Co., 1956.
Smalley, Beryl. *The Study of the Bible in the Middle Ages.*
  Notre Dame, In.: University of Notre Dame Press, 1964.

Index